Roni Cummings

The Self in the System
EXPANDING THE LIMITS
OF FAMILY THERAPY

The Self in the System

EXPANDING THE LIMITS
OF FAMILY THERAPY

By

Michael P. Nichols, Ph.D.

 BRUNNER/MAZEL *Publishers* • New York

Library of Congress Cataloging-in-Publication Data

Nichols, Michael P.
  The self in the system.

  Bibliography: p. 293
  Includes index.
  1. Family psychotherapy. I. Title. [DNLM:
1. Family Therapy. WM 430.5.F2 N62ls]
RC488.5.N533 1987   616.89'156   87-13773
ISBN 0-87630-472-2

Copyright © 1987 by Michael P. Nichols

Published by
BRUNNER/MAZEL, INC.
19 Union Square
New York, New York 10003

MANUFACTURED IN THE UNITED STATES OF AMERICA

10 9 8 7 6 5 4 3 2 1

To Jim Faraci and Jim Mullin
for lessons in sanity.

Contents

Preface

The advent of family therapy has revolutionized the way we think about human behavior and greatly improved our ability to resolve a host of perplexing clinical problems. Where once we thought of our patients as independent individuals, acting and reacting to others, yet basically separate and self-determining, we now see that people's lives are intertwined in complex ways. The family is more than a group of separate individuals; it is a system—a transcendent whole whose parts are coordinated in powerful if unseen ways. Unfortunately, this momentous discovery contained the seeds of its own distortion.

No longer do we recognize that the system is simply a useful metaphor for describing the way family members' lives are so richly interconnected. Now we accept the family systems model as a fundamental and unquestioned reality. In the process, we too often lose sight of a different reality: namely, that however much their behavior is coordinated, family members remain separate individuals. Our lives are bound together with the lives of others; still, we remain selves—flesh and blood persons, with private hopes and ambitions, motives and expectations, quirks and foibles, and potential for creative growth.

Family therapists discovered profound truths about systemic interactions, but forgot the lessons of depth psychology. If people were billiard balls, their interactions could be understood solely on the basis of systemic forces. The difference is that human beings interact on the basis of conscious and unconscious expectations of each other. However impossible it may be to understand people without considering their relationships, it is equally impossible to understand those relationships if we think only of external behavior without considering interior realities. At the heart of human experience is a central self, an "I," who feels, thinks, and acts—as well as interacts.

Family therapy was launched with a declaration of independence from traditional psychiatry. This separate and independent development made possible a rapid development of ideas and techniques, but it has also perpetuated an unfortunate divorce between family therapists and the rest of the field. As a result, family therapy deals with relationships but is arid with regard to personal experience. The family therapist may be like an anthropologist who observes the patterns of a culture without troubling to find out what goes on in the hearts and minds of the people.

The core of my argument is that family therapy has moved too far from the psychology of the individual, resulting in a wave of esoteric theorizing and a proliferation of mechanistic, highly technical interventions. Family therapy does require new ways of thinking, but the contemporary trend is toward theories so abstract that there is little room for human experience, for understanding, for personal responsibility, or for enhancing people's ability to solve their own problems.

The book is certainly not the first and only one to call for a reconciliation between systemic and psychological approaches to treatment. I want to make clear, therefore, my particular vision. What I do advocate is putting the self back in the system, both in theory and practice. What I *do not* advocate, however, is the kind of family therapy where the main emphasis is on individual personalities. Many of the object relations and psychoanalytic family therapies fall into this trap. The problem with these integrative approaches, from my point of view, is that by thinking first of intrapsychic problems, they underemphasize family interaction, which I believe is the essence of what family therapy is about.

A psychoanalyst surveying the contents of this book might justly conclude that my coverage of psychodynamics, self psychology, and object relations theory is incomplete. To this charge I must plead guilty. Rather than attempt a full-scale and formal discussion of these complex topics, I have deliberately kept my explanations brief, concentrating more on clinical application than on theoretical completeness. I have tailored my account to make it succinct and practical, because my aim is not to give a course on psychoanalytic theory but to demonstrate how a better understanding of individual minds can be incorporated into family therapy.

I do not subscribe to the point of view that psychodynamic problems are the *real* problems in family relationships. Happily, this myth, discredited by the pioneers of family therapy, is no longer much with us. Unfortunately, however, I think that many of the new psychoanalytic family therapies bring this kind of thinking in through the back door. No one, certainly no one who works with families, stands up to announce that intrapsychic personality dynamics are more important than interactional family dynamics. Nevertheless, I believe that many attempts to integrate psychoanalytic thinking and family methods lose sight of the basic insight of family therapy, namely that interactions and their triadic complications are the most powerful and immediate problem and remedy.

At this point I have criticized systemic thinkers for ignoring the self and criticized psychoanalytic family therapists for underutilizing the power of the family. Do I sound too critical?

This book contains a great deal of criticism. I hope that it does not come across as mean-spirited or destructive; I know that is not my intent. My saying this will not, however, make people happy to read my critical accounts of their work. One thing I would like to emphasize is that when I single out the work of particular authors to illustrate what I believe are excesses in the systemic

model, I have chosen only experienced and respected practitioners. It seems to me that it would be foolish to point out mistaken
thinking on the part of unrepresentative or not well-respected
therapists. My primary purpose is not to attack or even evaluate
these major figures, but to caution others against uncritically following their example. The truth is that I feel myself a better teacher than a critic.

The inspiration for this book does not come from thinking that I
have uncovered the Truth and that everyone else is misguided.
No, it was in my own work that I discovered the tendency to lose
sight of the self in the process of trying to outwit families. While
trying to correct my own errors, I began to look around the field,
where I saw others making what I thought were similar mistakes.
So, like most books, this one is partly an attempt to master something the author himself is wrestling with and partly an attempt to
reach out to others. My aim is to be constructive; my criticism is
done from love and respect for the field and my colleagues in it.

My primary purpose for writing this book is to remind family
therapists that we are working with persons not abstractions.
Some readers will be provoked by my critique into defending
radical systems thinking; some will be convinced that, yes, the
field has gone too far off on a tangent; and many clinicians will
find it refreshing as well as useful to think more of the human
nature of the persons we are all trying to reach.

Although this book begins with a critical analysis of the field, it
does not end there. Anyone who describes a problematic state of
affairs is under some obligation to provide remedies, and I will
offer an approach to clinical problems that takes into account individual and family dynamics. My thesis is that it is important to
analyze the system and often to work directly with it. But change
ultimately works through individuals within the system. We may
think about families—structured with boundaries and triangles—
and we may convene families. Yet, in a real sense there are no
families. The family is an abstraction. I will describe how to work
with the abstractions of family dynamics without getting lost in
them.

In Chapter 1, *Finding the Family and Losing the Self*, I describe how in the development of family therapy therapists lost sight of the psychology of the individual. I offer a critique of two corollary trends: one, techniquism (high-tech interventions designed for a quick fix); two, a flight into overly abstract thinking. Both of these trends, I suggest, obscure the reality of the individual persons who make up families *and* both trends are rooted in powerful emotional responses that families stir up in those who treat them. The implication of my analysis has to do with solutions—solutions to some of the vexing problems incurred by neglecting the psychology of the individual. From the start, my argument will point toward conducting family therapy that has maximum impact.

Chapter 2, *The Problem of Change*, takes up the question of how change really occurs in family therapy. Family therapists have dealt with the charge that they neglect individual psychodynamics and psychopathology by saying that what they do works. Yes and no. I will argue that sudden and decisive change does occur in some cases, yet even in these cases change takes place only when individual family members think and act differently. Moreover, as I will demonstrate with clinical examples, quick change may not last.

The remaining chapters are given over entirely to practical suggestions on technique.

The first phase of therapy is crucial. It begins the process of understanding and lays the groundwork for new and more productive ways of living. In Chapter 3, *Interaction*, I describe procedures for working with the family in action by promoting interactions and by uncovering triangular sequences, which are often overlooked when the family present themselves to "the doctor."

Sometimes even forceful and repeated pressure to change family transactions does not work. Even after weeks of trying, for example, a woman may be unable to stop attacking her husband and provoking him to retaliate. (A paradoxical directive may interrupt the sequence, but if something motivates her to provoke a fight, this maneuver won't stick any more than direct coaching will.) In another case, a man may make good progress in opening up his feelings to his wife only to retreat again to hurt withdrawal in the face of one critical comment. Change may, and often does, occur in discontinuous jumps, but no jolt to the system will re-solve a person's narcissistic vulnerability. Sometimes, something beneath the surface seems to prevent family members from changing their ways. I will emphasize reasons why they won't (often because they do not accept that the only person you can change is yourself) and can't (because of unresolved conflict or psychopathology) and I will offer ways to deal with these intra-psychic limits *in action*.

In Chapter 4, *Empathy*, I explain the enormous therapeutic val-ue of a deep understanding of another's experience, and I demon-strate how to convey empathy in such a way that it becomes part of the family's own style. Empathy serves two critical functions in family therapy. One, it encourages family members to open up to each other. Two, it gives individuals the courage they need to explore more deeply their own private experience. One of the hardest jobs a therapist does is remaining in the background and allowing private and conflicted material to unfold.

Empathy and silent listening, of course, are not all that is re-quired of a family therapist. In Chapter 5, *Assessment and Reassess-ment*, I emphasize the need to formulate a coherent overview of the entire family and, when necessary, an in-depth understand-ing of its members. A common error in all forms of therapy is to focus on one piece of a problem, coaxing and goading something that may not budge because it is stuck in a larger context. Even family therapists make this error when they narrow their attention to "problem-maintaining solutions," without taking into consider-ation their broader role in the family and their deeper roots in contradictory promptings.

The rather ponderous title of this chapter is my attempt to express the fact that assessment isn't something that we get over and done with at the beginning of therapy. It starts but does not end there. In family therapy, assessment should be from the out-side in. First we look at triangular problems. If resolving these solves *the* problem, there may be no need to go further. But a complete therapist must be able to shift attention to dyadic inter-actions and, when need be, to individuals. In the final analysis, only individual family members can change. When they can't or won't, it is useful to ask ourselves, Why not?

In Chapter 6, *Interactional Psychodynamics,* and Chapter 7, *Object Relations and Psychopathology,* I deal with topics that many family therapists deliberately neglect. It is not that they doubt that people have private layers of experience, but rather that they believe it is superfluous to delve deeper into personality dynamics. On the other hand, those who do pay attention to the workings of the psyche often neglect the power of interaction. As a result, even those who offer "integrative" models of family therapy unwittingly help to perpetuate the either-or thinking that has long characterized our field. The title *Interactional Psychodynamics* is the key to my perspective. The interaction of personal and family dynamics is circular. Unconscious patterns of expectation are laid down interpersonally, at an early age (or various early ages). They continue to affect and, in turn, be affected by contemporary patterns of interaction.

In these two chapters I offer brief summaries of Freudian conflict theory, self psychology, and object relations theory. Those well versed in psychoanalytic theory may find these summaries a useful refresher, while those to whom psychodynamic thinking is alien may be surprised to discover how useful some of these ideas can be. Both groups, I hope, will see how family members live lives of systematic self-restriction as long as they are too busy defending against anxiety and guilt to risk changing the ways they live together.

My main emphasis is on how to incorporate these ideas into the practice of family therapy. What are the practical clinical situations where psychodynamics are relevant? Where might even systems purists need to know something about hidden motivation? In answering these questions, I illustrate with detailed clinical examples how to use psychodynamic understanding in the context of a thoroughly interactional brand of family therapy.

In Chapter 8, *Understanding,* I explore one of the great neglected resources of family therapy. As long as we think of persons as caught up in systemic interactions that they cannot comprehend or control, we are likely to give short shrift to helping individuals understand their role in family problems. Too bad, because the best way to help families overcome their problems and avoid future problems is to help family members understand that what others do is a function of what they do. I will explain how to make effective interpretations of circular interactions and of unsuspected personal motives.

One of the ironies of family therapy is that the same people who belittle the power of interpretation tend to overestimate their own power to transform reality with framing and reframing.

In Chapter 9, *Resistance*, I examine what may be the most critical subject in family therapy. Resistance to change is the fundamental problem in all definitive therapies. But there are two unfortunate errors in approaching resistance: thinking of it as willful negativism and thinking of it as a temporary block to be breached. While there are instances of each (the father who refuses to attend therapy, young parents reluctant to stand firm in the face of temper tantrums), people persist in resisting therapeutic change for good reason. Everything we do, we do for a reason. The reasons for resisting are systemic (the family tries to preserve its stability), psychological (individuals are vulnerable and frightened of certain kinds of new experience), *and* interactional (as therapists we often provoke resistance unnecessarily). I will explain how and why individuals resist change in family relationships and what to do about it.

Ironically, while therapy is an interpersonal enterprise, I work alone; yet in writing, which is a hard and solitary activity, I am greatly dependent on my friends for advice and support. I owe thanks to many friends and colleagues who read and commented on portions of this manuscript. Among them are: Elsa Efran, Jay Efran, Rich Simon, Jack O'Connor, John Thibodeau, and Irv Hassenfeld.

This is a special book for me. Unlike previous things I have written, which were devoted to summary and analysis of other people's work, this book represents my own way of thinking about and doing therapy. Writing it was at once more risky and more rewarding. If I have managed to convey some of the excitement I feel about bringing back the personal equation into family therapy, I will be well rewarded.

The Self in the System
EXPANDING THE LIMITS
OF FAMILY THERAPY

1

Finding the Family and
Losing the Self

When I first met the Templetons (as I shall call them) they were a couple at their wits' end, futilely remonstrating with their son, Raymond, who had confided in the school guidance counselor that he wanted to die. The guidance counselor, who had been working with Raymond for three years, considered this a serious threat and felt that more intensive help than he could provide was called for. Accordingly, Mrs. Templeton called the clinic to make an appointment for Raymond. The Templetons were a close-knit family, and so when the clinic secretary asked the whole family to come for the intake appointment, Mrs. Templeton was neither surprised nor displeased.

Present in the first interview were: Raymond, shy and awkward; Mrs. Templeton, frightened and eager for help; Mr. Templeton, worried about his son but uneasy about participating; and myself, newly armed with the precepts of structural family therapy. The pattern that unfolded was one familiar to all family therapists, and one that I had been trained to anticipate and modify. Mother and son were enmeshed (overinvolved, preoccupied with each other), and father was distant. Held a little too close a little too long by his mother, Raymond had been slow to make friends. In school he was always closer to the teachers, and now in his junior year he was beginning to fear that he was doomed to loneliness. His shyness had turned him inward, and the other kids considered him a "momma's boy" and "teacher's pet."

When his hopes of a new friendship with a girl were dashed, he felt he just couldn't bear it any longer. He thought she liked him, but she laughed when he asked her out. For that moment, every trace of hope and confidence in his life was destroyed. Her laughter had crushed his heart.

My strategy was the customary one of improving the father-son relationship as a wedge to separate the enmeshed mother-son dyad, and then subsequently to bring the husband and wife closer together. Things went reasonably well. They were all cooperative and my interventions met with little resistance. They understood and accepted the direction of my endeavors and the crisis passed. I was relieved and pleased, but soon began to see that my efforts to restructure the family weren't really working. Mrs. Templeton made a real attempt to restrain her involvement with Raymond and to spend more time with her husband. But what could she do when Raymond came home from school moody and needed someone to talk to? For his part, Raymond was happy to spend more time with his dad, especially doing what he considered masculine things, like making furniture and going bowling. Mr. Templeton tried, too. He liked spending time with Raymond, but he was often so tired at the end of the day that he didn't feel like doing anything, and he wasn't much of a talker.

I worried. Why couldn't Mr. Templeton be more involved with his son? What were his private thoughts? The truth is, I didn't have the faintest idea.

The problem in the Templeton family is one I had encountered many times before: a dysfunctional structure that stubbornly resisted my efforts to introduce change. Is the solution more and better techniques? I used to think so. My approach was guided by the view that family members' behavior was a product of their interactions. Modifying a family's interactions nearly always leads to change, and often that is enough to get the family back on track.

Sometimes, however, inducing variations in the family's pattern produces only superficial change in behavior without really changing the quality of their relationships. If one does not get through to the individuals, such changes usually do not last. In some cases altering the pattern is enough, but when a family's problems reflect not just habit but personalities, individuals may not change as easily as we like to think. The problem is that the behavioral changes we introduce may not last unless we also work with the hearts and minds of the individual persons who make up the family. The presenting problem may recur or other ones may arise, not because of that old bugaboo, "symptom substitution," or because the family "needs a symptom," but because family members have not been moved to make lasting changes in themselves or in the way they relate to each other.

To reach Mr. Templeton I made allies of his wife and son: I encouraged her to pull back and give the father and son a chance to develop a relationship, and I taught Raymond how to befriend his dad by fitting in with his habits and moods. What I began to realize, though, was that to reach Mr. Templeton I would have to understand him better. The odd thing is that I wasn't used to trying to understand the individual members of the families I treated. Odd because I used to think a great deal about personalities when I practiced individual psychotherapy. And over the years I have thought a great deal about the personalities in my own family as I have tried to apply my family therapy experience to make me a better husband and father. But I just didn't think this way as a family therapist.

We tend to compartmentalize our understanding. When we talk to individuals privately, we generally listen with empathy. We care about how they feel, so we ask, and we listen. However, when we see families, we take a different view. We think about interactional patterns; that's what we look for and that's what we see. As soon as we categorize something—"it's disengagement"—it's hard to see it as anything else, hard to know how the person feels.

Moreover, with very little effort we tend to be more sensitive to what we ourselves have been through. I, for example, had some feeling for what it means to be a shy and lonely teenager. But I had very little idea of what was going on inside Mr. Templeton's head. Neither my deliberate attention to family structure nor my own reflexive ability to identify with familiar experience prepared me to understand his position. Only later, several months after I had terminated with the family, when Mr. Templeton came to see me by himself, did I begin to understand.

Family therapy has come a long way in a short time. Yet while we have expanded our understanding of family systems, we have moved too far away from the psychology of the individual. Just as I was unprepared to understand Mr. Templeton's difficulty with intimacy, family therapy as a discipline has neglected the self in the system.

Although each of us is embedded in systems, we are also separate. We are selves, individual persons with identities. The systems of which we are a part influence us in profound and unseen ways, but we are also, more or less, independent centers of initiative. As long as my efforts with the Templetons were confined to the structure of their interactions, I overlooked the motivation for their interactional problems. I saw only part of their reality—the observable interactions. What I did not see and, therefore, did not affect was their individual subjective realities.

Overemphasizing the family structure paints a passive picture of the self as caught up in a system that it is blind and powerless to resist. In some ways, people are remarkably elastic; in certain key respects, however, we remain consistently who we are despite changes in context. The self is a personality consisting of a pattern of traits that is deeply etched and difficult to modify. These ingrained and habitual ways of functioning emerge from an individual's entire developmental history. Whether or not a family will master or succumb to problems depends in part on the flexibility of its organization. But this flexibility is also a product of individual personalities, like Mr. Templeton's—a tightly-knit organization of attitudes, habits, and emotions that affect his capacity to cope with life's difficulties.

THE SELF IN THE SYSTEM

Once a radical new departure, family therapy has revolutionized our thinking and established itself as a dominant force in mental health. Family therapists have taught us that the family is more than a collection of separate individuals; it is a system, an organic whole whose parts function in a way that transcends their separate characteristics. We have learned to see the unity of the system by standing back, blurring our focus on individuals in order to see the whole. Unfortunately, in the process of stepping back far enough to see the whole system, family therapists sometimes lose sight of the individual.

Family therapists recognized that people are embedded in a social context, and thus corrected the psychology of separateness. But each of us is *both* separate and embedded. Neither a psychology of separateness nor one of embeddedness alone is fully adequate to explain human behavior or to serve as a guide for clinical practice.

Although it is not possible to understand people without taking into account their social context, notably the family, it is misleading to limit the focus to the surface of interactions—to social behavior divorced from inner experience. Personal relationships exist in the intersubjective experience of the participants, an experience shaped as much by memory and desire as by contemporary facts. The people we relate to are made of flesh and blood, but we filter our experience of them through cloudy images of expectation. Some of these expectations are built up over the course of a couple's, or a parent and child's, history together. Other images are ingrained in childhood. A woman like Mrs. Templeton who becomes enmeshed with her children is reacting not only to her husband's distance, but also to internalized images of what it means to be female and what it means to be a mother. Working with the whole system means not only considering all the members of the family, but also taking into account all of the personal dimensions of their experience.

Human behavior can be understood as embedded in a concentric series of systems: the structure of the mind, the nuclear family, the extended family, the community, the nation, and so on. A full description of human problems takes into account actors, behavior, and context. Clearly, the family is one of the most useful contexts within which to understand and influence behavior. But it is not the only one. Looking outward we may discover economic and social forces that must be reckoned with; looking inward we often find personal rigidities which will not readily yield to interactional influences.

Intervening at the level of the family context is often the quickest way to proceed. But not always. If a little girl refuses to go to school, the "phobia" may not be inside her head. It may be that her mother cannot accept the girl's going off to school and leaving her alone all day. On the other hand, the child may be bullied on the school bus or intimidated in the classroom. Family therapists have become adept at recognizing the complicating effects of diverse social agencies exerting uncoordinated influences on family problems. But they are less likely to recognize complicating dynamics of individuals—personal conflict, psychopathology, and failures of nerve.

The problems of people in crisis go deeper than systems analyses suggest. Each of us has a stable, relatively fixed personality, which includes, in addition to a set of coping skills, a matrix of enduring, though not always apparent, problems—our own inner anxieties and unconscious conflicts. The frustrated need for reassurance, the profound self-doubts, and the fear of natural human impulses are not merely the product of ongoing interactions. These are the results of earliest experience.

The hidden parts of our personalities are not simply suppressed. Since we are not isolated units, much of what we hide away from ourselves is projected onto other members of our families. A father smiles despite himself while discussing his son's delinquent behavior. A woman complains that her jealous husband won't let her spend time alone with her friends. These are signs of disowned impulses and restraints. The father's smile reveals his secret pleasure in the boy's rebellion; the woman's submission to her husband's demands suggests that she herself is conflicted about taking time for herself. Will negotiating with her husband resolve the woman's inner prohibitions against self-expression and pleasure? Probably not. If she recognizes her own doubts and fears, will her husband generously accede to her new self-expressiveness? Not likely. These impasses, like most human problems, exist in the psychology of persons *and* are played out in their interactions.

As I will argue, family therapy has moved too far from the psychology of the individual, resulting in a wave of esoteric theorizing and a proliferation of mechanistic, highly technical interventions. Family therapy does require new ways of thinking, but we need not abandon hard-won insights or common sense to do so. These insights are the accumulated understandings of our colleagues who use psychological models to analyze and treat human problems. Common sense tells us that, though we are joined together with others, we are still separate persons. The self is a center of initiative, not independent of others, but not determined by them either. This is not just an abstract point. If we do not give heed to the selves that make up families, we miss the reality of those we seek to help and we lose the leverage necessary to make them partners in a joint endeavor. As we shall see, family therapy's lack of attention to the self in the system has often led to unfortunate excesses in theory and technique.

At this point I will return to Mr. Templeton's story to illustrate that although family members' lives are so intertwined that what one does affects what the others do, change may be slow in coming as long as the what-one-does is deeply ingrained in habit.

Why couldn't Mr. Templeton be more involved with his son? Because he was busy fending off what he felt was his family's pressure to take over his life and swallow up his privacy.

He was a person who had never learned to let go, to float on the currents of the day. As a young man, he worked out a pattern of serious purpose and hard work that helped him achieve his professional goals, while at the same time compensating for his shyness and masking his anxiety. He organized his life so that nothing got in the way of success; he controlled his schedule the way he controlled his feelings, to control his uneasiness. Oh, he was capable of being sociable, alright. But on his time and on his terms. If he knew he was going to a party, he was prepared to make conversation and have fun. If he knew he was going on a date, he was ready to be open and close. But he was none of these things on the spur of the moment. Casual conversations and unexpected company were intrusions; fooling around and playing were frivolous. He didn't have time and, though he didn't know it, he didn't have the flexibility.

Self-containment and carefully rationed sociability may work for a single person; it *does not* work for a married one. When they met, he enjoyed her attention and she enjoyed giving it. He stood for a calmness and seriousness that she had missed and longed for. From the start of the marriage, though, she wanted more—more time, more attention, and more involvement. Why couldn't he understand? He wanted to be alone. Why couldn't she understand? It was a contest of wits and of wills. Isn't it a pity how often marriage, begun as a magnetic attraction, often becomes a contest of conflicting desires?

Then the babies came, adorable but consuming. They wanted to be held, fed, played with, tickled, cuddled, carried, changed. They reached out to him and he was won over, again enchanted. But they were too much. With their imperious demands they used up his tolerance. Gradually, they learned that mommy was more responsive, more available than daddy. And so a pattern, familiar to family therapists, emerged: the enmeshed mother and disengaged father. Sometimes he felt guilty when he pushed them away. He knew he did it, knew it while he was doing it, but he couldn't stop himself.

He was not a tranquil person, so he arranged to have his home a tranquil place. He was anxious and uneasy, so he favored preoccupying distractions. It made him good at working but bad at sitting around. At the end of the day, he wanted to take off his necktie, sit down, and read the paper. But just as he came home, the children were winding down like little clocks, fussing for their supper, quarreling with each other, and competing for his attention. It seemed that they saved up their disasters for him. "Billy scraped his knee." "Raymond broke your lamp." "The cat made doo-doo on the rug." Shit! why couldn't they leave him alone?

The family therapy brought about a short change in the pattern, long enough for Raymond to forget about killing himself; after a while, however, the familiar pattern reasserted itself. Mr. Templeton again pulled into himself. Knowing what he was doing made him feel guilty, yet it didn't stop his endless moping isolation. If this pattern were specific and limited to this case, a discussion might follow of dynamics and history. How did he become so anxious and how could it be resolved? And what about his wife's experience, and the polarizing effect they had on each other? The Templetons' story is so common, however, that it raises general issues. How do we bring about change? And how are our efforts related to the experience of the persons in the families we treat?

One might suspect I am advocating a return to individual psychotherapy—a reversion to pre-family therapy days when the primary forces shaping and maintaining behavior were believed to be located within individuals, and treatment was always segregated from families. Once, many therapists insisted—and many still do—that the only way to get to the bottom of human problems is to isolate them in the therapeutic relationship, a controlled environment where the therapist can serve as a blank screen, or provide unconditional positive regard, or reeducation, as he or she sees fit. But we do not get to the bottom of ourselves in isolation. No, I do not advocate a return to radical individualism. Nor do I intend to say merely that sometimes individual psychotherapy may be required to treat certain problems. My point is this: To provide effective and lasting treatment we need to be able to understand and motivate individuals, as well as to manipulate their interactions.

As we shall see, individual psychotherapy has inherent limits, which family therapy was developed to counteract. What family therapy added was an appreciation of, and a means of dealing with, the social forces acting on the lives of individuals with problems. Unfortunately, while adding this social dimension, family therapy has subtracted from our understanding of the individual

by repudiating depth psychology. In the following historical review we will see how and why family therapy came into being. We
will also see how certain key developments led to a fascination
with overly abstract theories and an overemphasis on techniquism. A brief tour of the history of psychotherapy and of family
therapy's divergence will demonstrate how these two approaches
became rivals in isolation from each other. While family therapists
were pursuing their discoveries with proud iconoclastic zeal, they
indulged in certain radical excesses that led to a growing isolation
from mainstream psychiatry. Ironically, the history that begins
with a naive neglect of systems forces culminates with a similarly
naive neglect of psychological forces.

PSYCHOTHERAPEUTIC SANCTUARY

Once psychotherapy was a private enterprise, conducted in
isolation from everyday pressures and routines. The consulting
room was a place of healing, yes, but equally important a place of
sanctuary, a refuge from a troubled and troubling world.

Buffeted about in love and work, unable to find comfort and
solace elsewhere, adults come to therapy looking to find lost satisfaction and meaning. Parents, worried about misbehavior, reticence, or lack of achievement, send their children for guidance
and direction. In many ways psychotherapy displaced the family's function of resolving the difficulties of everyday life. Once we
hid inside our family shells from the harshness of the outside
world; now psychotherapy is likely to provide our haven in a
heartless world.[1]

Plagued by anxiety and depression, or merely troubled and
uncertain, people turn toward psychotherapy, looking for help
and consolation. In the process, they often turn away from the
irritants that propel them into therapy. Chief among these aggravations are unhappy relationships—with friends and lovers, *and*
with the family. Our disorders are private ailments. When we
retreat to the safety of a synthetic relationship, the last thing most
of us want is to take our families with us.

The great healers shared and formalized this claustral approach—not only to provide a safe haven, but also to create a special atmosphere within which to practice their art. When Freud ventured to explore the dark forces of the mind, he needed a private setting, safe enough for the buried ghosts of childhood fantasy to emerge. To bring about cure through self-knowledge, he developed a strict code for practice. Free association, the couch, and the 50-minute hour were the instruments of that practice; but the essential ingredient, the precondition for analysis, was the totally private, one-to-one relationship between doctor and patient. All others were excluded.

Psychotherapists recognized the importance of family life and relationships in shaping the personality, but assumed that these forces were internalized and that intrapsychic personality dynamics become the dominant forces controlling behavior. Treatment can and should, therefore, be directed at the person and his or her personal makeup. This view of persons as separate entities, with families acting on them, is consistent with the way we experience ourselves. We recognize the influence of intimates—especially as obligation and constraint—but it is hard, very hard, to see that we are embedded in a network of relationships, that we are part of something larger than ourselves.

THE FAMILY AS AN ORGANIC WHOLE

Several converging developments in the 1950s led to a new view, namely that the family is a living system, an organic whole.[2] Hospital psychiatrists noticed that often when a patient improved someone else in the family got worse. As in the children's game of hide-and-seek, it does not matter so much who is "It" as it does that someone take the part in order for the game to continue. Few blamed the family for outright malevolence, and yet there was an invidious undercurrent to these observations. The discovery that symptoms move around in families was subtly rephrased: The family *needs* its symptoms.

Although practicing clinicians in hospitals and child guidance clinics prepared the way for family therapy, the most important breakthroughs were achieved in the 1950s by workers who were scientists first, healers second. The psychotherapist is a prescriber of a worldview and, like it or not, an actor in and a proponent of a social and political system. It is significant, but in retrospect not surprising, that the shift from seeing the family as a collection of separate selves to seeing it as an organic whole took place in the context of research on schizophrenia. The researcher is an iconoclast, a seeker of new discoveries, ready to challenge the accepted view of things. Those who spend their days treating psychological suffering are usually too busy and too harried applying familiar remedies to step back and reconsider the whole enterprise.

In Palo Alto, Gregory Bateson, Jay Haley, John Weakland, Don Jackson, and William Fry, studying communication, discovered that schizophrenia made sense in the context of pathological family communication. The patient is not crazy in some autonomous way, but an understandable extension of a crazy family environment. At Yale, Theodore Lidz found a striking pattern of instability and conflict in the families of schizophrenics. Family patterns of *marital skew* (pathological balance) and *marital schism* (open conflict) were more important than the psychology of the individual in shaping psychopathology. Murray Bowen, at the National Institute of Mental Health, hospitalized whole families for observation and treatment. In so doing, he implicitly located the problem of schizophrenia in an *undifferentiated family ego mass* and even extended it beyond the nuclear family to three generations. Lyman Wynne, at NIMH and later Rochester, linked intrapsychic psychopathology with the family context by saying that communication deviance in the family transmits thought disorder. *Pseudomutuality* described schizophrenic families as supraindividual entities and *the rubber fence* was a psychological membrane, like the skin, surrounding a living organism.

The excitement generated by these observations blurred the distinction between what the research teams observed and what they concluded. What they observed was that the behavior of schizophrenics *fit* with their families; what they concluded was far more momentous. First, it was implied that since schizophrenia fit (made sense) in the context of the family, then the family *must be the cause* of schizophrenia. In logic this inference is called "Jumping to Conclusions." A second conclusion, still with us, was even more important. All of these concepts—pseudomutuality, undifferentiated family ego mass—began to be seen as products of a "system" rather than as features of persons who share certain qualities because they live together. Thus was born a new creature, "the family system."

In retrospect, progress seems almost inevitable. A fact becomes known and in short order it is developed and put to use. No sooner did clinicians observe the complex interdigitation of family and patient than they made the family itself the patient.

Once the family became the patient, there was a need for new ways to think about and treat human problems. Two pivotal figures were responsible for brilliant advances in both directions. Unfortunately, the theoretical advances of one have led to overly abstract theorizing that has gotten too far away from an understanding of persons, while the technical artistry of the other has spawned a fascination with techniquism among his followers.

The Anthropologist and the Alienist

Though neither could be considered the founder of family therapy, Gregory Bateson and Milton Erickson had as profound an influence as any. But they represent two very different kinds of influence. Bateson, the anthropologist, was a man of science, a man of ideas. Erickson was a practitioner, a man of the healing arts. Moreover, their personal styles differed diametrically. Bateson was a scholar committed to detached observation; his goal was to observe and describe, with as little intrusion upon the data as possible. In contrast, Erickson believed passionately in intense engagement; his was the politics of control.

Erickson's legacy had both a positive and a negative influence on family therapy. On the positive side is his pragmatic, problem-solving approach, from which we get the important idea to offer help and then get out, letting families get on about their business, instead of having to incorporate a therapist as an expensive crutch. But Erickson's dazzling technical artistry also inspired a tradition of the quick fix, done *to* rather than done *with* families.

In the early years the search for understanding prevailed; today the pursuit of strategic influence is in the ascendency and Milton Erickson's stock has never been higher.

The anthropologist and the alienist, Bateson and Erickson, epitomize two traditions that represent a dynamic tension in our field. Bateson, the observer and theoretician, showed the way to understanding by careful, nonintrusive observation. Inspired by his anthropological approach, early family therapists spent a good deal of time listening and watching. They were willing to observe and to learn because they knew they were in *terra incognita* and they felt under no obligation to arrive armed with solutions. Unfortunately, many of us have gotten away from this receptive openness. So much has been written about family dynamics that we feel we should know what's going on, even before we look. And knowing in advance what we will find makes it all the easier to apply set strategies of intervention. Sadly, I encounter this posture even in beginning students, who take on attitudes of certainty to cover their insecurity.

Bateson is also the patron saint of the intellectual wing of family therapy. His ideas were so pregnant with possibility that they are still being explored in the most sophisticated writing in the field. Family therapists are beneficiaries of Bateson's example as a thinker who brought together ideas from many sources. On the other hand, we have followed him into realms of abstract systems thinking that sometimes makes us lose sight of persons and their problems. There was always a touch of the esoteric in Bateson's writing. Far-reaching ideas yes, but often couched in unnecessarily exotic language.

Why have family therapists gravitated toward Bateson's intellectual distance and Erickson's manipulative approach? What is it that we are so ready to get away from? Families. Not just any families, but rather the usually quite disturbed and disturbing ones who come to us. They are needy and so pressure us to take over. But they are frightened and so resist our direction. From the first, family therapists have had a paradoxical relationship to their clients: We are entreated for solutions, but confounded by obdurate inflexibility. Families may feel helpless, but they stubbornly resist change; healers need strong medicine because families are powerful. The family is our client *and* our opponent.

THE UNDECLARED WAR

Therapists first encountered the family system as a powerful adversary. Although we came to think of asylums as places of cruelty and detention, they were originally built to rescue the insane from persecution by their relatives and neighbors, from being locked away and tortured in the family attic.[3] Freud's discoveries indicted families as seducers of innocent children, and later as agents of cultural repression, the source of all guilt and anxiety. Since the natural child is oriented toward pure pleasure, the family must stand for antipleasure; the sheer joy of self-expression is choked off by sinister projections of parental superegos. If we grow up a little bit neurotic, unconsciously afraid of our natural drives, whom else do we blame except our parents?

Hospital psychiatrists also perceived patients as victimized by their families. Accordingly, except for purposes of footing the bill, families were kept at arm's length. Child guidance workers approached domestic life with a built-in prejudice. Their vision that flawed relations in the family held the key to psychopathology was blurred by their loyalty to their child patients, with whom they identified. Bent on saving the child, they saw mothers as enemies to be overcome and fathers as peripheral figures to be ignored. Researchers in child guidance clinics studied parental psychopathology as the cause of problems in children, and accused mothers of a suffocating influence on their offspring. David Levy denounced *maternal overprotectiveness,* and Frieda Fromm-Reichmann coined one of the most damning phrases in the literature of psychiatry, the *schizophrenogenic mother.*

The advent of family therapy may have been a scientific advance, but it also had moral and political dimensions. Previously, madness was ignored, ostracized, or locked up. Now it was located in the family where responsibility could be shared and cure made a group problem. Family therapists rescued schizophrenics from psychiatric invalidation by demonstrating that their crazy talk made sense as a desperate solution to desperate family situations. It wasn't the patient but the family system that was deranged. Family therapy aimed to humanize mental illness, but it created a nonhuman, mechanistic entity—the system—to do so.

In their efforts to make individual family members autonomous agents in their own right, practicing psychotherapists ran smack up against powerful family opposition to personal growth. The individual may want to get better, but the family may need someone to play the sick role. Some families apparently require a "scapegoat" to maintain their equilibrium. The patient's "sickness" is prerequisite to the family's precarious "health." This led Don Jackson to characterize families as "rule-governed, homeostatic systems."[4] The description of these conservative forces fostered the belief that domestic life imprisons people in predetermined roles.

The story of the family's resistance to the individual's growth is so familiar and the systems explanation so much a part of our thinking that it is difficult to observe this situation unfettered by the paradigms of family therapy. But we could describe what Jackson and others observed without invoking a new, nonhuman species. Improving psychotherapy patients met with family resistance because their intimates were used to them as they were—guilty, self-effacing, depressed, masochistic. Family and friends reacted badly to the new, more assertive persons, thus punishing them for changing. The changing, developing patients were a threat to the defensive order of things; small wonder they were attacked. If they changed back, as many did, it could have been described as regression, defeat, cowardice, or a failure of the therapist to help work through the changes. Instead, attention (as well as blame) was shifted to the family: "The family needs a sick member." Little noticed was how this description portrayed the recovered patient as helpless and passive. Instead of seeing a flight from progress as an appeasement of others, we saw it as inevitable.

The Bateson group's observations were objective and scientific, yet their language for describing family systems was combative and bellicose, often suggesting willful opposition: double bind, identified patient, family scapegoat, binder, victim, and so on. In Toward a Theory of Schizophrenia,[5] Bateson, Jackson, Haley, and Weakland argued that schizophrenia is a logical consequence of adapting to a context rife with conflicting messages; it is learned as a result of accommodating to the interactional demands of life in certain families. In plain English: Families drive people mad with their maddening communication. The point these investigators wished to make was that schizophrenia was a product of family organization. In the process, however, they emphasized the destructive power of families. Initially, this was expressed in the terms "binder" (usually the mother) and "victim." Subsequently, the suggestion of linear causation was corrected, but the belief of the times was that the family was the villain.

The negative attitude toward the family was not explicit and therefore was hard to refute. No one came forward to defend the institution of the family against its accusers because the charges were not plain. The idea that families were malevolent put family therapists in an adversarial stance—but it was unproclaimed combat. Jay Haley made the critique of the family even more pointed: What we think of as domestic tranquility is often a facade beneath which is a constant struggle for strategic advantage. Because these families were at once rigid—holding fast to their own ways—and slippery—hard to pin down—interviewing them became a struggle for control. Haley and Weakland, frustrated by evasions and shifting statements, sought Erickson's advice about how to pin patients down and force them to speak directly. The following remark from Haley betrays the adversarial attitude of some of the early family therapists. "You can catch them sometimes; if they have to contradict everybody, you can trap them in a contradictory impasse."[6]

Later, Bateson was honest enough to say what others had apparently felt when he confessed that he was "bored and disgusted" by "the dumb cruelty of the families which (as we used to say) 'contained' schizophrenia."[7]

The attack on the family found its most strident voice in R. D. Laing. What was presented as a humanistic and reformist protest came out as a virulent assault. The helpless child is a prisoner

whose only recourse is to develop a divided self, offering a compliant "false self" to appease his jailors, while hiding away the real
self that their tyranny threatens to annihilate.[8] Although Laing's
portrayal of the family as villain was dramatized to extremes—the
"concentration camp" of modern society—it was enormously
popular. The enthusiastic reception of Laing's assault on the institution of the family says something about our propensity for
blaming our families for our own self-doubt and uncertainty.

Even when family therapists got past the naive idea that patients are innocent victims of malevolent kinfolk, they felt themselves in opposition to families who obstinately resisted therapeutic efforts to change them. Don Jackson captured this combative
spirit when he said, "the peculiar communication devices the
family uses can be in turn used against them for therapeutic purposes. . . . "[9] Why "against them"?

This us-against-them attitude is a consequence of deemphasiz-
ing the human side of human beings. Sometimes we must recognize collective entities—family systems, communities, nations—
but we need not dehumanize them by forgetting that they are
made up of individuals. When we are sympathetic to and respectful of the individuals who make up families, we make them our
allies not our enemies.

Family therapists have learned to see nagging and withdrawal
as circular, but they must also learn to see them as human.
Thoughtful clinicians need to see through the nagging to the pain
behind it, and to understand the anxiety that motivates withdrawal. In other words, to the attitude of the systems thinker we must
add the attitude of a compassionate helper. Some apparently feel
that a sympathetic and solicitous attitude will lose them leverage.
It won't.

Neither total sympathetic immersion in a family's troubles nor
dispassionate distance puts us in the best position to help. As we
shall see, therapy goes best when we strike a balance between
emotional absorption, which renders us sympathetic but ineffec-
tual, and the distanced position of a systems engineer. The peril of
an excess of sympathy is losing perspective and feeling helpless;

the peril of authoritative distance is that it places the therapist in a parental position. The corollary is that clients are children, whose duty is to obey, but whose impulse is to rebel.

FAMILY THERAPY TAKES ON THE PSYCHIATRIC ESTABLISHMENT

Not only were family therapists avenging knights bent on rescuing innocent victims by slaying family dragons, they were also crusaders carrying out a holy war against the psychodynamic nonbelievers who still held most of the power. Inscribed on their banner was "General Systems Theory."

Outnumbered and surrounded by hostile critics, the champions of family therapy fought to win a place for their beliefs. Perhaps it was the vehemence of the resistance they encountered that pushed them into sounding somewhat self-righteous. Family therapists saw themselves as forward-looking modern progressives, in contrast to the antiquated, entrenched powers of psychiatry with their fossilized view of mental disorder, namely that emotional problems are firmly embedded inside people's heads. John Weakland demonstrates the attitude that the enlightened crusaders took toward the ignorant psychology of the past: "Put bluntly, a sizable part of our work on communication now appears related to digging ourselves out of individual-centered, depth-psychological views of behavior, problems, and therapy in which we originally were embedded, rather than to any elaborate creation of new ideas."[10] If the war against the family was undeclared, that against the psychiatric establishment was not.

Between the new crusaders and traditional psychiatrists there was agreement about nothing, not about the nature of the beast—"mental illness" or "communications deviance," "neurosis" or "family projection process," "personal problems" or "dysfunctional families," or whatever it should be called—nor about how to administer cure, analysis, or solution. Underlying these disagreements were fundamental conflicts about who should control the healing function.

The hostility between family therapists and psychodynamic therapists is primarily a thing of the past, related to a struggle for turf. Family therapy became firmly established in the 1960s, setting up its own training institutions and demonstrating effectiveness with some of the most vexing problems in psychiatry, including anorexia nervosa and acute psychosis in young adults. One reason family therapy gained acceptance from the psychiatric establishment is that it carved out its domain in areas traditionally neglected by the psychiatric establishment—services to children and the poor. Even the most critical opponents found it easier to accept family therapy when they no longer felt in competition for the same clientele. An unfortunate legacy of this early antagonism, however, is a continuing separation between the two schools of thought. We now have peace, but it is unfortunately only peaceful coexistence rather than respect and mutual enrichment.

As we shall see, family therapists can learn much about the families they treat by studying the latest developments in psychodynamics, especially in object relations theory and self psychology. Sometimes—not always, but sometimes—when a dysfunctional family transaction does not respond to our interactional interventions, it helps to focus on the individual. If we are going to see beneath the surface of interactions, we need to know where to look. Common sense and compassion for individuals are not enough.

In families, almost no extensive action is the simple result of group processes. Virtually all action is to some extent self-directed and planned. The process of interaction, which seems to take on a life of its own, is the product of personalities—personalities with ingrained expectations and hidden longings. Object relations theory sheds light on the nature of those expectations by demonstrating how early family experience becomes structured in the mind, organizing subsequent experience and giving private meaning to public interpersonal events. A man who grew up with a nagging mother has an inner image—object—of women as powerful and critical. This inner image will affect how he approaches and responds to women even years later. Held harshly by a rigid fear of nebulous disapproval, he becomes compliant and overeager to please—though perhaps unconsciously angry and resentful. It will certainly make him react all out of proportion to real criticism. Sometimes, the man arguing with his wife turns into a little boy screaming at his mother.

Both self psychology and object relations theory deal, in different ways, with the fundamental human need for attachment. While object relations theory deals with relatively fixed predispositions laid down early in life, self psychology deals with longings for attention and admiration which, because they are so tender, are so often suppressed. Underneath their tough-minded maturity or seeming detachment, most grown-ups are yearning for missing understanding. The unsuspected power of these longings makes some people clinging and dependent; others, too afraid of disappointment or rejection, seek satisfaction outside the family.

The longing to be special leads many people into a passionate pursuit of success, often neglecting their families in the process. The protean men and women of the eighties spend as much of their time in the office wars as at home with their families. Still, it is more often men who are driven to reach in vain for the brass ring of success—as though success had an effect like alcohol and they were drunk on adulation. The disengaged fathers we try so hard to lure back into their families may be too caught up chasing a fantasy to catch on to the real love that is available to them.

For all the light they have shed on the human condition, family therapists have also contributed to the false dichotomy of self and family. In order to work with families, these clinicians often suspend their awareness of the self. They enshrine the system in theory and in practice. As a result, the concept of the system has taken on mythic proportions.

I will now examine the development of systems thinking in family therapy to demonstrate how and why we have wandered off into unnecessary obscurantism and neglected the individual. I stress this point because I believe that it is time to rehumanize our notion of the family system.

FROM METAPHOR TO MYTH

The shift from working with individuals to working with families was discontinuous and required new ways of thinking. Therapists, unused to seeing whole families interacting, eagerly imported nonclinical models to help them conceptualize patterned interactions. Some, like John E. Bell, used group dynamics theory to work with families; but families turn out to be uniquely different from other small groups. Unlike groups of strangers, families have a history and a future together, which results in a sticky coherence and a shared set of assumptions so ingrained as to be invisible. Meanwhile, Bateson and his theoretically inclined colleagues turned to more abstract models that offered profound if recondite analogies of family life. Cybernetics and general systems theory provided useful metaphors, helping clinicians become aware of the large movements that we rarely appreciate in our own experience.

When we are puzzled by complex events, it helps to have some formula for ordering them. I remember the first time I saw a soccer game. It looked fun but chaotic; there didn't appear to be any order to it. Then somebody told me, "It's like basketball." "Oh, I get it!" Suddenly, I could see that the players weren't just running around pell mell; they moved up and down the field, passing the ball, avoiding interception, trying to put the ball in the opponents' basket—I mean goal.

Soccer is close enough to basketball so that using one as an analogue to the other seems trivial. More interesting things happen when we choose metaphors to make a point. The more complex and scientific the metaphor, the more likely it is to become institutionalized, and the more likely it is to carry side effects that were never imagined. This is true of many of the systems metaphors of family therapy.

Early family therapists used the concepts of general systems theory as a metaphor and a model of family functioning. Describing the family as a system helped them to see that a group of interacting personalities can function like one being, a coherent composite that behaves as an irreducible unit. Families then were said to be like systems in that the behavior of every member of the system is related to and dependent on the behavior of all the others. The triumph of this metaphor was so complete that we now take its presuppositions for granted. We no longer stare at family interactions with naive incomprehension; but when we compress them into a framework we impose, we are no longer free to let things be what they are. Now we fit events to a myth.

A myth is a construction that we forgot we constructed. Eventually, we cannot imagine any other way of thought. We forget that thinking of families as systems is just one way of thinking, and we take it as a fundamental reality. "Wait a minute," some readers may protest, "the family *really is* a system!" The possibility of debate about whether the family is a system or a collection of interacting personalities may leave us wondering, how do we discover reality? The truth is we don't discover reality, we invent it.

What do we see when we interview a family? Mrs. Jones complains about her three-year-old son, "His nursery school teacher says he's a behavior problem; he gets into trouble a lot, hitting and biting the other kids. *I* think he's very mature for his age. He's *so* smart. He wants to do everything his way. He argues with us whenever we try to say no." Meanwhile, the little boy crumples up drawing paper and throws it at his father. The father sits off to the side, ill at ease, apparently uninterested. When the boy takes a Pound Puppy away from his younger sister and she starts to cry, the father says, "Give it back," and when the boy ignores him he turns to complain to his wife.

What's going on here? It's a chaotic scene, but when we filter all of this through our selective perception, we see what we look for. Perhaps it is a "hyperactive child," or "poor parenting skills," or "a cross-generational coalition." The reality we discover is a construction of our own experience and pet theories. Young therapists, for example, often see children as victimized by cruel parents; Bowenians see triangles, structuralists see enmeshment, and brief therapists see families trying solutions that make things worse.

Every school of family therapy has its preferred way of describing family systems. Differences among these "brand name" constructions are often exaggerated to emphasize the uniqueness and originality of a particular approach, but underneath are a set of widely shared assumptions that most family therapists take as gospel truth.

THE CORE CONCEPTS OF FAMILY THERAPY

The postulates of systems theory are articles of faith to most family therapists. All of these ideas contain part of a useful reality, but each one also helps to obscure the reality of individual experience. They are so widely shared that they become confused with facts. Still they are assumptions and they have problematic as well as useful implications. No longer do we approach family interviews neutrally; we come armed with preconceptions that co-create the problems we see.

Among the core concepts of family therapy are the following:

1. *The family is the context of human problems and, like other groups, families have emergent properties that make them different from individual persons.* When we recognize that individuals have an exterior reality, we should not lose sight of the fact that they also have interior realities. The emergent properties of family groups affect but do not determine what people do. A woman whose husband and children pressure her into the role of selfless caregiver can either comply or refuse.

To act responsibly as selves and to encourage responsible action in our clients we must distinguish between that which individual persons *do* and that which merely *happens*, irrespective of their own agency. It is true that family influences are often obscure, but so also are our own intentions and our own actions obscure. We can best expand the range and freedom of human action by taking into account the two-sided reality of social influence and individual initiative. Moreover, these two realities (more properly, two ways of looking at reality) are never independent. Personal behavior and private states of mind have social antecedents and contexts, but the person is as much an organizer as an effect of those around him or her.

2. *Process, not content, reveals what is most significant about family interactions.* It is quite right that process, the way people interact, tells us more about how they function as a group than does what they talk about. Attending to the process of family conversations has a clarifying effect. Instead of getting lost in the details, we step back and see how they work. But the idea of process carries some additional baggage, namely that there is a superordinate group mechanism that is more significant and more powerful than the individual members of the group.

A useful distinction that captures the difference between my point of view and this one is that between *praxis* and *process.* Praxis refers to the engagement of an active subject with his or her environment ("a deed" in Greek), whereas process refers to the passive undergoing of an inevitable sequence of events by an object ("having occurred" from the Latin). "Resistance" and "negative feedback" are process; "avoiding frank discussion of how to discipline the children" and "giving up a new job to appease a spouse who is afraid to move" are praxis.

I am claiming that praxis is the more appropriate model for clinical work, and that mainstream family therapy follows an implicit process model. When people are seen as subject to processes (systemic forces) which go on regardless of their own agency and powers of initiation, they become victims instead of masters of their fate. From the notion of process we should gain an appreciation of regulating group influences without losing faith in the individual's ability to transform him or herself.

Exclusive focus on process also denies the validity of competing interests and the real basis for conflict. Family quarrels do not necessarily clear up when the combatants are taught how to communicate ("I statements" and all the rest). The weary combatants themselves know that the emotional ferocity of their arguments far exceeds the substantive issues, which could often be solved by a little logic, humor, or common sense. But this animosity is not just a by-product of "poor communication skills"; it is not an accident. In the warfare between husband and wife or between teenager and parents, the occasions for skirmish may be inconsequential, but the conflict is not.

The way a mother and daughter argue may complicate their differences, but teaching them to fight fair will not automatically resolve the differences. Focusing on process occasionally leads therapists to ignore the presenting problem. This danger is inherent in those therapies that look at underlying family dynamics (structure) and multiple generational process. When we shift from content to process, we see the horizontal flow of family life, but if we ignore the vertical dimension of personal experience, what appears to be clarity is, in fact, reductionistic.

3. Dyadic and triadic models of behavior are better than monadic ones. Family therapists discovered that the actions of one person can often be understood more fully in terms of interactions between that person and others. A child's fearfulness may not spring from anything inside the child as much as it does from the child's relationship with an anxious or punitive mother. But that dyad, in turn, may turn out to be part and parcel of a triad: The child's behavior reflects the relationship between mother and child, which is related to the relationship between husband and wife. Most people think of relationships in two-person terms: husband and wife, father and son, I-thou. But, as Murray Bowen pointed out, when we have problems in a relationship, we tend, automatically, to triangle in a third person. Such triadic thinking has practical as well as theoretical advantages. The quickest way to free the child from fear may be to free (or at least release) the child from the husband-wife tension.

But what of the residue of this tension? When we can intervene early in the child's history to restore the developmental environment to greater health, we probably do more good than we would probing the child's psyche. With adults who are currently involved in problematic interactions, the same may be true. Rectifying the interactions may do the most immediate good. However, dyadic and triadic thinking does not necessarily mean limiting the focus to behavior and to the present. To understand relationships fully we must recognize that interactions may be complicated by unconsciously misdirected desires and hostilities. Relationships in the present reflect relationships with others, past and present, real and imaginary.

Regardless of the conflicting effects of social relationships, at times a person acts in part from personal habit and for private reasons. An alcoholic and his drink, an overeater and her junk food, these people may be subject to a destructive social context, but they also have private battles, which only they can win or lose.

Less clear is the case of a neurotic and his or her anxiety. Is this a bodily based, asocial, psychic tension or is someone making the person anxious? We are inherently social; we are embedded in a matrix of relationships. But we are also persons in charge of our own lives. Shifting to a triadic view often brings to light important and unsuspected factors in human problems. However, clearing up triangular complications may or may not solve the problem. Sometimes it only clears the social field so that a person may be better able to get on with his or her personal struggle with life and its problems.

The concepts mentioned above are all assumptions imposed on the data. In all of these propositions there is a nucleus of truth, but they have been overelaborated, leading family therapists away from clinical observation and into a realm of unexamined myths.

SCIENTISM

Family interviews, first for scientific observation and later for treatment, are the source of our data about how families work. It is easy to underestimate the extraordinary advances made possible by observing whole families interacting. After all, don't we all live in families? And don't we therefore have a lifetime of understanding family dynamics? Not really. We are so wedded to viewing ourselves as individuals that it takes an outsider to see members of a family interacting as a structured whole.

Family therapists, naturalists on the human scene, discovered how individual behavior is shaped by patterned transactions that we don't often see. Systems concepts—feedback, circular causality, and so on—were useful devices that helped make complex phenomena predictable. But they did more as well. They gave the new discipline an aura of scientific respectability. This was necessary, in part, because there was great resistance to the development of family therapy—almost as great as the resistance to psychoanalysis.

Freud believed that clinical data alone could never be an adequate basis for a satisfactory theory of human behavior. He therefore tried to link his ideas with the well-established disciplines of medicine and biology. Thus, he postulated "drives"—biological forces—where he observed only the experience of drivenness—psychological tension. In part, this reflected the intellectual climate of his times, the 19th century determinism in which he was schooled.

But there was another reason why Freud emphasized the inseparable connection between mind and body. He was insecure. Since the data of psychoanalysis were produced by only a handful of analysts, it was prudent to be modest, even skeptical. Surely he was also anxious to defend his fledgling discipline from attack. So he emphasized the neurological connections, and even tried to spell them out in The Project for a Scientific Psychology. In fact, Freud developed a revolutionary new way of thinking about the human condition without logical connections to medicine or the natural sciences. His resort to scientism is not dissimilar to the common habit of bolstering one's argument by saying, "Everybody knows . . . ," or by citing authoritative pundits: "Well, Tom Wicker (or William Buckley) says. . . . "

Family therapists have not been immune from the tendency to bolster their enterprise with pretensions to high-sounding theory. The family therapy literature consists of: (a) clinical concepts, and (b) metapsychology. The concepts of crossgenerational coalitions, rigid boundaries, and symptom-maintaining sequences are clinical; they are, in other words, labels for what we observe when we watch families interacting. In contrast, there are nonclinical theories, such as general systems theory and cybernetics, which are abstract postulates introduced to make sense of clinical discoveries. It is important to keep the two discourses separate, or at least to recognize that they are separate. Otherwise we get into trouble; we leave clinical experience behind and wander off into an airy world of theoretical abstraction.

ESCAPE TO PROFUNDITY

There are at least two motivating forces that propel us from concrete observation to abstract theory. The first is pragmatic: a desire to make sense of complex data with a systematic statement of principles that organize and clarify. A second motive for theorizing is the sheer pleasure of contemplation. We delight in exercising our faculties and take pride in our intellectual accomplishments. But theorizing also serves a defensive function. Thinking about family therapy is often easier than doing family therapy. The urge to philosophize is impelled by a quest for predictable constancy. Abstractions are orderly and stable, less threatening than troublesome experience. When the going gets tough, we escape to profundity.

These two motives, pragmatic planning and the pleasure of contemplation, are related. Those of us who choose therapy as a profession are drawn to the helping role that being needed conveys, but we sometimes shrink from the anxiety of connection. Neediness, from a distance, draws us to give succor; up close, we may find that neediness overwhelming. Seeking distance from full immersion in the painful experience of our clients, we use systems thinking as a tool, a tool that clarifies but also establishes a barrier against painful emotional contact with the personal present.

We gravitate toward experience-distant concepts as a defensive and diversionary way of insulating ourselves from the chaotic experience of our client families. Increasingly, we accept traditional views that have become crystallized and resistant to change. And we pass them on in undigested complexity to give us a sense of convergent validation in the shared views of our teachers and colleagues. Sometimes, however, form masquerades as substance.

When family therapists want to show the flag, they say, "systemic." We are systemic thinkers, practicing systemic therapy; we

ask systemic questions, and expect systemic answers. "Systemic,"
like "psychodynamic," is a fine word which, because it is positively valued, has been appropriated by a major portion of the mental
health profession. (If one isn't psychodynamic, one is likely to be
systemic; some enterprising souls are both.) *Psychodynamic* is a
perfectly valid term, meaning psychoanalytic, though not necessarily Freudian; it has been corrupted to mean, roughly, a psychology that recognizes that all motives are not transparent. Like-
wise, *systemic* is often used to mean, merely, having to do with
families.

Not content to "think systemically," family therapists have
adopted the concept of "epistemology" to differentiate right
thinking (circular) from wrong thinking (linear). *Epistemology*,
which is the branch of philosophy that studies the development of
knowledge, has been adopted—it does sound impressive—to
mean "point of view." This usage originated with Bateson, whose
choice of words, along with his worthy ideas, have been
canonized.

Ironically, in many contexts where the term epistemology is
used, a more accurate term would be "psychology," meaning a
way of viewing human behavior. Thus "systemic epistemology"
usually means interactional psychology. Exactly why a term for
how we know has been adopted to describe *what* we know is
unclear, but it seems to be an important part of family therapy's
declaration of independence from its past. Unfortunately, the
loose usage is also an aspect of fuzzy thinking that often charac-
terizes dialogues about mental health.

James Coyne dubbed this kind of fuzzy thinking "epistobabble"[11]; Liddle and Saba called it "systemic chic."[12] It is a kind of
discourse that subordinates the meaning of words to their ability
to conjure up associations to scholarship and profundity. And it is
a style of expression that has become increasingly common.
Among the woolly terms used to describe a family systems perspective are: "cybernetic epistemology,"[13] "circular epistemology,"[14] "systemic epistemology,"[15] "ecological epistemology,"[16] and
"ecosystemic epistemology."[17] These puffed-up phrases have a
nice ring to them; they suggest weighty thoughts, but they cloud

over their subject, surrounding it with a haze of scholarliness while actually saying little.

This type of writing is not learned; it is jargon. Its appeal lies in the desire to appear knowledgeable, but its use encourages laziness. Examining ideas is hard work, especially when they are as complicated as human interactions. Covering up the confusion with phrases that sound technical is an easy way out. Once we fall into this habit, nothing but abstract nouns seem appropriate. At times, these discussions get hopelessly complicated. Here, for example, is a well-known family therapist pointing out that the concept of homeostasis is not useful for a therapy of change.

A theory of therapeutic change necessitates a description on this more complex level (the suprasystem), and a morphogenetic or ecosystemic epistemology is appropriate for such a theory. The clearing up of the homeostasis muddle paves the way for a theory of change using the concept of morphogenesis, a theory of change that does not need conceptual gymnastics to account for stability within a theory of changing systems. Stability is not the proper focus of an epistemology suitable for family therapy, and therefore stability is not a concern for a theory of change.[18]

At this point it may appear that I am carping, sniping at my colleagues simply because I object to their writing style. But the problem is more than a matter of style; it is also one of substance. The kind of writing that leaves behind the simple and direct and takes on airs of profundity, mystery, and powerful impersonal forces is part of a lingering defensiveness about the value of our work.

What has been the impact on the practice of family therapy of this fascination with the esoteric?

THE INFLATED POWER OF THE SYSTEM

The contemporary trend is toward theories so abstract that there is little room for human experience, for understanding, for responsibility, or for enhancing people's ability to solve their own problems. As "the new epistemology" grows ever more abstruse, clinicians lose sight of the experience-based concepts that can serve as blueprints to organize strategies in light of a family's structure. Instead, what we see in many quarters is a barrage of manipulative techniques designed to defeat a mechanical beast— "the family system."

The systems metaphors we bring to our everyday practice are, for the most part, so overpracticed and familiar, so taken for granted, that we are simply unaware of their existence. The metaphor of the system has become a shared myth. No longer do we act as if families were systems; now families *are* systems.

One of the myths of the system is that it is determinative rather than influential. Lynn Hoffman talks about mutual reaction processes, which show how people's behavior affects one another, in symmetrical or complementary ways. However, she slides from *affecting* to *controlling*: "The terms 'dominant' and 'submissive' are unfortunate because they suggest a power struggle rather than a systemic sequence that neither person has the power to resist." Note especially that *neither person has the power to resist*. She goes on to say that, "The beauty of the concept of complementary escalation is that it avoids the tendency to see such struggles in terms of individual motivation."[19] Avoiding blame and fault-finding is all to the good, but avoiding the possibility of self-determination is an invidious myth.

The danger here is the danger of mechanism. Interaction of family members is regarded as the mechanical interplay of causal forces. Here is Paul Dell, interpreting the ideas of Maturana and Varela:

> Every system (person, family, institution, etc.) has its own organization, its own coherent identity, that fully specifies how the system will behave in *any* and *every* situation. The system has no choice; it always functions in the way that it is organized to function. The system is what it is. Period.[20]

The language here is reminiscent of Werner Erhard, founder of EST, who urges participants to expand the range of their freedom by accepting the immovable facts of reality. But when family therapists think of people as puppets of the system, they think they have to pull the strings.

Systems thinking deals with action—really behavior—but often with little distinction between human action and physical movement. An act is seen as the causal outcome of a mechanistic interaction of elemental "systemic forces." It is the automatically caused outcome of mechanical (or biomechanical) processes. Therapy, therefore, can and should be arational. The truth is that action is also rational, mediated by individuals and their creation of meaning. Much of what we do is automatic and channeled by patterns of interaction. But although we do not always reflect and act rationally, we sometimes do.

We are not just links in a circular chain of events; we are people with names who experience ourselves as centers of initiative. Our most basic impulse is to protect our integrity. What's more, we are hopelessly absorbed with ourselves. Certainly, we are linked to others. Much of what we do is with other people in mind, some of what we do is with others, and once in a while for others. But the "we" who are the authors of the doing are single organisms, with hearts and minds and bodies all encased within our skin. So fundamental is this truth of human experience that we periodically have to be reminded of our intimate connection with others.

Family therapists taught us that our behavior is controlled in unseen but profound ways by the actions of those around us. Family rules and roles operate as invisible constraints influencing all that we do. The idea that people behave as they do because they are induced to live out defined roles can have a liberating effect; if one is playing a role it is possible to play a new one. For example, the attack on sexual stereotypes permits a broader definition of the self. Men can now be more feeling and social; women can be more enterprising and self-reliant. If overextended, however, this kind of thinking implies that the role is everything.

Systems thinking in the extreme dismisses selfhood as an illusion. The problem is when roles become reified and rigidified as prescribed determinants of behavior *and* as independent of personal agency on the one hand or wider family relations on the other. Systems thinkers have unfortunately implied that the role plays the person rather than the other way around. Whether they act in concert or separately, it is finally the selves in the system who must act to bring about change.

INTEGRATING PSYCHOLOGY AND SYSTEMS THINKING

As we have seen, in the process of overelaborating the metaphor of the system, family therapy has neglected the psychology of persons. The synthesis I am proposing is a more unified view of the family, one that incorporates personal as well as interactional forces. My aim is to describe a systematic alternative to those approaches that underemphasize the power of the person, that alternately assume noncooperation and then treat individuals as though they can be moved about like pawns on a chessboard. I am not, however, proposing a comprehensive new model of family therapy—we have enough of those already! My aim is more modest and more pragmatic than that.

I am not replacing anything, only adding. To the already well-developed concepts and methods of family therapy I will selectively introduce postulates and techniques from psychodynamic theory and practice. The aim of this modest reconceptualization is to produce more consistently effective clinical treatment and lasting improvement. I must emphasize: I *do not* advocate a complete integration of psychology and systems theory in practice. The result of such integrations is too often either a watered-down eclecticism, in which the muscle is taken out of both approaches, or an overly psychoanalytic family therapy, in which systemic ideas take a back seat to traditional psychoanalytic methods. Although the heading of this section employs the term "integrating," what I espouse is selective borrowing. Family therapists should continue to practice family therapy, not some hybrid model. But I think we must learn to shift attention to individual dynamics when family transactions get stuck because individual members are unwilling or unable to change.

In the remainder of this book I will suggest how to conduct family treatment using the best tools of family therapy and the most useful ideas from individual psychology, including, for example, object relations theory, empathy, and interpretation. I plan to develop my thesis in the most practical manner possible. For that reason I will present my ideas in the order that is most useful for clinical practice, rather than an order dictated by logic, such as assessment first, intervention later.

I begin my recommendations for practice, therefore, with a chapter on interaction, which I believe is the basic method of all successful family therapy. This is followed by a chapter on the use of empathy, which is the essential ingredient for understanding individuals and mobilizing them to change. Only then will I describe how to conceptualize family problems by using an integration of systems and psychological concepts. In the remaining chapters I will show how concepts from individual psychology can be used to reconceptualize and work better with many of the traditional concerns of family therapists, including framing and reframing, circular questioning, directives, and resistance.

But before we get into all that, we have to look at the problem of change.

2

The Problem of Change

Most discussions of change in family therapy are muddled by confusion over who changes. Therapists don't change, systems don't change; people change. To be more exact, therapists initiate change, systems undergo change, but individual persons must make changes. One consequence of ignoring the individual is the shifting of responsibility for change to the therapist. This is unfortunate because change ultimately works through individuals within the system. We may think about families—structured with boundaries and triangles—and we may convene families. Yet in a real sense there are no families. The family is an abstraction. Regardless of how many people are in the treatment room, the only person who can change is the individual.

Constructive change occurs when individual family members develop new perspectives that lead them to new actions. Therefore, therapeutic interventions must reach and motivate individuals. Because the actions of family members are coordinated in patterned interactions, therapists can sometimes effect change while thinking only in terms of interaction, of process instead of persons. Even then, however, the interventions succeed or fail to the extent that they mobilize persons to think and act differently.

Knowing this, therapists can concentrate their influence to encourage individual family members to accept responsibility for changing themselves, and to act on it.

The essential benefit of psychotherapy is that it adds something new—novel advice, perhaps, or a new way of looking at things. The fresh perspective that family therapy offers is that our lives are coordinated within our families such that what "they" do is a function of what we do. It is an enormous insight, and it puts us in charge of our own lives. The man who complains that his wife spends all her time with the children can stop complaining and get more of her attention by approaching her through the children; his spending more time with them frees her to become available to him. To "get it" in family therapy is to realize that, while we are inescapably bound together, we are ultimately free— free to get what we want and need out of family life. This is different from saying that "We are all in it together" or, more doctrinaire, that "We are all part of one system."

Paradoxically, family therapy's great potential for change carries with it the greatest impediment to change. Having the crucial actors in our lives together makes it possible to resolve problems at their source. But whenever several parties to a problem are present together, there is the danger of diffusing responsibility. Change is stalled if everyone waits for someone else to initiate it. Therapists inadvertently play into this built-in exculpation when they think only of systems instead of persons.

Done well, family therapy is a dialectical balancing act, conducted so that interpersonal changes will not be stymied by individual psychological rigidities, and personal changes will not meet with unyielding family constraints. Sometimes we can produce a good effect by working on one person's frozen conception of what has to be and limited conception of what can be. A single mother who grasps the fact that she is afraid to discipline her daughter because she has no other love in her life is capable of transforming both her life and her daughter's life. Sometimes we can work exclusively with family interactions. Simply provoking parents to insist that their reluctant five-year-old get on the school bus may resolve the child's "school phobia," with no need for any of them to understand the possible function of the child's remaining home with mother. Human dilemmas, however, are often sufficiently complex that working with both rigid mind sets *and* rigid interactional patterns is the wisest course.

People come to therapy because they are stuck. When they arrive at our office, they may be unable to recognize or act on options that might release them from their dilemmas. Their behavior is constricted and so is their experience. How can we help them?

LOOKING FOR LEVERAGE

Inevitably, the enthusiasm of seeing how problems fit into the family context gives way to the hard reality that changing these patterns is terribly difficult. When family therapy first came along, some people worried about the danger of upsetting the fragile equilibrium of families. Don't worry. The truth is it takes dynamite to change family interactions.

Like individuals, families cling to the familiar and resist precisely those solutions that mean breaking old habits. The person who has been told to relax more is by nature the person least likely to do so. Similarly, families too much together or too much apart, or too strict or too lenient, will not readily alter these accustomed patterns, even when they become dysfunctional. Bumping up against the enormous conservative forces of the family necessitated the development of something that would give leverage. Unfortunately, many family therapists have gravitated toward techniquism, manipulative ploys designed to provoke change, which often fail to mobilize individual persons to overcome their personal rigidities. It is not enough that these techniques "work"—a gun to the head "works"—the problem is that their impact may not last.

I will now describe in more detail how the mechanistic view of families has led to a mechanistic approach to treatment. My purpose is more pragmatic than esthetic; the point is not to scold family therapists for being "manipulative," but to demonstrate that we can provide more effective treatment by putting the self back into the system.

Tricks of the Trade

Strategic therapists openly acknowledge their willingness to be manipulative. For them therapy is a power struggle and they set out to win it using an arsenal of tactical maneuvers. For this reason their work has been the focal point of debates about the ethics of manipulation. In fact, as Jay Haley pointed out long ago, all therapies are manipulative in the sense that they endeavor to use clever and artful means to change people. "Manipulation" is a buzzword, toxic because it conjures up images of influence that is fraudulent (to manipulate the stock market) or exploitive (to manipulate one's friends). The question is not whether family therapists are manipulative, but in whose interests they work and how effective they are.

A couple in their mid forties argue about how to handle their bulimic daughter. The father is for sympathy and understanding; the mother is for being firm and setting limits. Unfortunately, they don't get anywhere because neither one listens to the other. The woman talks in a scolding schoolmarmish voice, and the husband listens about as well as a schoolboy being bawled out. The therapist intervenes: "He doesn't understand that you can be subtle, patient, and sympathetic." It is a manipulative ploy, designed to break the pattern by provoking the woman to prove that she can be "subtle." It may work. But if you think of two people with personalities and of what they are doing, you could be more direct. You could interpret what is going on so that, rather than being provoked into a temporary break in the pattern, the couple has the possibility of understanding what each of them is doing, and the possibility of acting more thoughtfully, now and in the future. For example: "He doesn't hear you because although you feel worried you show only anger, and he gets too upset by the anger to hear the concern and worry underneath."

Every approach to family treatment is based upon a strategy for effecting change. Reframing and paradoxical directives are obviously manipulative devices, but so too are the interpretations of psychoanalysts, the personal disclosures of experientialists, and the enactments of structural family therapists. Some of these interventions are so powerful and clever that we may be beguiled into becoming interventionists instead of therapists. Inherent in our more cunning techniques is the lure of the shortcut—anything to avoid grappling with persons and their enormous difficulty in changing.

Will one interpretation, like the one in the example above, transform a family from one that acts out of habit and impulse into one that acts wisely and thoughtfully? Of course not. The point is that the intervention aims to make the family members collaborators in their own therapy; it shows them what they are doing— and, more important, why—and thus helps put them in charge of their own lives. Direct interventions—interpretations, empathic comments, explanations—are not more powerful than indirect ones. Quite the contrary. Direct interventions are more likely to require repetition and working through. The difference is that they aim at individuals, whose personal rigidities impede functional problem solving, and whose personal responsibility it is to overcome ineffective ways of behaving.

Family therapists in the 1980s have become increasingly fascinated with high-tech interventions, but, although current technology is more sophisticated, the impulse to circumvent resistance instead of resolving it has been a part of family therapy from the start.

Some clinicians imported devices from individual therapy into family work. Experiential family therapists employed a number of structured exercises, including role playing, family drawings, psychodrama, family sculpting, and guided fantasies. As introduced in the human potential movement, these techniques were effective in promoting emotional catharsis during individual sessions and weekend encounter groups. In these settings, where people are isolated from their natural context, provocative techniques not only helped overcome defenses against emotional expression, they also introduced life into the consulting room.

Since family therapy brings life itself into the consulting room, why were these experiential techniques needed? Cathartic techniques helped participants in encounter groups to loosen up to overcome emotional insensibility. Shutting up when real adversaries are present may be very sensible—cowardly, perhaps, but sensible. In family meetings much is held back. But the reason has more to do with deliberate avoidance of conflict than with excessive emotional restraint.

Expressive techniques seem like a way to open family members to their experience, but gimmicks won't trick conflicted emotions out of hiding (thank goodness). The emotions that do emerge during structured exercises tend to be weepy ones—old losses, shared hurts, forebodings—not anger or conflict. Using artificial means to introduce novelty and excitement into family sessions seems unnecessary and distracting. Often these procedures were practiced without much idea of family dynamics. Today, although still used occasionally (by Peggy Papp, for example), the experiential approach has largely given way to methods that stay closer to what the family brings—their problems and attempts to solve them.

Today, few family therapists are sufficiently innocent of family dynamics to believe that simply helping people express their feelings will resolve many family problems. Most family clinicians are aware of dysfunctional boundaries, pathological triangles, and systemic resistances, and most use techniques borrowed from structural family therapy, Bowenian therapy, and strategic therapy to deal with these complexities. The point remains, though, that most rely on a limited set of devices to produce change.

By the 1980s, family therapy techniques had become increasingly sophisticated. Circular questioning, rituals, pretend techniques, the debate, paradoxical injunctions, the invariant prescription—these are examples of the state of the art. All of these techniques were developed by experienced teams of family therapists in the course of trying to treat particularly difficult cases. The invariant prescription, for example, was first tried in desperation with a family containing a very sick daughter, a chronic psychotic with anorexia nervosa. After meeting several times with the whole family and failing to make a dent in their enmeshment,

Mara Selvini Palazzoli and her colleagues asked the parents to attend one session without their children. In this session they were assigned the task of taking an unscheduled outing—anywhere, just something alone together—and leaving a note for the children, saying only, "We are out for the evening." If asked later where they had gone, the parents were to say simply, "This concerns only us." The prescription proved effective in this case and subsequently with a whole series of families.

Once discovered, innovative techniques become the subject of journal articles and workshop presentations.

PLAYING TO THE AUDIENCE

More and more teaching is now done in workshops. Even national conventions, conceived as forums for the exchange of ideas, have increasingly become a super series of workshops. The enormous appetite for workshops reflects a thirst for retraining and a continuing need for infusions of energy in the practice of a profession notorious for its burnout rate. But just as the television camera helps make the news it sets out to report, the public exposure of family therapy has had an unforeseen effect on practice. The medium transforms the message, putting a premium on drama and action.

The field of family therapy is still dominated by charismatic personalities whose clients, working clinicians, sit in the audience at workshops. Workshop participants are often overburdened by difficult jobs and hungry for help with refractory cases. They come eager for inspiration, and they find it. Like their patients, these therapists look for techniques that will make them successful. Unfortunately, it is not possible to demonstrate on the stage patience, modest goals, and a slow process of understanding. When we watch, we want to see what the therapists do; so they do more. The needs of the audience dictate an emphasis on daring and unusual interventions.

Here is an example of one of family therapy's most respected therapists, Maurizio Andolfi, performing—there's no other word for it—at a recent workshop.

The family was a black family with a mother and father and four children. The eight-year-old daughter, identified as the patient, was a bedwetter. . . . Andolfi . . . was ready in a hurry with pronouncements. The identified patient, he said, is like her mother. "She's got your anger. Maybe when you were pregnant she was swimming in your anger—in your belly." Assuming that the little girl is angry (bad, not mad) has two implications: Make her stop, or help her with her feelings. Andolfi raced off in both directions. He asked the little girl how many mattresses she had ruined (5), and then instructed her to ruin them faster by crapping in them too. The little girl didn't understand the word "crapping" (but the audience did). Other than pursuing his constructions (wetting = anger) most of Andolfi's efforts were directed toward getting the mother's mother to take part in the therapy. Then, after implying that the bedwetting was angry defiance, he told the little girl *not* to stop wetting until her parents bring their relatives in. The little girl just looked at him with scared eyes.[1]

Provocative? Yes. Effective? Who knows, because the consultant did not have to face the family again. But what about the context? Were we seeing Andolfi the therapist, or a different Andolfi— Andolfi the teacher, or perhaps Andolfi the performer?

We study the great therapists, not as therapists but as teachers. Those who flocked to Phoenix to learn from Milton Erickson in the last years of his life witnessed his favorite teaching devices— permissive indirect suggestions, metaphors, and analogies—and assumed these represented his therapy. But it is an unbalanced view. Many of his more straightforward and confrontational techniques were missing—not because he didn't use them, but because they were not suitable to his audience. At workshops, presenters emphasize what is dramatic and unique about their work. It suits their own needs and it makes good theater.

Among the most popular workshop circuit riders—Virginia Satir, for example, or Bill O'Hanlon—are engaging personalities whose energy and charisma infect the audience, recharging the batteries of the participants. Their vitality and enthusiasm are infectious and the audience wants to take these energizing quali-

ties home with them. What they do bring back are notebooks
filled with specific techniques, thus furthering the idea of the
universal value of specific interventions.

When they return to their home clinics, many family therapists
will try out their newly acquired techniques with a team of colleagues. Once the team of observers broke through the one-way
mirror to advise the therapist how to conduct the session, therapy
became even more strategic and technique-centered. Working
with a team adds to the therapist's leverage, providing multiple
perspectives and the possibility of bolstering the therapist's directives by referring to the concurrence (or split opinion) of the unseen experts. On the other hand, the therapist who works with a
team becomes somewhat passive, sizing up the family but waiting
for the team to provide ammunition in the form of a decisive
technique—the silver bullet.

The most compelling and popular interventions are then widely imitated. But even a "good technique" is only a description of
what someone did in a particular context. When Selvini Palazzoli
applies her invariant prescription, or a team at Ackerman utilizes
"the debate," they have a lot going for them: the prestige of their
institution, their own careful assessment, the position of leverage
that they gain before applying their technique, and the personal
power of experienced clinicians. The most renowned family therapists are not only good clinicians, they also have a special personal quality. Call it flair or panache. Or better yet, flash. Much of this
unfortunately gets lost when novice family therapists try to apply
these techniques.

We emulate the powerful by imitating their techniques, but we
are not them. Flashy techniques may lead to breakthroughs if the
groundwork is done. But authors and speakers say little about the
amount of training or supervision or preparation needed to apply
their models. Instead, they emphasize the power of the technique
and they find a receptive audience that is always hoping to find
rapid and, more to the point, effortless cures. The current emphasis on techniquism leaves the impression that difficult human
problems can be vanquished in a flash if only one is sufficiently clever. The idea that change must be provoked rather than

inspired is related to the idea that people are pawns of the system.

BREAKING THE SYMPTOMATIC CYCLE

The early form of communications family therapy partook of was the appealing but naive view that the way to solve problems is to talk things over. This sometimes works, but not often with families troubled enough to consult a therapist. Most of the time, "talking things over" means only laying out the competing positions. Resolving conflict may come, not through talk, but through reflection, compromise, and willingness to accept the rights of others. Pointing out problems in communication—"I notice that whenever I ask you a question you look to your mother before answering"—led to acknowledgment ("uh huh") but not much change.

Say that a couple is quarrelling about how to discipline their small son. Imagine (it isn't hard) that they aren't getting anywhere. The father says, "That boy is spoiled rotten; he needs a good spanking." The mother says, "You're too hard on him; leave him alone. We get along fine until you come home cranky from the office." If attempting to improve their communication to make it more problem-solving and less name-calling doesn't work, we can conclude that the system is homeostatic, and that the direct approach won't work. *Or* we can conclude that the problem lies in the persons, and must be brought out and explored. Why is the woman afraid of her husband's anger, for example? Why are the two of them so preoccupied with the child? In response to impasses like this one, therapists might have become more confrontive or empathic; instead they became more clever.

Patterned interactions were seen as "homeostatic cycles" or "feedback loops" and the goal became "breaking the symptomatic cycle."[2] These metaphors captured the recursive and automatic character of family interactions but suggested that human action is a mechanical process, which (a) can be derailed by one decisive move, and (b) can be changed more effectively by an outsider— the therapist as engineer—than by the actors themselves.

Sometimes the metaphor of "breaking the cycle" is apt. If a woman once stands up to her bullying husband, she may never again shrink back to subservient submission. This can be described as second-order change that reorganizes the structure of the family.[3] More often, however, lasting resolution of family problems requires sustained, persistent, and conscious effort on the part of family members. Sometimes therapeutic intervention does produce a sudden breakthrough, but the old pattern reasserts itself—actually, family members reestablish it. When this happens, judging success depends upon who is judging and when. Consider the following:

An overinvolved, controlling mother is locked in battle with her adolescent son. They fight over the most trivial things—he forgets to take out the garbage, he slams the door when he is angry, and he stays out riding his bicycle 15 minutes past his 7:30 curfew. The father is peripheral, which makes the mother even more harried and angry. The therapist intervenes to disengage mother and son: "You are tired, depressed. All this fighting has worn you out." Mother agrees. "Let him (husband) take over the discipline for a while. I will meet with these two (father and son) next to see if the discipline is working." By the following session an extraordinary change had taken place. Everything was calm and peaceful. Mother was rested, enjoying herself. Father and son were getting to know each other and finding that they liked one another. Success. Fini.

Of course the success was short-lived. "Of course," because most family therapists would anticipate, or at least be alert for, the rebound that followed. Despite the fact that the son's behavior had undergone a remarkable transformation, the mother, who was temporarily cut off from the only emotionally sustaining relationship in her life, reasserted her control like a steel coil springing back into place. There are a number of things the therapist might have done to prevent this. He had broken the cardinal rule of: Never work with only one subsystem of a family. The point of the example is to illustrate the limits of "breaking the cycle." Cycles are not mechanical, nor are they simply habit. They represent motivated patterns that serve the psychic economy of everyone involved.

But wait a minute. Are human problems in the psyche or in the system? As a result of professional factionalism, writing in the field emphasizes *either* interactional *or* intrapsychic intervention as the solution to the dilemmas of life. From my perspective, psychological change is worked out in interaction between the individual and the family group. Some therapists chose to approach this interaction from the individual side, and treat the group as a taken-for-granted stage on which individual action is played out. Others stepped back and tried to choreograph the group interactions, leaving the private complexities of the individual actors out of their calculations.

Contrasting individuals with systems is unfortunate because it posits separateness where there is interaction. As long as we limit ourselves to narrow alternative models, we are tempted to rely on all-purpose techniques. Leaving the self out of the system implies that individuals cannot change and, therefore, therapists must do it for them. Recognizing the interaction between self and system, on the other hand, broadens the scope of our understanding and decreases our reliance on techniquism.

It is important to note that talking about the "interaction" between self and the family is only a matter of convenience. It is phenomenologically correct since it fits the facts of experience, but it is logically incorrect. Psychological and systems explanations do not, in fact, deal with different phenomena; they are different levels of discourse on the same theme, human behavior and relationships. Sometimes it is useful to think in terms of one level of description, sometimes another.

Different levels of analysis do not compete. Psychological theories are not better, or worse, than systemic ones. Otherwise we should all study to become molecular biologists, and stop wasting time with mere behavior. Of course, in another sense, psychological and interactional models *do* compete. They compete for our allegiance, for in truth most of us gravitate toward one system of understanding or the other. Since neither model, psychological or systemic, is right or wrong, only more or less useful in different circumstances, the wisest course is to move back and forth across models. Each theory is useful for various situations that arise in practice. An accomplished clinician needs a rich assortment of perspectives *and* the ability to respond flexibly. Theories do not and cannot prescribe what we do with our families on a moment-to-moment basis. But wide knowledge permits therapists to improvise with more force than common sense.

What is missing from many contemporary approaches to family therapy is an appreciation of psychodynamics, which are related as cause and effect to family dynamics. Narrow focus on technique is the result of trying to bypass resistance and personal conflict. Whatever success is achieved by circumventing defenses, systemic or psychological, may not last without altering the conditions upon which the defenses are based. To understand what holds our clients in unproductive cycles—and to help them understand—we sometimes need to look into personal experience, thoughts, and feelings, as well as behavior, and past as well as present interactions. Just as looking only at the borderline character of an adolescent in an unhappy family ignores all that the parents may be doing to provoke her angry outbursts, looking only at their interactions ignores how and why she responds with such emotional excess to their provocations.

We have seen how family therapists have neglected the psychology of the individual, drifting off instead to mechanical models of the system and mechanical methods for fixing it. Just as the effects of our treatment of patients may not last unless we arm them with some awareness of each other's motives and how to achieve their purposes more productively, so we may not be able to alter our own one-sided approaches unless we understand our own motivation for distancing ourselves from psychological experience. Many of the pioneering tricks of the trade have been modified, but they still describe a need for power. The need for power was not just a phase in the history of family therapy; it is something we all face in working with families.

"TELL US WHAT TO DO!"

Families come to therapy full of anxiety, full of pain. It isn't easy to apply for psychiatric treatment. Therapy is expensive, time-consuming, trying, and, like it or not, still stigmatized. As long as we continue to ignore the self, we will not recognize the pain, will not respond with informed compassion, and will not help individuals understand and overcome their defensiveness. When frightened and uncertain families resist our efforts to change them, we can say that "the system resists change," or we can say that individual family members want relief but avoid at all costs the difficult and painful work of changing their own behavior.

By the time they ask for help, many people have given up on themselves and are ready for an expert to take over. Even those who say, "Therapy is a waste of time; you have to solve your own problems," may have the same longing for dependence; they've simply learned to hide it away. Others appear trained to ask for assistance. Many families with inadequate personal and economic resources turn automatically to outsiders to handle their problems. Therapists who work in public clinics are familiar with these families, products of a culture of social interventionism. One often gets the impression that the family members are children and the various agency workers are the parents. Whether they come readily or reluctantly, families invest in us the same authority they would in a physician or a priest. They turn to us and we take over. Rather than accept the reduced authority of a helper or a Socratic teacher, we find ways to live out the roles they project onto us.

Facing the complex and shifting demands of troubled families clamoring for help makes it clear that one needs to "do something." One something to do is to gently shift the responsibility back where it belongs; if the family is stuck, help them to figure out how to get unstuck. But it is also possible to be beguiled by the promise of techniquism: We have only to find the right technique, the definitive procedure, and any problem will yield before it. Families yearn for magic and we oblige.

YEARNING FOR MAGIC

We associate magic with the primitive mind,[4] but at times of crisis we all become a little primitive. When getting unstuck seems impossible, or at least beyond our capacity, we yearn for magic solutions. Baffled and uncertain, people resort to magic for easy answers to hard problems. Often the very fact that people look for magical relief is an indication that they are not ready to do what is necessary to achieve results. Inexperienced therapists often learn this the hard way.

Many years ago a newly married couple came to see me. She was a Playboy bunny, he was obese. They both wanted me to help him lose weight. When I met with him individually, he told me that he wanted to go on a diet but he couldn't. So, would I hypnotize him and entrance him into thinking that French fries and Pepsi Colas taste bad? Implicit in his request was the idea that he was powerless to resist his taste buds. Fresh out of clever strategies to engage him in the hard work of controlling his own behavior, I agreed to his request. I hypnotized him and told him that his favorite foods tasted greasy and sickeningly sweet (they do, by the way). Under the influence of my suggestions, he stopped eating his bêtes noires for a couple of weeks, lost a few pounds, and then went back to his old habits. It's not just that there aren't any quick fixes to hard problems. The problem is that I was lured into trying to solve his problem for him—the way family therapists are when they try to operate on systems rather than work with a group of individual persons.

Magic may not lead to lasting cures, but that doesn't seem to diminish its hold on the imagination. We may look condescendingly on the mumbo jumbo incantations of witch doctors, but the logic, the heroes, the deeds of myth survive even in an age of skepticism and disillusionment. Today, in order for magic not to strain our credulity, it must pass as scientific. An example of this modern-day magic is Neurolinguistic Programming. NLP offers a variety of quick tricks to help people control their behavior using cognitive strategies. Bandler and Grinder talk about achieving control over "the brain"—a nice metaphor for self-control, rich with pseudo-scientific status. The brain, like "the system," is mechanistic and therefore control can be achieved mechanically.

To many family therapists, Milton Erickson stands for magic. But if he was a wizard, he was so only in a metaphorical way. He was unquestionably a therapeutic genius, a master of clinical artistry with much to teach. In trying to emulate him, some clinicians make the mistake of trying to separate what he did from who he was. Erickson was not someone who gave hypnotic suggestions, but someone who gave suggestions in a hypnotic way. Intuitive sensitivity cannot be reduced to a formula. Even when therapy becomes highly cerebral and technical, as family therapy often does, it is a mistake to underestimate the importance and power of the therapeutic relationship. It isn't just magic that people want; it is a magician.

Client families induce therapists to play magician because they long for a magically protective relationship. Even the most resolute self-reliance gives way in prolonged periods of personal stress. Beleaguered by the pressure of unsolved problems and with personal coping strategies used up, peoples' resources run low and they look for someone to take over. Families, especially those cut off from a network of kin, soon exhaust the number of people on whom to shift their burdens. When this happens, they turn to experts, full of hope, not only for solutions but also for someone to lean on.

The intensity of the hunger for magical dependency is due to the fact that the magical relationship is striven for as a substitute for missing segments of the family's own resourcefulness. Young families learn not only how to cope, but also that they *can* cope— they are competent. The less secure they are as individuals and the shakier their sense of family pride, the greater is the tendency to depend on experts and to look for magical solutions.

We find a complementary expression of this idealization in the rescue fantasies common to members of the helping professions. Mistaking idealization for respect confuses honest admiration with the distorted projection of fantasied power. Many therapists attempt to capitalize on their clients' idealization, realizing that it lends power to their directives, but ignoring that the complement of the powerful therapist is a humble and insignificant family. Authoritarianism bothers us least when we are the ones deferred to.

The same wish for a magically protective relationship that impels patients to search for a strong, self-assured authority causes therapists to long for an all-powerful expert, someone to borrow strength from.

Decisive and forceful techniques are often useful, sometimes even essential. The right move at the right time may provide a quick, bold solution to festering problems that otherwise might grow worse with time. A carefully designed ritual, an artful reframing, or a confrontation delivered with intensity may create a breakthrough, but they are only part of a long process.

A quick intervention may bring about a dynamic attenuation in the conditions that create pathological patterns. Sending a rebellious teenager off to boarding school may interrupt an escalating battle with his parents. Yet precipitating factors often persist and endure. Problems of immediate adjustment are susceptible to immediate cure, but only a minority of difficulties are of this nature. After the problem becomes internalized—in persons and in their relationships—simple cures of this type are often impossible.

To illustrate how dynamic intrapsychic and systemic forces may make quick change impossible, or at least not lasting, consider again the case of the obese man married to the Playboy bunny. Perhaps his overeating was a regressive attempt to soothe himself in order to counteract feelings of being unloved and worthless. Maybe his mother was a woman who proved her worth and exercised her control by feeding her family. Still, her oldest son defied her. She said, "Eat, eat," but he ran off to be with his friends. Watching all this, and afraid of incurring his mother's wrath, my patient, eager to please, ate, ate. If he was an obese child, his mind may have been filled with grandiose daydreams—his way of compensating for the inevitable humiliations fat children suffer in the schoolyard culture. Once again he'd eat to provide himself with missing nurture. Thus, a familiar vicious cycle may have been set in motion: Overeating provided temporary relief from frustration and depression, but the resulting obesity led to more self-loathing—and thus to a greater need for relief.

Or, to cite a systemic explanation, his wife may criticize him for being "a fat slob," while continuing to stock the kitchen with goodies and prepare him lavish, high-calorie meals. Without knowing it, she may encourage his overeating because it helps perpetuate a relationship in which she is the beautiful young girl and he is the nonsexual older man. Obviously, these two explanations are not mutually exclusive. Sometimes, by the way, there are hidden forces at work, neither systemic nor psychological. I know of one very sad case in which a bright, attractive girl of 14 nearly died of starvation despite several weeks of family therapy, until it was discovered that she was suffering from Crohn's disease.

Chronic circumstances cannot be changed at will. What is wrong with highly technical solutions is that they reduce therapy to a formula. They emphasize doing for and doing to people, neglecting personal responsibility and difficulty in breaking out of interpersonal patterns. The new technology encourages therapists to take responsibility, when what they should be doing is giving it.

The pioneers of family therapy sought to rescue patients from the Freudian vision of the person as ruled by unconscious forces in the form of inexorable repetitions of the past. Family therapists saw the unconscious as an integral part of the psychiatric mystification that obscures personal responsibility. Most were vigorously opposed to the idea that people are like marionettes, driven against their will by dark forces of the unconscious. Ironically, despite their general antipathy to the idea of unconscious motivation, family therapists have created their own version of a nonconscious agency: "the system."

RESPONSIBILITY

Now, instead of attributing responsibility to the unconscious— "She shoplifted because of an unconscious need for punishment"—we attribute blame to the system—"Her shoplifting served the systemic function of uniting her parents in concern."

So, in spite of their diametrical opposition on many points, psychoanalysts and family therapists treat the individual as the plaything of powerful forces, internal or external, and as having little agency.

Felix Guattari even challenges the idea that the individual is a separate entity: "The concept of individual unity strikes me as misleading. To claim on the basis of such a unity to be able to centre a system of interactions between behaviours arising in fact out of heterogeneous components that cannot unequivocally be located in one person appears to me to be an illusion."[5]

Much good results from systems explanations. Realigning family relationships may, for example, be effective in helping a teenager stop stealing (as may also helping her understand and think through her wish for punishment). An unfortunate side effect of systems explanations, however, is a tendency to blur personal responsibility. Neither the system nor the unconscious actually steals; the person does—and she can stop.

There *are* dynamic intrapsychic and systemic forces which operate outside the bounds of awareness and they *do* define limits within which we are free—and responsible—to act. However, there is much more room to maneuver within these limits than is generally assumed. My intention is not to oversimplify the classic issue of free will versus determinism by recognizing only one of these two truths. Rather, I wish to make a case for the clinical utility of mobilizing people's resolve to solve their own problems. Ordinary terms for conscious intention, like "resolve," "willpower," "determination," and "perseverance," may seem out of place, even quaint, in sophisticated discussions of family dynamics. Nevertheless, only by acting differently do people change, and psychotherapists, to do any good, must eventually influence their patients' "willpower," "determination," and "perseverance."

In the following case we will see how a systemic focus—process instead of praxis—tempts us to forget individuals and their personal responsibility for change.

    It was just after New Year's Day when Noel and Lillian came into my office. Both of them were giving me meaningful glances, which I, not being a mind reader, could not decipher. For a little over a year I had been trying to help them with what they said was the only significant problem in their relationship: her parents/his inlaws. He was jealous of her attention to them, which he thought was excessive, and wanted her to devote less time to them and more to him. She thought his jealousy was unreasonable, but tried to work out a compromise so that she could spend time with her parents without making him feel neglected. Now, following the holiday that so often leads to disappointment, I assumed that their grumpy silence signaled a failure to pass this test of their compromises. I was not, however, going to break the silence.

After a few moments, Lillian said, "We haven't been speaking for a couple of days—in case you couldn't guess." Me: "Oh?" More silence. Finally I broke the silence, but instead of simply (taking responsibility for) initiating the discussion, I pointed out that neither one of them was willing to: "Frankly, I'm a little worried, not that you had a problem, but that neither one of you seems willing to take responsibility for working it out." (Couples wish they didn't have problems; therapists wish they would learn how to resolve them afterwards.)

It turned out that they had survived the holidays in remarkably good shape, including several visits to and from Lillian's parents. She had made a point of getting Noel's consent in advance to any plans that involved both of them—including, for example, a firm agreement about what time they would leave her parents' house on Christmas day—and he had resigned himself to the visits and tried to be cheerful. Everything had gone well until the Sunday two days before our session. A series of mishaps culminating in a water pipe bursting in the laundry room led to hurt and angry feelings. Both of them had been under a great deal of pressure and when things started breaking down each felt wronged and misunderstood. Instead of talking about it or yelling at each other, the way most of us do at some point, they suffered in silence.

That there were reasons for the couple's silence is obvious. Both of them were afraid of aggression and dependent on each other; as a couple they didn't have much practice fighting fairly. Much was to be gained, moreover, by remaining silent. Above all there is the pleasure of being right and knowing that the other person is wrong. Noel and Lillian may have been hurt and angry, but at least they got to savor the delicious satisfaction of being innocently wronged. Some people find it hard to forgo the dubious pleasure of sulking for the messy and uncertain alternative of hashing things out.

In intervening, I had a choice: Either promote the unfinished argument and help them figure out what goes on when they argue that makes them want to avoid it, or emphasize that they have it within their power—each one of them—to break such deadlocks by simply trying to talk it out. I chose the latter course and left them to work through their own differences, which they did, not perfectly, perhaps, but effectively.

In therapy, people who are stuck begin to realize that the suffering they have been passively enduring is partly a result of their own doing—their own inaction and misguided action. Regardless of the kind of therapy, even the most action-oriented, people begin to get glimpses of themselves, their personal fears, their destructive habits, and their collective need to work things out. The woman who complains that her husband won't allow her any independence learns that she *is* free, but must overcome her habit of caving in when he says, "Sure, but what about me and the kids?" The man whose wife has become, in his words, "an hysterical shrew" realizes that if he were to relieve her of some of the responsibility for the children she would be more peaceful and more loving.

These realizations may come like a flash of illumination or a fleeting glimmer. In any case, realization means nothing unless it is translated into responsible action. There's the rub. The woman whose husband manipulates her with guilt knows it, "but can't overcome her upbringing." The man whose wife needs help is too bitter about "how unfair it is that he married a woman less competent than his mother" to make changes that would give him peace of mind. We could say that personal realizations mean nothing because systems resist change. This implies that much of what we regard as human emotion, personal initiative, even altruism, is meaningless mechanics. Now, instead of being programmed into our genes, it is the result of "systemic forces." An alternative idea is that change is hard and requires a struggle. It's not that people cannot change themselves, but that to do so they must fight habit and inertia and fear. Here is an example.

Mrs. Kaye was referred to the clinic by her minister, who felt that her bouts of depression might necessitate medication or even hospitalization.

Mrs. Kaye's husband brought her to the intake interview. When the resident asked her to come into the consultation room, Mr. Kaye asked, "Did you want to see both of us or just her?" "What would you prefer?" Mrs. Kaye answered, "I'd like to speak to you by myself first, then you can talk to him." "Fine."

Mrs. Kaye complained of having "mood swings" every few days. She had trouble falling asleep, was tired all the time, and sometimes broke down in tears, even at work. She related this to a recent stormy divorce. Two years ago she discovered that her husband was having an affair and she immediately filed for divorce. It was a contentious divorce with fights about property and custody of the children. Although she was awarded custody of all three children, her husband kidnapped their 14-year-old daughter and took her to live with him in Florida. Now the daughter no longer even writes.

Mrs. Kaye also spoke of her recent marriage to Ned. She loved him all right, but they were having "adjustment problems." She described him as the opposite of her first husband who was a devil, drank a lot, cursed all the time, and sometimes slapped her around. Ned is almost too perfect. Like her, he's very religious, but he doesn't seem to have any faults. "He's *so nice!* I should be happy. I don't know what's wrong with me. Maybe I don't deserve him."

Mr. Kaye described a similar history—the divorce, the kidnapping, and the remarriage—but his description of the "adjustment problems" was quite different. According to him, she was depressed and did cry a lot, but she also had furious explosions of temper. She got upset, often for no reason, and screamed at him, smashed things, and stormed out of the house. Once she even drove the car into the garage door.

It was a striking discrepancy: She emphasized her hurt and depression, he emphasized her explosive temper. We decided to see them together.

Midway through the first conjoint session an interchange

took place that revealed a great deal about the Kayes, about their interactions, and about their separate personalities. All of a sudden Mrs. Kaye started to cry. There didn't seem to be any reason for it; they had been talking about how well they got along most of the time when her face broke and she started sobbing. He just sat there. Facial muscles tense, holding onto the chair, and holding back whatever comfort he might be able to offer. I said, "She's really upset, I think she needs you." Then he barraged her with questions: "What's wrong, honey?"
"I . . . don't know. . . ."
"What is it? What's the matter? Don't cry."
"I'm sorry. . . . I don't know what's the matter."

Here was a textbook example of an obsessive compulsive trying to comfort an hysteric. She was upset, which comes easily because her feelings are close to the surface. But she didn't have a focused idea of why. He, too, was upset. When she cries he cannot imagine that it could be anything but about him, so he feels guilty and accused; his trying to comfort her takes the form of asking her to reassure him. "What's the matter?" means "Tell me that it isn't my fault." He confirmed his dilemma by saying that he doesn't know what to do when she gets upset. "Sometimes she says, 'Leave me alone,' but then if I do she says I don't love her."

The couple's pattern could be described behaviorally: she cries; he crowds her; she tells him to leave her alone; he does; she gets mad and then sad, so she cries. A richer description includes something about what each of them feels and why. She cries because she is going through a difficult time. She misses her daughter and feels rejected; she also finds it difficult to get used to a new husband who is so different from her old one. So she cries. But she is also a person who feels things without always being able to put them into words. When she gets upset, she needs to accept and express her feelings even if she doesn't know at the moment why she is upset. At these moments her husband could comfort her by just being there, holding her perhaps, but certainly not by demanding that she explain herself, or that she stop crying.

He understood when I explained all this; the problem was changing it. Rather than trying to figure out some way to provoke him to respond differently, I asked him to think about the pattern and why he found it so hard to change his role in it.

That night he sat in his chair going over and over it in his mind. He was sure he was right, even if she didn't understand. He went over all the reasons he was right and all the reasons she was wrong. ("You can't get to the bottom of things unless you first figure out what's wrong.")

As he sat thinking, or rather brooding, all of a sudden he had an image of her crying. And for some reason he was shocked. It was hard to think of himself as wrong, hard and painful, too. But he could see it now. All she wanted was for him to love her. Why should her crying make him feel attacked? The answer made him ashamed. He was afraid of her, afraid of her criticism, afraid of her disapproval, afraid of her nagging. He sat looking at the fire for a long time, thinking.

The next few days when she cried he just held her. It was great. Instead of feeling threatened, he felt strong. He liked taking care of her. But once in a while she did get mad at him. And slowly he started to withdraw again. The maddening thing was he could see what he was doing. Saw himself punishing her with silence. He could be close when she was friendly and warm or when she was sad and helpless. But he just couldn't (wouldn't) take it when she got mad.

Here is a good example of how personal insight can be derived in a family context. Seeing them separately would narrowly circumscribe the focus of attention. While many individual therapists would suspect unexpressed anger beneath Mrs. Kaye's depression, few who saw the husband alone would think to advise him to respond to the hurt behind his wife's anger.

What happens next depends on a lot of things. She could stay depressed, stabilize it by seeing a series of therapists, or mask it with drinking. Each of them could freeze the distance between them by taking up other interests. One of the children could become a problem that uses up most of their energy. Et cetera, et cetera. But he could break the pattern of attack and withdrawal *all by himself*. She could, too, of course, but if he waits for that to happen, he will simply be giving up on his own responsibility.

One consequence of the belief that people are more or less helpless to change their own lives is that someone must do it for them. To say that the therapist is responsible promotes a constructive emphasis on solving problems and alleviating suffering. However, truth does not always lie with one or another of two apparently dichotomous alternatives. Neither the therapist nor the client is responsible for change—both are. Therapists are responsible for doing everything they can—including mobilizing people to get busy solving their own problems. When we adopt the position that the therapist is chiefly responsible for change, we are inadvertently taking up the medical model. One of the ways that the psychological model differs from the medical model is in placing more responsibility for change on the patient. Whereas successful surgery depends primarily upon the diagnostic acumen and technical skill of the surgeon, successful psychotherapy depends upon an interaction between the healer and those who would be healed. My point is not to absolve therapists of responsibility, but to encourage them to inspire it in their clients.

"You Go First"

One of the great advantages of family therapy is that, by bringing together all the participants in the family drama, we can see what part each individual plays in the family's problems. This broader vantage is, however, a double-edged sword. Once the family is understood as structured by interactional dynamics that follow their own logic, it becomes possible to predict and interdict problems that otherwise might remain a mystery. But, as we have seen, ignoring individual dynamics in favor of interactional dynamics leads therapists to take over, shifting from technique to technique until they find a way to force the family to change. Even if we resist the temptation to take over and we put the responsibility for solving problems in the family where it belongs, there is yet another problem. Once responsibility for change is placed in the family, individual family members pass it around like a hot potato.

Inevitably, family members in treatment discover what goes on between themselves. Even though they've heard it before, they hear each other's side, perhaps a little more clearly now, and they begin to see some of the reciprocity in their actions. But it is hard, very hard, to give up waiting for others to change. Patients in individual therapy may have the solace of believing that others (especially spouses and parents) are cruel and wrong; still it is clear who must change. But when responsibility is diffused throughout the group, family members often wait for someone else to go first. Nowhere is this more true than in couples therapy, where most spouses feel bitter and resentful at that loved-and-hated person who, maddeningly, selfishly, seems to withhold the little consideration they need. Nowhere is this feeling more painful than in the bedroom, as the following example illustrates.

One of the chief aggravations between Cindy and Joe was sex. Sad, isn't it, the way something that can bring such pleasure causes so much pain.

Their impasse is one familiar to family therapists (and to most members of the human race): He was the pursuer, she the distancer. (The roles may vary, but the pattern is distressingly common.) They didn't really need anyone to tell them that. Still, discussing the pattern in therapy made it crystal clear to him that his grabbing her in bed without any preliminaries only annoyed her—even though once in a great while it led to intercourse.

For her part, Cindy could see that the longer she avoided him and pushed him away, the more desperate he got and the more aggressively he pursued her. Like paunchy people at New Year's, they resolved to change. "Damn it, I'm not going to bang up against her anymore. I'll just hug her gently with my arms and wait for her to soften." "I guess I'll have to initiate things once in a while, so he doesn't become so aggressive."

Their resolution lasted about as long as most diets. Not long. What kept them stuck was that, unlike most dieters who must help themselves, each knew that the other one could resolve everything by changing. "He heard what the doctor said, didn't he? He could solve everything just by being a little gentler and going a little slower." "Damn it, why doesn't she come over and touch me? Then I wouldn't have to attack her."

I've seen impasses like the one between Cindy and Joe hundreds of times. You have, too. Sometimes there are complications (in them or between them) that can be ferreted out to make things easier. Often, however, the two will stay stuck until one of them just changes. Knowing this does not mean that we as therapists cannot help. But it suggests that we can help by putting the pressure on them to do what is within their power, rather than by trying to skirt around the issue or trying to solve it for them.

We know that people who do not wish to be in therapy or who have strong reservations about its efficacy tend not to benefit. For this reason, many therapists will decline court-ordered referrals and refuse to see people who only "want to see what therapy is like." What we sometimes forget is that in family therapy *most* of the participants don't want to be there. For one thing, they "know" that the identified patient is the one with the problem. For another, they doubt that the others will change. "I don't think my husband will come (and I know for damn sure the bastard won't cooperate)."

One way to respond to the absence of commitment to change is to assume that conscious intention is (a) impossible to mobilize and (b) useless, and therefore to work around it, using indirect and covert means of manipulation. An alternative response is to begin by accepting whatever motivation there is, but at a later point to confront people with their need to accept personal responsibility for change.

When we translate the problem of change from the abstract (who is responsible) to the practical (how we as therapists can maximize our influence), we move to considerations of technique. The rest of this book will be devoted to showing how the principles discussed in these opening chapters are introduced into the consulting room. To begin with, however, it is necessary to activate the system.

3

Interaction

Although I have been talking about the need to reintroduce psychology into family therapy, we cannot understand the self in isolation. We must look at the self in context *and* in action. At the same time that the actual mechanics of family relationships are exposed in dialogue, they are also available, directly, for constructive intervention. Working with interaction is the *sine qua non* of effective family therapy—not verbal descriptions, but actual conversations about what counts.

THE SELF IN ACTION

The problem of change discussed in Chapter 2 is based on a theory of human action: Behavior is influenced by contemporary interactional forces and by personal habits, motives, and defenses. Lasting change takes place through a spiraling process of altered (*interpersonal*) interactions and enriched (*personal*) understanding. A therapist who works with both individual experience and family relationships must shift focus to concentrate sometimes on the interpersonal (*the system*) and sometimes on the personal (*the self*). By alternating perspectives, the clinician can move

65

across models to effect change. Because "the system" and "the self" are, in fact, only different ways to describe people's lives, one cannot separate them; neither model is right or wrong, but both are more or less useful in different circumstances. Pragmatically, the most efficient way to conduct family therapy is to concentrate first on systems dynamics, postponing more detailed attention to the selves in the system until it becomes necessary.

A system is a related group of elements plus the way they function together. A family is a related group of persons plus the way they function together. As with other groups, the dynamics of the family are revealed by the way they interact. Thinking of the family as a system means thinking about persons in action, paying more attention to the interactions than to the persons. The human beings lurking in the family system do not, however, disappear. The "elements" in the family system are complex personalities, and their dialogues are affected by converging streams of personal and interpersonal influences. In addition to their manifest interchanges, the persons themselves are simultaneously struggling with latent possibilities of action and interaction: anger and affection, withheld or partially expressed; expectations, accurate or distorted; and projections, fended off or lived out. In time, I will take up these complex subjects, but since my aim is pragmatic I will begin by describing how to mobilize these complex person interchanges—how, in other words, to set the self in motion.

The following example illustrates the clarifying effect of observing interactions.

> Mrs. Lee called to say that she was worried and upset, and wanted to arrange for an appointment. She was having an affair and didn't want her husband to know about it. I agreed to see her alone.
>
> She was anxious and guilty. Infidelity wasn't her style; it went against all that she expected of herself. "Besides," she said, "I don't really know how it happened. There isn't anything wrong with my marriage. It was just one of those things. Bob, the man, is one of my husband's friends. One night about

two months ago we had a party. It got quite late . . . I had been drinking more than usual. . . . When I went into the kitchen to get some ice, there was Bob, grinning at me. He said, 'This is a terrific party, and you're a terrific lady.' He wanted to give me a friendly hug. I didn't see any harm in it, but when he put his arms around me, I felt him growing excited. All of a sudden I couldn't catch my breath; my heart was racing. I was scared, but I didn't want to let go. Then he kissed me. My God, what a kiss! I felt like a teenager again, hot enough to melt. But I realized that what we were doing was crazy. So I went back to the party, forgetting my ice.

"He called the next day. I agreed to meet him for coffee because I wanted to make it clear that there would be no repeat of what happened. I told him, but he didn't listen. And then my heart started racing again. I wasn't thinking anymore, I just wanted to be alone with him. We went back to his house and were all over each other as soon as we got in the door.

"Since then I've seen him six or seven times. Most of the time we can't even really be alone. So we go for a ride and talk, sometimes go to the park and fool around a little in the parking lot. But now I want it to stop. I *don't* want to ruin my marriage. It's a good marriage."

I'm sympathetic toward most patients; this one I really liked. She was energetic and intelligent, and frankly I was glad to hear that she didn't want to jeopardize her family. What didn't make sense, though, was that she thought nothing was wrong with her marriage. Most people, even if they don't have affairs, have some complaints about their spouses. For three sessions we talked about her affair, what she saw in Bob—he listened, really listened—and how she felt about being unfaithful. She decided to break it off and did so. Since my agreement was to help her determine what to do about the affair and she had terminated it, I asked, "Is there anything else?" "Yes," she said, "I want to understand what happened. I don't want it to ever happen again."

Having an extramarital affair and not having any complaints about her husband suggested repression. Sexual passion that had apparently been buried for years was disinterred in an affair where there were none of the taboos of family life—nor the conditioning of years of habit. After we talked for a while, she suddenly came out with, "I know what's wrong with my marriage. It's boring. We don't do much together and we don't have much to say to each other. The worst thing is that he doesn't express his feelings. He's just not much of a talker. That's what was so attractive about Bob." So. Finally, we had found the problem: it was her husband. By the way, I was tempted to accept her version of the relationship. She was a lovely, engaging woman, and if her husband didn't want to be with her, he must be dull as dishwater. My better judgment made me suggest that we have a few sessions together to talk things over.

So, saying she was unhappy and didn't know why, she invited her husband to the next session. He came, though I could see he wasn't thrilled about the idea. He knew she was unhappy. He thought it was just something she was going through and had accepted the lie that she needed time to be by herself.

Right off, she told him she was unhappy with their relationship. "All you ever seem to want to do is go to work. When you come home, you don't want to talk to me; you *never* express your feelings."

"I know, I'm just not much of a talker."

Even though they agreed, I wanted to see it happen, so I suggested that she talk with him about how he felt about the marriage. "Okay," she said, and shyly he began.

"I'm pretty satisfied with everything. I like our house, I like the kids, and I guess I love you. Still . . . sometimes I wish you weren't so critical about how much money I bring home."

No sooner did he say this, his first statement of feeling, than she interrupted with: "Bullshit! I wouldn't say anything if you would see that your partners are losers and the only way you'll ever get ahead is to quit the firm."

It was a remarkable transformation. Suddenly this lovely woman, who had been such a pleasure to talk to, turned into a shrew. He shut right up. "See? He just won't express his feelings." I did see, and I saw why. What at first was a mystery (a marriage with nothing wrong) and then a flaw in the husband's character (a dull person, not much of a talker) was revealed in interaction to be a problem between husband and wife—when she criticized, he folded his tent.

Only by seeing the couple together did their problem become clear: She nags—he withdraws—she nags—he withdraws, and so on. They are partners in a "game without end" that neither perceived until her playing around with someone else put the marriage in jeopardy.

The process of interaction between Mr. and Mrs. Lee, which seems to take on a life of its own, is still the product of persons— persons conscious or unconscious of the possibilities of interaction, persons who see these possibilities and act blindly, impulsively, deliberately, creatively, or stupidly, depending upon their own attitudes and flexibility. Even in this simple interchange, the partners show signs of complex layers of experience. There is, for example, the wife's reluctance to face her dissatisfaction, complemented by the husband's apparent acceptance of the status quo. The couple's stake in maintaining the manifest surface of their relationship may seduce us into ignoring the emotional, wishful, and fantasy-ridden aspects of their performance. We might ask: Why does this man need his wife to play the role of a harsh jailor? Why does this woman undercut her husband's independence?

These questions take us into the realm of projective identification. But we do not have to go there yet. I will begin, in writing as in practice, by bypassing some of this complexity, holding it in abeyance for later consideration. Family relationships are layered like an onion, and it is only necessary to peel away enough of the layering to satisfy the family's desire for change.

THE POWER OF EMPIRICAL OBSERVATION

It is tempting to believe that we can discover what goes on in a relationship by simply asking. Even though it seems obvious that asking one party to a relationship to describe what goes on gives only one side of the story, therapists continue to do so—and accept what they hear as valid or assume that they can infer what actually happens. Experience reduces but doesn't eliminate surprises.

A colleague who had for two years been treating in individual therapy a 29-year-old bulimic woman asked me to evaluate

the family and to consider the possibility of treating them while
he continued to see the young woman. Given the severity of
the presenting problem, I expected to see sharply-defined patterns of family relationship, especially enmeshment and
triangulation.

Cheryl, the daughter, describes experiencing no pleasure.
Nothing brings her any joy. Instead, she seems motivated primarily to do what she considers good or wholesome. She is
emaciated and frail, much too weak to work, but she does manage to do a little volunteer work in the library. To her, appetites
are not something to be enjoyed, but to subdue; indulgence
beyond a certain point makes her feel guilty and disgusted. She
spends from one to three hours every day vomiting, or trying
to.

Cheryl's mother says that her daughter is "very capable" and
then cites one or two trivial accomplishments—she was a good
artist in grade school—revealing her value of competence, but
also her extreme denial and infantilization.

Mom: Cheryl seemed happy as a kid.
Cheryl: I didn't have any friends.
Mom: We're very proud of how smart you are.
Cheryl: You never praised me when I was growing up. All I ever
   heard was how well Sarah was doing.

So. Bitterness and misunderstanding were clear, but what
about current relationships? I was reasonably certain that the
parents, or at least one of them, would be actively overinvolved
in Cheryl's life.

Therapist: Can you tell me a little about yourself? Where do you
   live and how do you spend your time?
Cheryl: I live in an apartment on Quail Street. I don't do much
   of anything. A little volunteer work in the library. Once a
   week I go to meetings of a feminist group that I belong to,
   and twice a week I go to see Dr. Bergin. Dr. Bergin wants me
   to go back to school, but I'm not ready for that yet. I want to
   get my head together before starting another program.
Therapist: How often do you see your parents?
Cheryl: Oh, about once a month.

Therapist: What do you think about Cheryl's situation?

Mom: We worry about her, of course, but we leave her pretty much alone. She has to lead her own life, and we're pretty busy with the business.

Dad: We try not to get involved. But she knows we love her.

Here was a striking lack of parental overinvolvement in their daughter's life. In fact, on the basis of this session, I could see nothing structurally wrong with this family. Since Dr. Bergin was obviously a central person in Cheryl's life—perhaps her only significant relationship—I asked him to join us for the second consultation session.

Dad: Well, what did you figure out about us?

Therapist: Not much. Cheryl, have you thought of anything important that we didn't get to last time?

Cheryl: My dad and I used to have a lot of arguments. He's very conservative and I'm a radical feminist.

Dad: The trouble with you is that you aren't willing to listen to anyone else's opinion. You always have to be—

Dr. Bergin: (Cutting in) They always argue. They don't understand each other.

Cheryl: That's right, you can't talk to him.

Dr. Bergin: (Trying to avoid an argument) Have you completed those forms I gave you for food stamps? You're going to have to learn to manage your money better. Do you remember the budget we worked out?

Cheryl: Oh yes, but. . . .

Dr. Bergin's interruption of the father-daughter argument was striking and unsuspected. It blocked conflict, but keeps father and daughter from working out their differences. Moreover, by protecting Cheryl from conflict, Dr. Bergin implies that she cannot fend for herself. As the session went on, this initial impression was confirmed. No longer in her parents' household, Cheryl had nonetheless become embroiled in an enmeshed relationship with her therapist, who not only listened and counseled her, but assumed a very directive and controlling relationship with her, thus keeping her in a position of helpless dependency.

As is often the case, the pattern of enmeshment between Dr. Bergin and Cheryl became clear only when all the significant members of the "family" were present *and* were given the chance to interact freely, so that the pattern of relationship was manifest.

Family interactions can be investigated in one of two ways, rationally or empirically. Assuming that people behave pretty much as they say they do, we can find out how they interact by asking them. From their answers and from what we know about other families with similar complaints, we can deduce much of what is problematic in their mode of relatedness. This is the rational (drawing conclusions from inferences) approach.

Alternatively, making no such assumptions, we can investigate the life of a particular family by empirical observation. To see their dynamics actually taking place, it is necessary to watch them interacting. Observing them at home without being noticed might give us a truer picture, but the dialogues that take place in the consulting room take on patterns similar to those outside. Family interactions in the presence of a therapist may be constrained at first, but once family members start conversations about what matters, accustomed dynamics take over and the transactions become genuine and passionate.

THE LIMITS OF CIRCULAR QUESTIONING

An alternative strategy relies on an interrogatory dialogue between the therapist and family members. Often these dialogues are conducted so as to uncover descriptions of interaction and to suggest change. *Circular questioning* has recently become popular as a way to discover interactional patterns without actually seeing them. Introduced by the Milan Associates[1] and popularized in this country by Peggy Penn,[2] circular questioning is designed to get around the obvious distortion that occurs when you ask family members directly about their relationships. Instead, one asks a third family member to comment on the relationship between another two.

According to Selvini Palazzoli, "One will readily agree that it is far more fruitful, in that it is effective in overcoming resistance, to ask a son, 'Tell us how you see the relationship between your sister and your mother,' than to ask the mother directly about *her* relationship with her daughter."[3] Perhaps, but it is just as likely to substitute one bias for another. Human nature inclines us to present ourselves in a favorable light while complaining about others.

Asking the son to comment on his mother and sister's relationship tells you less about that relationship than about whose side he is on. Thus, one of the strengths of this technique is its power to uncover reports of coalition. When the therapist asks questions about who does what, when—"What does your father do when mother stays crying in her room?"—circular questioning tracks family members' behavior around problems and reveals what they believe and are willing to report about their behavior. Questions can be designed to ask about changes that have taken place: "Who is closer to father now that he is retired?" Or even about changes that might take place: "If your sister goes off to college, who will be more lonely, your mother or your father?"

Circular questioning is such a useful way to gather information that it is easy to overlook some of the premises upon which this technique is based. Therapists who conduct sessions by asking questions, rather than allowing people to speak and interact freely, place themselves in a central and controlling position. In defining circular questioning, the Milan Associates emphasize the (circular) interaction between the family members as witnesses and the therapist as interrogator: "By circularity we mean the capacity of the therapist to conduct his investigation on the basis of feedback from the family in response to the information he solicits about relationships and, therefore, about difference and change."[4]

Peggy Penn emphasizes the power of circular questioning to uncover and demonstrate to family members their patterns of interaction: "The patterns that circular questioning punctuates in conducting the session become isomorphic to, or a structural equivalent of, the ontogeny of the problem in the family. The aim of circular questioning is to fix the point in the history of the system when important coalitions underwent a shift and the consequent adaptation to that shift became problematic for the family."[5]

Circular questions are useful questions, but questions are a poor substitute for observed interactions. Interactions provide a more vivid and accurate picture of family relationships by showing instead of telling. Moreover, relationship problems revealed in interaction can be solved in interaction. That is, family members can be helped to change their own way of working together, and be held accountable. Relying on clever questioning puts the therapist in charge and leaves him or her there. As long as questioning is the primary mode of data collection, everything is under the therapist's control. This implies that the therapist is like a detective who will expose secrets and solve problems.

Many clinicians believe that control and detective work are necessary. The case against working with interaction is that simply letting family members talk over their problems is letting them do the same old thing they do at home. Therapists interested in behavioral sequences doubt that these interchanges will give them enough information to figure out what maintains problems—or prevents their solution. Those who believe that people need to overcome emotional reactivity sufficiently, not only to talk but also to listen and begin to recognize their own role in family upsets, believe that unregulated conversations will only replicate destructive arguments without showing the way to their resolution. In short, many family therapists think that working with interaction is naive and outdated, like treating a family with group therapy. Interactions are thought to produce insufficient information and undue chaos.

That which is described, as opposed to reenacted, is the result of a selection that eliminates some of the most important elements. When the selection is controlled by the therapist's questions, the agenda will be the therapist's and what emerges will be in terms of what the therapist is looking for. The family will disclose, more or less of, the content that the therapist introduces. The resulting process of interaction will reveal as much about the family's response to the therapist as about their response to each other.

Suppose, for example, that a therapist is interested in the nature of a couple's relationship. Asking them about it—"What do you two do together?" "What does he do that annoys you?"— limits the field of inquiry to specific content issues and may reveal more about the couple's candor than about their intimacy. Simply asking them to discuss one of these issues doesn't free the interaction from the therapist's domination. To do so it is necessary to discover (take the cover off) something that the couple wishes to discuss—perhaps something that they have been avoiding but that *they* bring up. Then you invite them to discuss it, and you stand back out of the way.

Questioning family members about their relationships also limits the participation and understanding of the selves in the system, focusing primarily on cognition. One can remember and report only on what has been consciously experienced. All of us have vast reservoirs of inchoate experience, thoughts and feelings and images and memories and intentions, which are as obscure to us as to others. Some of our experience we know well; we claim it and are willing to report it. Other aspects of experience flow just below the surface of consciousness. Past hurts make us hold back. "He wouldn't understand. . . ." "She would be angry. . . ." As a consequence, the experience festers. There is shame, yes, anger, maybe. But more than that, there is not knowing, not understanding, and therefore not being whole and accepting of oneself—and remaining incomplete with the others. This material will not emerge under questioning, but it will be felt and be manifest under the influence of live and authentic family dialogues.

Why does unconscious material emerge more effectively in interaction than under questioning? It is because certain emotions and impulses are not quite conscious. They are triggered not by inquiry but by evocative and provocative remarks made in the heat of family arguments. A boy's account, or his mother's account, of their conflict may tell a story about control, respect, freedom, and defiance. But, even when one listens carefully, it may be unclear what is and what isn't fair.

Other dimensions of their conflict won't even come to light unless you actually witness their disputes. Some of these other dimensions are systemic. Perhaps when the boy and his mother argue, the father—*but only if he is present*—becomes enraged and attacks the boy. Among the material that emerges in the drama of actual conversation are latent thoughts and feelings. Personalities are not one-dimensional. When she yells at him, he manifests tremendous anxiety. You can see it, and you can see how his upset blots out her words. He doesn't follow her instructions—one of her main complaints—because he remembers only the anxiety.

Here's an alternative explanation, using self psychology rather than drive psychology. The mother yells at her son, and in the process demeans him. "No one would put up with what I put up from you! You are a disgusting person, you don't know how to get along with anybody, no wonder your only friends are losers." His face reddens. She is talking about his behavior, but he is aware only of his anger, his narcissistic rage. ("It's not fair! She's such a bitch! When will this yelling be over?") Once again, he does not really hear her. But the therapist who observes the interaction can see this and can see why it takes place: In trying to explain herself, the boy's mother is tearing down his fragile self-esteem.

I once had a patient at the V.A., a handsome, gray-haired man, but depressed. I remember being especially affected by him. I guess he reminded me of my father. He was a new car salesman, smooth and articulate. He was taking medication, but it didn't seem to lift his depression, so I was assigned as a psychology trainee. My efforts to help were fairly naive. I knew I wanted to help, but I didn't really know how. I met with him daily and we talked about one thing and another. He taught me about the car business, how tough it was, and how the customer can get the best deal (by going to three dealers and playing one against the other). Mostly I just tried to be supportive—sympathetic and attentive. From time to time he mentioned his wife. I got the idea that the marriage—the second for both of them—was a good one, but that they quarreled from time to time and he couldn't stand it. So I asked if she would attend some of our sessions.

Under questioning, both of them remained calm and gave me details of some of their conflicts. It all seemed pretty mundane. But after two or three sessions, they loosened up and began to interact more freely in my presence, not because I knew enough to be inactive, but because I didn't yet know anything else. When they talked he became extremely regressed. There was nothing subtle about it, he was plainly a little boy talking to his mother and they both seemed to enjoy it. She asked him if he was being a good boy in the hospital. He said yes. But when she said, "When you get home, Mommy'll make you a goodies breakfast," he became enraged. Her using their pet language in front of me was too humiliating for him. With a shock, I realized that this man, whom I thought of as a father figure, was actually a regressed and immature little boy. But I would have suspected none of this had I not seen the two of them in interaction.

There are two kinds of interactions in family therapy, those that occur spontaneously and those directed by the therapist. Just as we reveal ourselves more honestly in what we volunteer in unguarded moments than in response to questions, families often show their truest colors in little scenes acted out on the way to the consulting room or in unpremeditated disagreements. Parents nagging ineffectively at children misbehaving, couples quarreling, children interrupting their parents—these interactions are among the most reliable indicators of what goes on in the family. But they are tough to work with. They tend to occur more quickly in chaotic families and they are usually related to ingrained features of the family's mode of relatedness. Spontaneous interactions may reveal more, *but* they are harder to work with.

SPONTANEOUS INTERCHANGES

Richard Chan (age 16) called to request help for problems with "interpersonal relationships." Because he was still living at home I said that I wanted to see the whole family, at least for the first session. He didn't seem to like the idea, but agreed to ask his mother. His father lived in a city 150 miles away and Richard didn't think it would be possible for him to attend. I insisted, saying that I needed to hear from everyone. Three weeks and several phone calls later, we scheduled a meeting for a Saturday morning. The family that greeted me in the waiting room consisted of a somber and dignified Chinese gentleman in his 50s, a harried-looking occidental woman of about 45, and their son, Richard, who seemed American in everything but his facial features.

I thanked them for making the effort to meet together, and then asked, "Who would like to begin?"

Richard spoke sarcastically to his mother, "Why don't you start, you're the one with all the complaints." That was about the last thing anyone said without being interrupted.

Mrs. Chan said, pointing to her son, "It's that guy, he wants total freedom—"

She was immediately cut off by Richard who was ready with a counterattack: "I just want—" But he didn't get a chance to finish either.

Like most therapists I am disconcerted by this kind of chaotic squabbling. My temptation is to take control, to forcefully quiet them down and insist that they take turns. I waited, however, until I could see more clearly who interrupted whom and when.

Sitting back (which took some effort), I noticed that what at first appeared merely chaotic was, in fact, patterned chaos. Richard was full of complaints about his mother, and she about him. "He never . . ." and "She always . . ." The content was familiar: He wanted freedom, she wanted respect. Mr. Chan was on the side of authority, yet his more moderate position placed him somewhere between his son and his wife. The form of the discussion was more interesting than its content.

Richard and his mother did not merely argue their opposing points of view, they seemed positively glued together. Regardless of who was speaking, these two addressed themselves to each other. When I asked them questions, they responded in a deliberately provocative manner, with barbed comments and rhetorical questions, expertly baiting one another. They fought, but it was a little like the play fighting of puppies: snarling and growling and nipping, but no real biting. Just the opposite were the occasional cracks between the parents, which showed a poisonous hostility. She called him a "liar" and said the boy's problems were "all your fault." He said little, and even when he tried, Richard intruded himself, quickly turning the discussion back to himself.

Here then were the dynamics: conflict between an adolescent

and his mother serving to diffuse a more virulent conflict between the parents, and yet made worse by the parents' inability
to form a united front. It was easy to see; unfortunately, the
easier structural problems are to see, the harder they are to
solve. Redirecting the interaction along more productive lines
reveals how ingrained the problems are at the same time it
begins to solve them.

Therapist: I don't think you are going to get anywhere convincing Richard that he should take a year of remedial study
before college, unless you two parents talk over your differences and come up with an agreed-upon position. And I
don't think you can do that without keeping Richard from
interrupting you.

Mrs. Chan: (With stinging vituperation) You liar! You tell me
one thing and you tell him another. I thought you agreed that
the boy was not prepared for college.

Mr. Chan: (Very controlled) Yes, I agree, but I do not believe that
we are in a position to force the boy to take a year of remedia-
tion unless he is willing. Since he is not, why not let him
apply to college and find out for himself that they will not
accept him?

Mrs. Chan: You cruel bastard! Why make him suffer? He would
be *devastated*. You don't know how depressed he was when
he failed French last year—

Richard: (Breaking in) I was not—

Mrs. Chan: You were . . .

Therapist: It's easier to let him interrupt than to finish your discussion.

Mrs. Chan: You *never* take a stand. That's why we have all these
problems in the first place. You aren't willing to discipline the
boy; that's why he is an *unmanageable spoiled brat*. You're never around. Where were you when I had my sex discrimina-
tion hearing? Off traveling, that's where. I get nothing from
you! The only support I got was from the boy. I had to go to
court all alone. Except for the boy, I had no one. (Sobbing)
You aren't a husband, you aren't a father; what are you!

Mr. Chan: (Long suffering) I agree that he needs more preparation, but what can we do if he refuses?

Richard: I can—

Therapist: (Waves his hand to silence Richard).

For the most part it is best to let the parents silence an intrusive child, but until they learn how they may need help.

In this example we can see how spontaneous interchanges reveal troubled patterns of family interaction. At the same time, they provide the material for therapeutic intervention. The therapist first observes the pattern, waiting long enough until the roles of all the players become clear, and then intervenes to probe the family's flexibility. With most families—and certainly for beginning therapists—it is more useful to work with carefully orchestrated interactions. Working with enactments is still empirical, but more like the experimental method than naturalistic observation. By initiating and directing family conversations, the therapist gains selectivity and leverage. The therapist selects particular transactions—often ones that are otherwise dormant—and is therefore in a position to control their intensity and duration.

ENACTMENTS

The term "enactment" is Minuchin's and I will draw upon his teaching for many of the ideas in this section. According to Minuchin, "Enactment is the technique by which the therapist asks the family to dance in his presence." Moreover, "The person is his dance."[6] Minuchin's metaphor of the dance, with the therapist as choreographer, is instructive. It captures the essence of the self in interaction, and the therapist's ability to direct and observe the interactions. From my own point of view, however, Minuchin takes poetic license to overstate the unity of the dancer and the dance. Family dialogues reveal habits of dealing with other members of the family—the self in action—but attention to individual personalities may be required not only to mobilize interactions, but also to transform them. The dancers think and feel as well as dance.

The first step is to build an alliance of understanding between the therapist and every member of the family. This means speaking to each one and finding out how he or she feels about being present and what he or she thinks about the presenting problem. This is, of course, how most clinicians begin. But I mean something other than Minuchin's "joining" or strategic therapists' attempt to elicit verbal descriptions of problem-maintaining sequences. I mean entering people's minds, not showing understanding, but really understanding.

Family members come to therapy expecting to talk to a professional expert—to be understood—not to interact with each other. Beginning therapists often err by skipping lightly over these inquiries and then pushing family members into premature interaction. The result is failure to connect with the individuals and resistance from the group.

Telling people to "just talk it over" underestimates them. Put technically, it mobilizes resistance; in ordinary language, it ignores the natural reticence to disclose private feelings and open up family conflict in front of a stranger. This superficial and hurried approach illustrates a naive attitude to the psychology of persons. The following is an example of superficial conversation with family members and an overhasty attempt to get them to interact.

The Nelsons were referred to the clinic by their daughter's school vice principal after Terri had threatened to kill herself with a knife. The family was seen first in the crisis unit, where the intake interviewer concluded that there was no immediate risk of suicide and therefore no need of hospitalization. A brief note from that interview explained that Terri, age 16, was a good student, but shy. She got along well with her teachers, but the other kids considered her "stuck up" and "Miss know-it-all." The therapist entered the session assuming that mother and daughter were enmeshed and father disengaged.

Mother: We're very worried about Terri. We know that she has trouble getting along with the kids at school, but we had no idea that she felt so bad.
Therapist: Terri, can you talk with your folks about what happened?
Terri: Not really . . . I'm afraid they won't understand.

Therapist: Go ahead and try; tell your parents how they can help.

Terri: Well . . . I wish I could spend more time with you guys. You know, go out once in a while instead of staying cooped up in the house all the time.

Mother: What do you want to do?

Terri: I don't know . . . go to the movies or just go to the mall. I know those things cost money, but I just wish we could do them once in a while.

Therapist: (Assuming mother-daughter enmeshment, pushes father and daughter to talk.) Talk to your Dad, tell him what you want to do with him. You should be closer to your Dad.

Father and daughter comply, entering into a desultory conversation without much feeling, but also without any interruption from the mother, which raises some doubt about the assumed enmeshment. Mothers enmeshed with their children while fathers remain on the periphery are so common that the pattern can almost be assumed. Almost. Moreover, in this family where the daughter had threatened to take her life, the conversation about going to the movies seems to be missing some of the important issues for the members of the family.

Here is a short excerpt of the same family after the therapist was encouraged by his supervisor to "spend more time talking with each one of them; really put yourself in their shoes and imagine how they feel."

Therapist: Terri, you must have been feeling pretty desperate to think about killing yourself.

Terri: I guess so . . .

Therapist: Can you tell me about it?

Terri: Well . . . Nobody likes me at school. Kids who dress like me (very conservative) and want to learn something aren't very popular. I'm used to that. But there's this boy, he's new, and his friends told me that he likes me, but he's shy too. So I asked him if he wanted to do homework together, and he said he did. He comes from Pennsylvania and they don't have the same math we do, so we did homework together three or four times, and I really got my hopes up. Maybe we could be friends. And then I didn't see him for a couple of days. I didn't know what happened. And then when I finally did see him, he told me that he had a new girlfriend. I shouldn't have gotten my hopes up like that. If it happens it happens; but it's best not to count on anything.

Here Terri reveals more about her loneliness, and more about her defensive tendency toward denial and rationalization. The therapist's mindset determines the richness of the material. Therapists with preplanned strategies—looking for behavioral sequences surrounding problems, or in a rush to promote interactions—will likely be in such a hurry to intervene that they won't get more than what family members readily reveal. The therapist learns more here by working slowly, listening carefully, and avoiding premature assumptions. He is preparing the way for an interaction, but this time the interaction will be more revealing because Terri has been encouraged to open up more than briefly. Next the therapist turns to Terri's parents to find out what they think about her story.

Therapist: (Looking at both parents) What do you think about what Terri has said?

Father: I know how you feel. It's hard to make friends. But don't be in a hurry. If things don't work out this time, maybe they will the next time. You just have to be patient.

Mother: The main thing is to keep your grades up. Don't let little things get you down or distract you from doing a good job.

When the interaction is allowed to unfold with less direction from the therapist, denial seems more prominent than enmeshment. The parents listen, briefly, but then counsel suppression and offer trite suggestions. Their need for comfort would trivialize the daughter's anguish, leaving her only a faded and anemic relationship with them.

At this juncture the therapist has a number of options—point out the denial, encourage the parents to listen more but refrain from offering suggestions. He chose instead to talk more to the parents, asking them about their own adolescent years and whether or not they were lonely. In the process of describing their own youth, both parents mentioned but brushed aside similar battles with loneliness. The therapist gently countered their avoidance by reflecting their feelings and returning to the subject of loneliness when they tried to avoid it. As a result of inquiring more thoroughly into each family member's experience the therapist uncovered the theme of loneliness and denial, which then made it possible to move the interaction to a more feelingful and productive level.

> *Therapist*: I guess then you know something about how Terri is feeling. My suggestion is to help her express her feelings to you, ask her to talk about what happened, but, if you can, try to avoid giving her suggestions. After all, you had to discover your own solutions. Terri does too.

Making Interactions Real

Many of the mistakes in working with interaction involve their initiation. As we have seen, premature assumptions lead therapists to short-circuit the process of uncovering and connecting. Another common difficulty is giving vague suggestions to "talk things over." This well-intentioned suggestion often sounds to family members as though the therapist's plan is to encourage the family to talk out and solve their own problems. Since they have likely tried this already, they naturally resist repeating their failures. Some families are so talkative that they willingly engage in conversation no matter what the therapist says. With more reticent families, however, giving premature and vague directions to "talk things over" puts them on guard. Therapy then becomes a contest: They think the therapist wants them to do everything; they want help. One consequence of the resulting poor interactions is that in many quarters family therapists eschew working with interaction.

In order to initiate an interaction, three things are necessary. First, as I have said, it is important to give the participants a chance to explain their views to the therapist. Second, it is necessary to develop a specific issue to talk about. Third, the therapist must explain clearly and precisely what the issue is, who should discuss it, and why. Once the therapist has heard from each of the family members, he or she will have some idea of which the problematic relationships are. For example, if a father complains that he cannot talk to his son, the therapist may wish to find out if this is so, and why, by having the two talk in the session. Remember, though, that without a specific issue and a rationale the discussion may fall flat. Here is a common example.

Therapist: What seems to be the problem?
Father: It's him; he's gotten so snotty that no one can talk to him anymore.
Therapist: Why don't you talk to him now?
Father: About what?
Therapist: Anything.
Father: Why don't you ever listen to me?
Son: (Silence.)

The problem with such abortive enactments is not only that they fail to go anywhere, but also that they confirm to family members the futility of trying to talk. In a case like the one above, it is necessary to hear from both participants and then uncover a specific issue for them to talk about.

Therapist: What seems to be the problem?
Father: It's him; he's gotten so snotty that no one can talk to him anymore.
Therapist: What do you think about what your father just said?
Son: Who cares?
Therapist: I guess you don't think there's much hope of improving things.
Son: They just want to run my life. They never let me do anything, and they're always poking their nose into my business. They don't like my friends, what I do, or the way I dress. So, who cares?
Therapist: So, they don't respect your privacy and they don't give you enough freedom, and you don't think talking will change any of that. Is that right?
Son: You got it.

Now that both father and son have explained how they feel, the therapist can talk with either one of them long enough to uncover specific complaints, which the other can respond to.

Therapist: What are some of the things that you can't talk to your son about?

Father: You can't talk to him about anything! He wants everything his own way. He shows no respect to his mother and me, he's always shirking his responsibilities around the house, he never gets his homework done, he hangs around with a bunch of losers. . . .

Therapist: What are his responsibilities around the house?

Father: Not much, *believe* me. He's supposed to shovel the driveway when it snows, which he does, most of the time, clean his room, which he *never* does, and take out the garbage. Do you think that's a lot to ask?

Therapist: Your father says you never clean your room, can you respond to him?

Often, this is enough. But sometimes it is necessary to go a little further, to stand up and turn the chairs toward each other, and to emphasize the importance of the discussion.

Therapist: Let me turn you toward each other a bit. That's right. You two need to talk this over. You say no one can talk to him, and I think that's important. We need to understand that and do something about it. And you say they don't give you any respect. If you want respect at your age, you're going to have to start expressing your point of view like an adult. Now, respond to what your father said about your never cleaning your room.

Another mistake is interrupting interactions too quickly—before the self is fully revealed. Sometimes we are drawn in by content; sometimes we rush too quickly to teach process. Both errors reflect impatience and overcontrol. The following case shows how interruptions are often the product of naivete.

Mr. and Mrs. Mollenkamp were in a couples group for recovering alcoholics and their spouses. Mr. Mollenkamp's individual counselor had recommended the couples group to help the couple bring their differences to the surface and learn to talk them out. As long as they continued to avoid each other and Mr. Mollenkamp nursed his resentments in private, the counselor felt that his client was at continuing risk to resume drinking. In a session shortly before Christmas, Mrs. Mollenkamp said that she was worried about an upcoming holiday dinner at her family's house.

Mrs. Mollenkamp: I'm worried. I know you don't like being there and I don't like you to have to deal with all that pressure.

Mr. Mollenkamp: Don't worry. One thing I know for sure is *I won't drink*. There is absolutely no possibility of that.

Mrs. Mollenkamp: I know, but I don't like you to have all that tension. You remember what happened last year.

Mr. Mollenkamp: Don't worry.

At this point, the therapist (worried) interrupted.

Therapist: I have a suggestion. If you feel tense, why don't the two of you go for a walk. That's what my husband and I do when we go someplace and we aren't having a good time. We just get up and go out for a walk.

Mrs. Mollenkamp: That's a good idea.

It may be a good idea, but it misses the point. A couple who avoid each other, a couple who never go for a walk together, are a couple who need to open up and overcome barriers of avoidance that are keeping the two partners apart. They need to have a talk before they go for a walk.

The Mollenkamps' interaction is a model of their relationship; if they have trouble relating they will have trouble interacting, and vice versa. If we can get them to interact in the session, we can help them relate outside. The advantage to working with interactions is that we can observe selves in action, transform the interactions, and work through the changes.

By "work through" I mean help them open avoided and suppressed feelings, talk over their conflicts, and start to resolve them. This is change from the outside in. We begin by strengthening the boundary around the couple—concretely, by sitting them down to talk, and then not interrupting. This puts pressure on them to open up. Beginners assume that bringing avoidant people together can be pleasant. Usually it is not. They avoid each other for a reason. Bringing them together will bring out the conflicts they have been avoiding.

When this happens, the therapist must be prepared to help them work through their difficulties. Otherwise they will resume avoiding each other. Working through involves helping them overcome resistance to talking—interactional habits and psychological defenses. It also means keeping pressure on them to keep going, while at the same time providing some support to help them. Or, to put it negatively, the therapist stays out of the way except to block avoidance and to soften the most destructive arguments.

CLEARING THE INTERACTIONAL FIELD

Behavior is determined by far more complex processes than the well-intentioned advice to the Mollenkamps suggests. If action is viewed as the product of psyche *and* system—interactional pressure and personal ways of thinking, feeling, and acting—then symptomatic behavior may not be resolved without change in persons which leads to altered interactions.

When we have mobilized family interactions, it is possible to observe what impedes functional relating. These impediments can be of two sorts: interactional (interruptions, arguments) and psychological (fear of intimacy, unwillingness to compromise). Although these two sorts of problems are never separate, we can approach them sequentially. The first step is to clear the field of interactional obstructions. Once we resolve the influence of the group, what's left is the person, his or her shortcomings, characteristic rigidities, and psychopathology. Problems in interaction can occur in one or more of three levels: the self, the dyad, or a triangle. What the following example attempts to demonstrate is that we cannot sort out these various levels when we rush in to take over.

Mrs. Caspari asked the clinic to evaluate her five-year-old son, Nicky, "because the school says there's something wrong with him." With her permission, I called Nicky's teacher who told me that even though the boy was in a preschool class with four-year-olds, he behaved much younger than the other children. He wouldn't come into the room unless his mother took him, he didn't pay attention to the teacher, and many days he would spend the morning just curled up in the cubby where he hangs his coat. The teacher felt that he was depressed and immature, and said that if things didn't improve he would be held back a grade for the second time.

Mrs. Caspari was very apprehensive about coming to the consultation. She called three times before the first session: to ask if everyone really had to attend, to say that she didn't understand because there were never any problems at home, and finally to ask me, "What should I tell the boys about why we're coming?" My answers were: Yes, Oh, and I don't know.

The first interview was conducted by a child psychiatry fellow while I observed behind the one-way mirror.

Therapist: Hello, Nicky, did Mommy tell you why you were coming here?

Nicky: (Barely audible) I don't know.

Mrs. Caspari: I told him that we had to go to the doctor, but not to worry.

Therapist: I see. I gather that you were surprised when Nicky's teacher said he was having trouble in school.

Mr. Caspari: We certainly were. We don't have any kind of problems at home. They're good boys, they mind and everybody's happy. Nicky is fine at home. He's a good boy. He helps me out at the restaurant, don't you Nicky? Tell the doctor how you help me make the pizzas. (Nicky smiles at his father and then goes back to playing with Legos on the floor.)

Mrs. Caspari: Carmie, I wish you wouldn't let him near that pizza oven. I don't want him to get hurt. Sometimes you forget, he's just a little boy.

Mr. Caspari: (Mumbles) Yeah, sure (and then shuts up).

Mrs. Caspari: Nicky's our baby, our youngest, and he's a good boy.

Therapist: It sounds like, Mrs. Caspari, you and your husband have some different ideas about what Nicky can do, what he's old enough for, and what he's too young for.

Mrs. Caspari: No, no, it's just that Carmie, he sometimes gets carried away. When he was a little boy he had to work in the restaurant. He don't understand, Nicky's too young to be in that kitchen.

Therapist: Mr. Caspari, your wife says that you don't realize how young Nicky is. Talk with her about that. She thinks Nicky is too young, and you think he's old enough to help out. You need to talk it over with her.

Mr. Caspari: (Voicing a long-held but seldom expressed opinion) The trouble is, you baby the boy. He's five years old. When I was five I was already helping out in the kitchen, rolling the dough, spreading the sauce. You don't realize, if you treat him like a baby he's going to act like a baby.

Mrs. Caspari: What do you know about my boys! You're never home! And you *dare* to criticize me? You don't know nothing about children!

Therapist: (Upset by the sudden and unexpected explosion) Wait a minute, wait a minute! Everybody calm down. I can see that you both feel strongly about this, but we won't get anywhere with all this shouting. Why don't you both take turns, and instead of saying what you think about the other person, just say how you feel.

Arguments are aggravating. When family members argue about their problems, it is tempting to interrupt, offering them solutions or at least better ways to communicate. At some point it may be necessary to intervene, but that point comes later than many therapists think. Two people may be calling each other names, they may not seem to be getting anywhere, but as long as they are still talking, they are communicating.

Much is gained by allowing interactions to continue long enough to see what really happens in the family, rather than letting them go only a short while before intervening in a rush to set things right. By letting these dialogues go beyond the point where the family is tempted to break off, the therapist sees much that otherwise might not emerge (including triangular complications) *and* tests the family's resources for getting past the point at which they are stuck. This begins to put pressure on family members to resolve their own conflicts. As they learn that the therapist will not come to their rescue, they have more time and motivation to get beyond where they have been.

The time to intervene is when the discussion actually breaks down. This point—when they actually stop talking—reveals the nature of the interactional dysfunction. By allowing the conversation to go until the pair actually give up, the therapist will discover that either a third person interrupts or that they break off when they reach a repetitive dysfunctional sequence.

TRIANGLES

When family dialogues touch on troublesome issues, the emotional temperature rises and a third person breaks in to cool it down. Whether the entrance of the third person seems intrusive or reasonable, it almost invariably prevents the conversation from reaching resolution. The first two allow it, even welcome the distraction, because it relieves them of the anxious risk of having things out.

Virtually all family therapists are aware of the role triangles play in preventing people from solving their problems. Those who rely on their own questions to discover problem-maintaining sequences search to uncover descriptions of dysfunctional triangles. A therapy of interaction flushes triangles out of hiding and forces them into the foreground.

Working with interaction doesn't mean just letting people talk; it means finding important and unresolved issues and then pushing two key people to hash out their competing positions. Inevitably it is a confrontation. Whether the topic is as familiar a subject of unresolved squabbling as, say, parents nagging at their children, or as loaded a subject as the dormant conflict between the parents, asking the two parties to face each other is confrontational and triggers the family's pattern of automatic reaction. In response to rising anxiety, a third person enters the dialogue.

We see triangular intrusion into spontaneous interchanges—the husband who butts into an argument between his wife and his son to tell her to "be firm"—and as derailing incomplete enactments. A mother complains that her two children are always quarrelling. When the therapist asks the kids to discuss with each other how they can learn to stop fighting, they start to criticize and blame each other. As soon as they get heated, mother tries to pacify them—"Be nice, children"—avoiding the confrontation and preventing its resolution.

Often therapists (other therapists, of course) also interrupt dialogues before they are finished. A woman complains that her husband never spends any time with her. In response, he says that they never have any fun when they're together, and the woman starts to cry. The therapist comments on how upset she must be, offers her a tissue, and asks her how she feels. When therapists interrupt, it is usually with the best intentions. The therapist in this example may have been moved by compassion, but it is a compassion that prevents the wife from expressing and bearing honest feeling, the husband from offering solace, and the couple from continuing their discussion.

To work effectively with interactions, therapists should follow *The Principle of Minimal Intervention*. (If there isn't such a principle there should be.) The twosome may have much to learn about communicating and we may have much to teach. But their way is not our way. They may get along nicely without making "I statements." The best results are achieved by pushing them to rely on their own resources, intervening only just enough—just enough to help them get moving when they get stuck.

One of the reasons why families become dependent on therapists and are able to bring discussions to a satisfactory conclusion only during weekly therapy sessions is that most therapists are too active, intervening before it is necessary, teaching and preaching instead of helping people work things out in their own fashion. If you have something of earth-shattering importance to teach a couple—for example, that a father should learn to listen to his small daughter's feelings—the time to offer this advice is after the twosome has had a reasonably successful discussion. The alternative, interrupting with "helpful advice," conveys the idea that they are wrong and you are right. It also confirms their fear that dialogues must be conducted in a certain way or they won't succeed. Meddling is meddling. Here is a slightly longer example.

Tim Butler was 21, unemployed, and living at home with his mother when he decided to kill himself. One sunny spring morning, as soon as his mother left for work, he drank a half a bottle of vodka and then went into the garage, started his car, and passed out. Hours later his mother returned home and found him unconscious on the front seat. The car had stalled.

Tim spent 45 days in the hospital. Upon discharge he was referred for psychiatric follow-up to manage his antidepressant medication and for family therapy to help disengage him from a smothering mother.

Present in the first session were Tim, his mother, and his father, who although divorced from Tim's mother for four years was believed to represent an important and underused resource for Tim. Tim, pale and fragile-looking, sat next to his mother. Mr. Butler, dressed in a shiny, blue polyester suit, sat at some distance from both of them, odd man out. The therapist asked them to describe their reactions to and opinions about Tim's recent attempt to take his life. Tim said little. He spoke softly about feeling hopeless, glancing at his mother to calculate the effect his words might be having on her. Mrs. Butler was sympathetic. To her, Tim was a sensitive boy, someone who needed special understanding and time to find his way.

Mr. Butler had a different idea. The boy was "spoiled," his mother "overprotected" him; he should be forced to go out and work. "Stop feeling sorry for yourself, get out and work, then you'll have something to live for." Here was a man like Archie Bunker, a redblooded, thickheaded American. Still, if Tim could learn to talk to his father, maybe he would be less tied to his mother.

Therapist: Mr. Butler, you seem to have some strong ideas about what Tim should do. Does he understand your point of view?

Mr. Butler: No, we hardly ever talk. His mother thinks I'm just another dumb working stiff. (They exchange looks.)

Therapist: Why don't you talk to him now, explain your point of
view to him? After all, shouldn't a father and son understand
each other?
Mr. Butler: I don't think he wants to hear it. He don't care what
I think.
Therapist: Go ahead, give it a try.

Cheek muscles tensed, frowning with the unaccustomed effort
of teaching his son what he knew about life, Mr. Butler tells him
that a man has to be strong. There are important things to do. It
is a ponderous lecture, filled with words like *sensible* and *responsible*. The boy sits restlessly, half listening, half preparing his
response. According to Mr. Butler, life is a grim business.

The therapist, not liking this message, not liking Mr. Butler's
way, interrupts with some helpful advice—in the process, echo-
ing Mrs. Butler's criticisms, which are part of the reason Mr.
Butler continues to remain uninvolved. He listens as the therapist suggests that he be more gentle and make more of an effort
to understand the boy. "Try to understand how he is feeling.
Maybe he's not ready to go out to work." But Mr. Butler has
heard all this before, from his wife. He mumbles about the
therapist maybe being right and then withdraws into brooding
silence.

The mistake in the example above is simple: well-intentioned
triangulation on the part of the therapist. Other common mistakes
involve confusion over the purpose of enactments and lack of
clarity in setting them up.

Roger (35) and Peggy (36) married one year after she divorced
her first husband. Living with them were Peggy's daughters,
Tina (11) and Gina (5). Peggy was also pregnant. They were
referred to the clinic by Peggy's gynecologist who felt the couple was having problems of adjustment.

Roger and Peggy got along famously. The problem was the
children. Now that Peggy was working, the girls had more
responsibility around the house, but they wouldn't cooperate,
and the ensuing arguments made everyone miserable.

The therapist was a graduate student in social work. In the
following session, she attempted to set up an interaction to
begin to deal with the problem of enmeshment.

Therapist: Talk with the children about what you expect from them.

Roger: When I ask her (points to Tina) to do the dishes, she always says she has homework.

Therapist: Talk *to her* about it.

Roger: I asked you to empty the dishwasher—which is a five-minute job.

Tina: Well, I did it.

Peggy: (Interrupting) After you banged around in the kitchen, letting everybody know how miserable you were.

Tina: I didn't bang them around. *Mom!* You always say that.

Peggy: What about your homework?

Tina: I did some!

Roger: (Breaking in) Since it was Wednesday and you didn't do the vacuuming. . . .

Tina: I did it! Every time I have a friend over, you say, "Do your chores."

Peggy: Your friends have to do their chores before they even leave the house. Nobody *around here* even picks up clothes. We all have hampers.

Gina: You have brown, I have white.

Therapist: I notice that you let Gina jump in. . . .

The parents digress to talk about what a good girl Gina is, ignoring the therapist's point. She tries again.

Therapist: You're talking about chores and roles—washing the dishes and picking up the clothes. Have you guys (indicating Peggy and Roger) had a chance to talk these things over?

Peggy: Well I took a part-time job for Christmas and it's disgusting when you come home one day and everything's clean and then you come home the next day and you figure maybe it will be just the same—clean—and it's not; it looks like a disaster area. And you got to start all over. I've got to the conclusion that I don't care what it looks like. They can trip all over it as far as I'm concerned.

Therapist: Well, have you guys talked with each other?

Peggy: I go on my little rampages for a moment and then calm down.

Roger: You can't discuss things and say, "What are we going to do about it?" or "Let us help you clean up." The only thing that changes is her; the house is always the same. Some days she goes on a rampage, some days not. Maybe something else is bothering her.

Tina: It's not all our stuff. A lot of it is Roger's, his shoes and socks and books and stuff.

Yes, they are enmeshed, but the therapist makes two mistakes, one conceptual, one technical. Conceptually: An enactment is a dialogue, meaning a conversation between two people. The question is, can Roger speak to his stepchildren? Will they listen? Will Peggy allow him to talk with her daughters or will she break in? Technically: The enactment must be clearly structured. Two people should be asked to talk about something specific and the others should be told to listen (in other words, shut up). Once the enactment is set up, the therapist is in position to see what stops it—who talks out of turn.

In the session above, the therapist is vague about who should talk to whom, apparently indicating that both parents should talk to the older girl, but expecting them to keep the small daughter out of the conversation. As a result, Peggy's intrusion is neither seen nor dealt with as such. Later, when the therapist asks tentatively, "Have you guys talked this over?" she is on the right track, but Roger and Peggy ignore her. State what you see or what you want family members to do clearly and directly. If they ignore you, say it again.

Triangulation can be, and usually is, described as a property of systems. According to Murray Bowen, "The triangle, a three-person emotional configuration, is the molecule or the basic building block of any emotional system, whether it is in the family or any other group. The triangle is the smallest stable relationship system."[7] But triangulation can also be described as a property of persons, as something they do rather than something that happens to them. Involved are two different actions: interrupting and allowing it. The psychology of persons contains a number of concepts that are relevant to explaining triangulation, including dependency, conflict avoidance, lack of understanding, and oedipal wishes. These psychic dynamics can be investigated in the inner object world of individual minds or externally in relationships structured to maintain them. Later we will look more at the psychological factors responsible for triangulation; here I will concentrate on what to do about it, working with interaction.

The family therapist's job is like that of a traffic cop, directing the flow of conversation, worrying less about where people are going than that they take turns and avoid collisions. Another metaphor I often use in teaching is that family dialogues should be conducted like a boxing match with the therapist as referee. At first, two principals may avoid each other altogether. Afraid they might get hurt, they stay out of the ring, or duck out when the first blow is struck, or depend upon someone else to enter into the fray.

The therapist's job is to get them—two at a time—into the ring and let them have at each other. Avoid the temptation to interrupt the proceedings with lengthy discourses about the Marquis of Queensbury rules. Just keep intruders on the sidelines, and if one of the combatants cries foul or tries to leave the ring, simply give him or her a push back in the right direction.

Here are a few brief examples of a therapist merely prodding people to keep talking.

Her: You *never* listen to my feelings!
Him: "Never?!" See, doc? she always exaggerates.
Me: Fine, tell her.

Wife (8 1/2 months pregnant): Maybe I shouldn't say this but I guess I'm a little worried about being stuck in the house all day with an infant. You're always so worn out when you come home, and you expect me to be sympathetic. I feel like I'm going to have to be everybody's mother.
Husband: Cathy . . . I'm not saying that having a baby is the easiest thing in the world, but you act like I'm out having fun all day. One thing you've got to understand is that men just aren't interested in little babies. Who's going to get more attention, a fish who just looks at you and opens and shuts its mouth or a dog that comes over and climbs on you and wants to play?
Wife: A baby isn't a fish! How can you say that?

Therapist: Good, keep expressing your feelings, but don't forget: Understanding how the other person feels doesn't mean giving in.

Mother: You never want to talk to me. All you ever want to do is sit in front of the stupid television.
Father: (Long silence) I'm afraid you don't care about me and what I'm doing. All you want to talk about is the kids. The kids did this, the kids did that—(She breaks down in tears and his face drops like a kid who just broke the living room window.)
Therapist: Alright, so she's upset. That doesn't mean you have to stop talking—(to her) does it?
Mother: (Sniffling) No.

Just like that? Yes—not always, perhaps, but often. While it is true that many family conflicts are anchored in long-standing personal reactions and family interactions, many more might be solved if people would only stop running away. Many dialogues never take place. The teenager who "can't talk to her parents" probably doesn't spend much time trying; the man whose wife "spends all her time with the children" makes little effort to tell her how he feels, preferring the pleasure of resentment to the uncertain results of honest communication.

Other conversations recur as predictably as the common cold on vacations, but because they are painful they don't last long enough to get anywhere. Most people run away when they get anxious. Left alone, they carefully avoid getting too close to certain painful conclusions. At home, when conversation heats up, they change the subject or walk away.

MAKING IT SAFE TO OPEN UP

The problem of blockaded communication may be thought of as "systemic resistance" or "homeostasis." But an alternate, and more useful, construction is that people avoid conflict unless they feel protected. Those who fear that they cannot protect themselves (like the couples who only fight in public) may open up in the presence of a parent figure like a therapist. In therapy they can't walk away because the door is closed, at least for an hour. This structured confinement makes it possible to extend the limits of never-started and half-finished conversations.

The following case illustrates a slightly, but only slightly, more complicated example of prodding people to open up and work out their own problems.

When I first saw Irv in individual therapy his complaint was loneliness. He moved from a large city he liked to a small one that he didn't like in order to follow a career opportunity. It was, he thought, a mistake. The new city was "cold," people were "clannish" and "provincial." Feeling sorry for himself, he spent his evenings in his apartment drinking beer, where the only people he met were locked inside the television set. My treatment consisted of little more than encouraging him to go out and meet people, and helping him to understand some of the reasons why he was afraid to do so. Soon after he met Megan, he thanked me and said goodbye.

Two months later Irv called and asked me to see him and Megan together. They were thinking about getting married but he was concerned about their recurrent arguments. The main point of contention was her going out to a bar with her girlfriends. They talked about it and talked about it but somehow couldn't resolve the conflict. The real problem, they thought, must be something deeper than communication. I wondered.

When I asked them to talk it over, Irv said he was worried about her. She shouldn't be drinking so much; why did she need to see all these other people anyway? Why couldn't she agree to go to the bar only once every other week, and then only with him? In reply she mumbled something about wanting to have fun, and then started negotiating with him about how often she should have some time with her friends.

To say that a problem is "deeper" than communication implies that it is rooted in the unconscious (or the system) and that talking won't get at it. But it isn't always necessary to invoke unconscious motivation or homeostatic systemic forces. Irv and Megan's problem was "deeper" only in the sense that they weren't saying all that was on their minds. They kept repeating their argument because neither one ever heard what was really bothering the other one.

Megan was 26 and single. She had lived with her parents all her life up until four months ago. She wanted to feel free. Irv was 34, had been living alone for years, and wanted her to move in with him. Their discussions stayed within a limited range. What didn't get talked about was his insecurity and jealousy, or her wanting to be her own boss. He assumed a paternal tone, and she adopted the same deferential manner she used at home. My intervention was simple. I pushed them to keep talking, urged her not to pretend to agree to do something that she really didn't want to do, and suggested that he talk about what he was afraid of rather than what she "should do."

Megan told him that she wanted to be her own boss, she didn't want to move out of her father's house and straight into Irv's. He told her that he was afraid she would see her old boyfriend in the bar. I pointed out that if Megan allowed him to tell her where to go she would always feel stuck and resentful. He got the message. And I told Irv that he wouldn't ever feel secure as long as he thought his security depended on keeping her on a short leash. There were, of course, reasons why Irv and Megan held back some of what they felt, but it didn't seem necessary to analyze their avoidance. Once they opened up, they were able to work things out. The relationship didn't need an overhaul, only a tune-up.

As any family therapist (or anyone who has lived in a family) knows, some dialogues get stuck and stay stuck. Even when the avoidant parties are brought together, and others kept out of it, the conversations just don't seem to get anywhere. Instead, the couple bogs down in bickering and self-justification. They talk but don't listen. These impasses lead many clinicians to take over. Some do so by frequent interruptions, others give up altogether on communication as a vehicle to solve problems.

An alternative solution is to open up deeper levels of experience, to get past defensive positioning to the often more vulnerable feelings underneath. Individual therapists have described the need to provide a "holding environment"—an envelope of warmth and support within which it is safe to explore the secrets of the heart. Family therapy provides a holding environment for the whole family—a place where it is easier to open up and harder not to. But the risks are greater. If a woman tells her husband that she sometimes wishes he were dead, he's not likely to ask her, "What comes to mind?" Family therapists must therefore be more active than individual therapists, but the activity can be to push family members into opening up more rather than to take over for them.

Individual therapy permits deep involvement, but there is a temptation to treat the tools of healing—immersion in feelings, the past, and fantasy—as ends rather than means. The counter problem in family therapy is to stay stuck on the surface in present behavioral reality, which drowns out unconscious aspects, creating external confirmation of inner object-images. When children or spouses are recruited to fill unconscious roles, family dialogues can be like shadowboxing in the dark. You cannot make real contact when you are fighting your own shadow.

Individual therapy provides a holding environment, but that environment is artificial and can be symbiotic. Family therapy is more real, but more risky, so many people stay on the surface. It may be necessary to go below the surface—to find out, for example, why a father cannot let go of his daughter.

Imagine a father who intrudes into his daughter's conversation with her husband. The father can be said to be enmeshed with his daughter and therefore should be blocked. While it may be possible to keep him out of the daughter/son-in-law conversation in a therapy session merely by giving him another job ("Listen, and see if they can settle it"), he is unlikely to stay out of it until he learns to see himself and (in this case) his daughter as separate and distinct and until he begins to realize that his child is *not* as anxious, dependent, or shy as he has felt himself to be. Breaking endless family arguments may mean getting to the felt experience behind the words—the dancers' feelings, not just their steps. But families seduce therapists into taking overt reality as the ultimate reality.

There are many ways to break repetitive cycles of interaction using only the material before you, but sometimes the best way is going deeper, past defensive maneuvering to the heart of the matter. Opening up deeper levels of experience is especially important in couples work, where the fact that a couple request or accept work on the relationship makes looking at triangles less important. When the field is cleared of triangles, the only complications left are those arising from the psychology of the two persons in dialogue. They've already acknowledged that "it's us," so it is more important to get a fuller, richer picture of the "us" than to isolate them from interference. The following vignette illustrates how opening up privately inflected experience can help couples through impasses in their relationship.

A couple in their forties came to therapy because of repeated quarrelling. At the same time they called they had not been speaking to each other for two months. In a session four weeks into treatment, she spoke of wanting to buy a house. He is reluctant. The subject has been on their minds for some time, but like many couples, they avoid the discussion to avoid the conflicts that go with it.

Their commitment to therapy (it seemed like the last resort) and the presence of the therapist give them courage to open difficult issues. When they begin, they do so in repetitious terms: He says what he usually says, she says what she usually says in response, and so on. . . .

Her: I want to move.
Him: Okay, but I don't want to live under the pressure of a big mortgage.

In a familiar pattern, she gets angry and criticizes him for implying that she is impulsive and irresponsible. ("What are you saying!") He responds with ever more obsessional doubting. ("I know, but what about. . . ?") She is "sick and tired" of living "in squalor"; she wants to "enjoy life." He wonders whether they can afford a new house, worries that they will be in debt, and doesn't want to take any chances.

As the discussion goes back and forth, the therapist becomes frustrated because it seems that a little checking would clarify many of the practical aspects of their argument. A realtor could tell them what they could get for their house, how much the house they want would cost, interest rates, and probably even come up with an estimate of their new monthly mortgage payment. ("Why don't they check it out, instead of attacking each other's personality?")

Not certain but assuming the issue may have something to do with unstated, more personal themes, the therapist talks separately with each of them in an effort to get deeper into their feelings.

She cries and says she feels stuck and trapped. "We're locked indoors. Everything is so serious with you. We can't do this, we can't do that, we don't even have any friends anymore."

He says he feels negated. "You can't just disagree, you have to attack me. I always end up feeling that you just don't like who I am."

So, we have surfaced some deep resentments and concerns. Just voicing them can be therapeutic. Experiencing deep worries—as worries, not attacks—and sharing them brings people closer to understanding. But at this point I risk oversimplification—replacing one myth, that people are puppets of the system, for another, the humanistic myth that if people will only open up, all will be well. Well, it won't. People hide away their tender feelings because *they* are tender. Family members are guarded with each other for a reason. The more unexamined and unexpressed are feelings, the more vulnerable people are to unkind responses. It isn't just what someone says that counts, but how people respond.

In the process of describing interactions as mobilizing the self in action, I have twice emphasized the need for understanding and support: first, to initiate enactments ("building an alliance of understanding"); second to provide a "holding environment" safe enough to help family members overcome their fears of opening up to each other. In the following chapter I will explain how therapists can use understanding and support to explore deeper into the psychology of the self in the system *and* to teach family members how to enhance their own relationships through empathy.

4

Empathy

Empathy is as essential for engaging individuals in honest and full participation in family therapy as interaction is for mobilizing group processes. Interaction sets the system in motion; empathy brings out the elusive self.

It is impossible to overestimate the motivational significance of the need for understanding and acceptance. This is true in therapy and in everyday family life. Troubled family members experience therapy as an attempt to undermine their identity. It is hard to give up one's identity and patterns of behavior until new ones are available. And it certainly doesn't feel safe to give up the old world unless you trust the therapist enough to guide you to a new one. A reticent father may begin to talk about his unhappy child, but unless he finds some understanding he may not talk openly or long. The therapist's empathic response helps family members feel understood and accepted enough to become engaged in the process of therapy, and encourages them to express long-felt but incompletely understood and seldom voiced aspects of their experience. Everyone needs an ally at times of stress.

Viewed from the outside, family members often seem maddeningly, stubbornly unwilling to change. From this perspective, it seems reasonable to provoke them into doing what they don't seem to want to, using strategies to manipulate rather than to inspire change. If we assume that "systemic forces" make it impossible for people to change of their own accord, then it seems to follow that the best results can be achieved by standing outside the system to contrive interventions. When family therapists take up an overdistanced emotional position, they do so to protect themselves from being trapped in the family's narrow and unproductive view of their problems *and* to protect themselves from feeling the family's pain.

Family therapists are a sensitive lot. That's why they choose helping as a profession. Yet something makes them ready to deliberately mute this sensitivity, or rather deemphasize it, in favor of a more calculating approach. The healing attitude has given way to detective work for personal as well as programmatic reasons. As therapists, we often recapitulate our own personal evolution in our careers. In adolescence, we are in full touch with life; we see everything and feel intensely. This exposure leaves us open to wonder and pleasure, but also to countless hurts. So, gradually we seal over our sensibility. We feel less and we are more equipped for practical life. A similar pattern describes our development as therapists.

When I first started seeing families, I felt with my patients, making me compassionate but often overwhelmed. Gradually, I concentrated on the tactics of change, and slowly I anesthetized myself to the awful anxieties and disappointments my clients suffered. This is not altogether unhealthy. Too much sympathy leaves us without objective perspective. If we feel too much with our patients, we may not see through their defenses or find a way out of their dilemmas.

Hardheaded, detached observation helps us see systems in action, but can lead us to confuse living persons—wanting, thinking, and feeling people—with moving objects. In unhappy families, people are cut off from understanding and sympathy. These people develop whole reservoirs of feeling that they believe their families don't know about and don't care about. The resulting resentment can fester and is often preoccupying. When they come to therapy, families are anxious and defensive, but also hopeful—hopeful for a fresh start, hopeful that here is someone who will understand them at last. Being understood makes life bearable, and cooperation and compromise possible. In the absence of empathy, everybody loses.

Some people are hard to empathize with. How do you empathize with someone who does horrible things? How do you "understand" the woman who beats her children or the man who molests a little girl? It isn't easy. A woman came to see me recently because she was depressed. Two weeks previously the state police had come to her house in the middle of the night to arrest her husband. Their 15-year-old daughter had run away to the police barracks and told them that her father had repeatedly forced her to have anal and oral sex with him. His wife hadn't suspected. She was numb, horrified.

Hearing the story, so was I. You don't blame me? However, unless I could get over my disgust enough to try to understand what happened—what led this man to do what he did—I doubt that I could provide very effective help. Like the court, I would probably be prejudiced in favor of expelling this man forever from his family—and that's not my right to decide.

It's hard to understand what is alien to our experience. At a recent disposition meeting in our clinic, a psychiatric resident reported his intake session with a 22-year-old single mother from the wrong side of the tracks. Her presenting complaint—"I've been losing control with my baby, hitting her, and I'm afraid I might hurt her"—provoked a long and heated argument. The law says we should report "even a suspicion" of child abuse. Most of the staff members insisted that we immediately report the case to the child protective agency. But, despite my own fears—for the child's safety as well as for my own culpability—I decided to interview the woman myself before informing the authorities. I needed more facts about what exactly she was doing and I also felt that if I could understand her, not just her feelings but why she had trouble controlling the little girl, I could help.

Fortunately, I *was* able to understand. She so desperately wanted her little girl's affection that she found it hard to set and enforce rules. And I was able to help her realize that her daughter would love her at least as well if she took charge.

Short of such dramatic examples of child molestation and beating, most family therapists have trouble empathizing with certain types of people, especially domineering and controlling mothers, while they tend to overempathize with others, often misunderstood adolescents. Here is an example from my own practice. When I referred to this case in Chapter 2, I implied that excluding the mother was an error of calculation, perhaps, but I think the root problem was my inability to empathize with this woman.

The Sullivans were one of those families with a domineering mother and an emotionally absent father. This family was worse than usual. Mrs. Sullivan was a real harridan. She berated her husband, attacked her children, and took control of the session. I knew enough not to oppose her openly, so I tried to "join" her by pretending to sympathize with her. I knew I would lose in any argument with her. So I used her complaint that she had all the responsibility as an excuse to get the husband more involved. I convinced her that she was "not only worn out, but depressed" (that wasn't too hard), and therefore I would meet with her husband and the "problem child" for a few sessions. "Unbalancing?" Maybe. Looking back I think I excluded her because I didn't understand her and didn't like her. Or, tried to exclude her. My strategy backfired when she reacted to my attempt to put her husband in charge of discipline like a bear protecting her cubs. It's probably accurate to say that the system was reverting to the familiar status quo, but I think it is also true that she knew I didn't like her and was trying to usurp her position in the family.

How do you empathize with people you can't understand? Part of the problem is confusing empathy with sympathy. But there is a crucial difference. Sympathy is more limited and limiting; it means to feel the same as, rather than to be understanding. It is an emotion that makes us suffer *with* unhappy people, and that feeling motivates us to avoid them or do *for* them. Nor does empathy mean, as many students think, actively prizing, valuing, praising, supporting, and encouraging patients. It means understanding. The difference can be illustrated in response to a hypothetical patient who says, "It's not fair. I work all day, just like he does, but when I come home at night, he still expects me to do all the cooking and all the cleaning." A sympathetic therapist might say, "You're right, it's not fair. He should help out." An empathic response would understand, accept, and sensitively interpret the patient's need for support. For example: "It's frustrating, isn't it? And I gather that, more even than having to do all the work, it hurts to feel that he doesn't understand, and doesn't care. But I also get the idea that something makes you hesitate to demand a change."

WHAT EMPATHY MEANS AND WHY IT IS CRUCIAL

Empathy has been defined variously as "the inner experience of sharing in and comprehending the momentary psychological state of another person,"[1] "vicarious introspection,"[2] and "emotional knowing."[3] Like the more familiar term "understanding," empathy entails both comprehension and acceptance. Empathy is a natural human capacity that becomes layered over by nonempathic forms of cognition. Just as we put blinders on horses to prevent them from being distracted on the way to the finish line, we blunt our own seeing and feeling in favor of getting and doing. One small example: The first time you drive to a new job you probably notice the houses along the way, the trees, and the changing of the seasons. Later, you notice only whether the traffic lights are red or green—sometimes not even that.

Empathy is primarily a tool for understanding, and it is achieved by open and receptive listening. Empathy is particularly important if we view persons as more complicated than the surface manifestations of their behavior. If we reduce human action to behavior and family life to behavioral interaction, then there would be little need for empathy. If, on the other hand, we comprehend that people's behavior depends very much on psychic and emotional events, then empathy, which is the means to gain knowledge and understanding of the mind and feelings of another person, becomes very important.

The pioneers of family therapy made discoveries about family relationships that most of us miss as long as we are caught up in the emotions of everyday life. In the process of discovery, systems thinkers deliberately suspended their empathic concern for the individual in order to take a larger perspective. The family systems point of view is a little like seeing patterns and harmony emerge as you view the landscape of a community from the window of an airplane. From the sky, you can see order and design where previously you saw only confusion and separateness. Adopting an empathic point of view means returning to earth, where people live, for a closer look.

The empathic point of view—openness to the inner experience of others—is a counterweight to free family therapists from what has increasingly become an elaborate and elegant, but also mechanistic, systems model. Empathy is not confined to any one school of psychotherapy. Here, for example, is Cloé Madanes, one of the most daring and ingenious of the strategic therapists, explaining the importance of empathy:

> I think we all have problems empathizing with people who represent the weaker aspect of ourselves. So if I have a weak mother in a session or a weak wife that gets mistreated by a man, I have trouble identifying with them because I don't like to see them in myself. To deal intelligently with a client, the important thing isn't distance but the ability to feel that I am her. So if it's painful to feel that I am her, I will have trouble developing the relationship I need. I will then tend to have trouble engaging and motivating her.[4]

If we can at least understand the people we work with—what they really want, what are their private feelings, what drives them to do what they do, and what are the fears that hold them back—a great deal has been accomplished. It may not sound like much, but it's more succor than most people get at home. Moreover, once they discover that they are in the presence of a receptive listener, most people feel stronger—strong enough to fight for what they want and strong enough to be receptive to what others in the family want.

The disengaged father, for example, is not merely "not participating"; he is actively engaged—feeling angry, perhaps, and brooding about nobody caring what he thinks. The first step toward making room in his mind for something other than his private reservoir of resentment is getting him to say what is on his mind. If someone seems willing to understand and convinces him of that, he may stop stewing in his own vexation and start talking.

However much individuals in a family may be concerned about and involved with one another, they are still largely preoccupied with their own agendas: personal concerns, idiosyncratic perceptions, quirky inhibitions, strongly held opinions, and secret (and not so secret) wishes. Even (or especially) if unspoken, such personal agendas are aggressively defended. The persistent pressure of these subjective urges works a dynamic claim on the mind and a thrust toward action in a personal direction which may conflict with collective aims of the family. The individual's personal motives may represent a secret rebellion against the need to grow up and renounce the self-centered pursuit of his or her own desires.

Ordinarily, many of one's feelings and desires are private. They separate the individual from the group. Shared opinions and wishes, on the other hand, are a step toward mutual understanding. Secrets shared by everybody are no longer secret—and no longer act as unseen blocks to cooperative change. A receptive, empathic response encourages people to share their motives and perceptions. Therefore, we must pay particular attention to empathy, our own and that of other family members, if we are to treat persons, not just collections of nameless, faceless cogs in a machine.

Empathy is enjoying a fashionable acceptance in psychoanalysis where it has lately been advocated as a corrective to the more austere and cool traditional analytic stance. Actually, empathy has been around a long time. In 1942, Fliess advised therapists "to step into [the patient's] shoes, and to obtain in this way an inside knowledge that is almost first-hand. The common name for such a procedure is empathy."[5] In *The Psychoanalytic Theory of Neurosis* (1945), Fenichel quotes Reik, who maintained that empathy consists of two acts: "a) an identification with the other person, and

b) an awareness of one's own feelings after the identification, and in this way an awareness of the object's feelings."[6] Later, Carl Rogers founded his whole approach to treatment on empathy.[7] In client-centered therapy the therapist listens with benevolent understanding—"unconditional positive regard"—to help people rediscover their true feelings.

Thanks to the popularity of self psychology, empathy is much in vogue, but it is sometimes reduced to a superficial sensitivity and a trite and false, patronizing, shallow comment: "I understand," "Don't feel so bad; you're a good person," "Things will work out." Like cotton candy, the saccharine approach to patients is sweet, but lacks substance. Empathy does not mean condescending kindness from a patronizing therapist, but rather a sincere understanding of what the person is experiencing and some appreciation of how it feels to that person.

Empathy is a great tool of understanding, but it is not magic. Indeed, advocating empathy can degenerate into the idea that therapy cures through kindness, respect for the patient, and love. This is an incredible conceit considering the complexity of individual needs and family problems. Moreover, the emotional capacity of most therapists is no better than the average person's. That therapists can be loving is due to the fact that patients impinge relatively little on their lives, which only points up the limited and artificial nature of the therapeutic relationship.

Individual therapy is sometimes described as a developmental remedy. If mommy and daddy were not loving enough to nurture a secure base of self-esteem, the therapist will. Therapists who try to repair "developmental arrests" believe that what was missed is still missing and that it needs to be provided in roughly the original form. Therapy, then, is described in mother-infant terms, recreating the world of the nursery with "holding," "containment," and even "good mothering." But our grown-up patients are not really infants in adult bodies. They are adults, some of whose developmental capacity for relatedness was warped and who now have needs for an adult version of these needs—something real, something authentic.

Family therapy is about the present and about real relationships. It is not up to the therapist to provide missing support, it is
up to the family. An empathic therapist acknowledges what family members say and thus confirms their experience. In this way,
the therapist vitalizes by emotional participation and reflection
what clients sometimes experience as inchoate. In the long run,
though, it isn't the therapist's understanding that counts, it is the
understanding that family members develop for one another.

Family members can enrich their own lives by getting beyond
solipsistic experience. Most people, however, are fixed in their
own singular, idiosyncratic perceptions, and hope they can impose their personal vision on others. They stay that way until they
are heard and understood. Unfortunately, as long as right and
wrong are "me" and "you," the result is permanent stalemate and
permanent bitterness. Let me illustrate this with an example.

Elizabeth had her suspicions but preferred not to think about
them. When Derek suddenly announced that he had to spend
Labor Day "checking the progress on their ski lodge," she could
no longer remain silent. She confronted him. He confessed and
moved out. I saw them three weeks later when they were in the
process of trying to put their relationship back together.

Elizabeth, seven months pregnant, was bitter and hurt. She
wanted him back, but she also wanted some reassurance that
he would not repeat his infidelity. Derek felt enough guilt to
deny it. He said, "I'm sorry that I hurt you, but I am not about
to put on a hair shirt and brand myself with a scarlet A." The
sad part was that they both seemed to understand the other's
point of view—only they couldn't, wouldn't, admit it.

"If only she would stop condemning me and start putting
the past in the past, then everything would be okay." Meanwhile, "If only he would start letting me talk about my feelings
and stop trying to make me out a shrew. . . . " They said as
well as thought these things but, since neither listened, the
other's statements became background noise, as meaningless
as Muzak. They tried to be active and constructive, but the form
it took—repeating their own points of view—left them feeling
passive, resentful, victims.

Remember the Chinese finger puzzle? We played with it when we were kids. It was a tube of woven raffia, and you stuck one finger into each end. As long as you tried to yank your fingers out, the raffia only held them tighter. The trick, easily discovered, was to relax and stop pulling, then the raffia would let go. Unfortunately Elizabeth and Derek were playing too serious a game to risk letting go. Each of them wanted to win, meaning be right, and therefore felt the need to make the other one wrong. So they did what couples often do: they shut up, preferring to avoid the subject of their feelings rather than suffer the arguing and recriminations.

Over the years, couples hide away their feelings. Not all of them, of course, but enough. These silent areas fester and assume more than their share of importance, eventually perhaps becoming preoccupations. If Derek and Elizabeth never talk about the affair, they will find it hard to forget. Guilt flourishes when we hide away important parts of ourselves. Anger, too. The more we hide, the more guilty and angry we feel.

People live in their own personal and subjective worlds. To meet, truly meet, means that they must open up this part of themselves, feel it, and share it. And it must be received. Much of the time we hide away our real feelings, sometimes even from ourselves. As a result, the transactions of family therapy, like the transactions of everyday life, often consist of defensive shadows dancing with each other.

Often the best way to support people is to help them face what they don't want to face. As therapists, we sometimes have our own reluctance to face facts. When Derek and Elizabeth were in the process of repairing their relationship, she wanted him to talk about his impulse to fool around outside the marriage. He was willing, but I tried to smooth it over, redefine what he was saying to take the sting out. For example, when he said he thought he might "just be the kind of person who never settles down," I asked him, "When you *used to* think that, did you think of it as natural or maybe as a sign of immaturity?" It was not an innocent question. I guess I just don't want to think of people as unwilling to be faithful. But, in order to understand Derek, I had to realize that was *my* fear, not his, and as it turned out, not so much his wife's fear. She said, "I can understand him having those feelings, but I want him to talk about it."

The therapist's empathy is a bridge to enrich relationships in the present. Being in the presence of an empathic therapist reactivates the hope of responsiveness to self. That is why family members turn to the therapist even when they are asked to talk to each other. The therapist's acceptance and support provide a transition to help develop possibilities for relationship previously unavailable or unutilized in the family. For example, the therapist's empathy for Derek's previously unacknowledged feelings of not being appreciated and his need to prove his worth through conquest has two effects which seem paradoxical. Elizabeth, who may have regarded his behavior as willful, stubborn, and mean, may now regard it as necessary, or at least driven. He did what he did because of how he felt and what he thought. Action seemed at the time the only possible reaction. He could not do otherwise, *then*, even though someone else might have.

At the same time, this enlargement of Derek's subjective experience brings with it a greater sense of freedom of choice. To be conscious of his feelings and to have them acknowledged takes away some of their driving push. Now he begins to experience himself as the author of his actions, both in the past and in the future. Empathy makes it possible for her to understand the inevitability of his past actions, and for him to imagine alternatives.

Aren't all therapists empathic? No. Humane and compassionate, perhaps, but among family therapists empathy often gives way to a calculating techniquism. It is hard to feel and show understanding when you are in a rush to change people.

Another thing that makes empathy difficult is the sense of powerlessness that sometimes motivates us to act a bossy show of power*full*ness. Rather than empathize with a family's hopelessness and helplessness, we sometimes rush in to make it go away. This is an action-discharge form of denying our own feelings of pessimism. Busy, active techniques can be an attempt to substitute action for empathy.

TECHNIQUISM AND DETACHMENT

It's hard being a therapist. Not only are we exposed to a great deal of human unhappiness, we are also expected to relieve it. People often ask, "Isn't it painful to listen to people's problems all day long?" Yes, it is. But what makes it bearable, for me at any rate, is the sense that I can understand and help. In fact, when I am treating a family that I don't think I'm helping, I feel exhausted and drained. I believe that too many family therapists respond to this anxiety by taking control; I recommend trying harder to understand.

We come to our profession with intuitive empathic skills. But we also have a need to master the threatening influx of anxiety that listening to other people's problems exposes us to. This anxiety interferes with empathy and drives us toward detachment and techniquism. I believe that it is this pressure—an instinctive aversion to sitting still in the face of human suffering—that propels therapists to look for the quick fix. Solving problems is in itself satisfying and worthwhile, but we are also driven to solve them by the desire to keep the world of painful experience at arm's length. Family therapy has slid into a preference for quick-action solutions that aim to cover up as quickly as possible the emotional pain that is part of every human life. It is the number one occupational hazard of our trade.

The same one-way mirror that allows observers to see what is going on also screens out painful feelings. Therapists who sit on the hot side of the radiant shield are exposed to swirling emotions, but tend to hold back, waiting for consultation and guidance from behind the screen. Not all family therapists have the luxury of working with a team of colleagues behind a one-way mirror, but in a broad sense the field is guided by the leading figures who figuratively sit behind mirrors. We all wait for their input.

Techniquism is not confined to family therapy, but it seems particularly prevalent among therapists who treat more difficult cases. We have become so absorbed with techniques that our relationships with patients have become depersonalized. Gestures are made. But real empathy is not the same as faked feeling, the cranked-up sentimentality of one who feels nothing of his or her patients' lives, but pretends to do so.

It is generally unwise to fake compassion you do not feel. The problem is not so much with being a phony, but with failing to ask sensitive questions to draw out the client's dilemma. Saying, for example, "I don't quite understand. Can you tell me what it's been like?" conveys an honest wish to understand. A false mask of sympathetic concern—"Oh, I understand"—can shield us from contact with real human suffering every bit as effectively as whiz-bang techniquism.

Seasoned and skillful therapists are committed to an approach rather than bound to a technique. As the term "positive connotation" suggests, even a strategic approach does not preclude appreciating and valuing clients simply for who they are. A narrow concern with technique—even positive connotation as a disingenuous ploy—inevitably seems to distance us from our clients. The clinical technician is analogous to the compulsive punster. When a person makes a pun in a social situation—regardless of how clever the pun and its author—the joker has momentarily drawn back, making connections he would not think of if he were fully involved in the social moment.

The clinician enamored of technique may become an excellent teacher or consultant, but probably not an effective therapist. For that it is necessary to be willing to undergo long, careful immersion in the hopes, joys, and disasters of unhappy people.

Empathy, if it is to serve any practical function, means understanding what the other person is struggling to express. Unfortunately, the desire to reform and change people is inimical to understanding them. You can hardly listen and take in anything like the full richness of a patient's experience if you are only waiting to pounce on him like a cat on a mouse. (Incidentally, cats know little about mice except where they hide and which way they run.) When we focus narrowly on who does what to whom, we may forget that the whos and the whoms are as real and complex as we are ourselves.

Almost no one doubts that compassion is a good thing; its worth is transparent and needs no defense. But many family therapists need to remind themselves to work harder at being empathic. At a certain point—when we grow sure of our skills and limits—we can stop thinking of clients as adversaries and begin thinking of them as *patients,* people who suffer and come seeking help.

HOW TO ACHIEVE EMPATHY

Therapists vary in their naturally endowed sensitivity to others. Some people can read another person's motives, intentions, feelings, anxieties, and hesitations more readily than others. But sensitivity alone doesn't make a good therapist, any more than intelligence alone makes a successful student. Real curiosity and genuine compassion may be personal gifts, but empathy is not a passive experience. All therapists must work at it.

Regardless of the approach to treatment, it is unlikely to be effective if it doesn't meet the person's basic need for affirmation. The therapist who intervenes to change people before understanding and affirming them is indistinguishable from the destructive parent who rejected and criticized them. Such "therapy" is another instance of nonresponsiveness, a failure to value people for who they are, and an attempt to discredit or disqualify their experience of reality. Strong patients will rebel, weak ones may be traumatized.

The empathic therapist offers a bond of understanding in a deep sense. It is more than the friendly sympathy you might get from an aunt; it is the deeper resonance of understanding you feel when a trusted friend reveals something rather complicated and personal. Perhaps you may remember a time when you were troubled and a friend put a hand on your shoulder. It is a reassuring experience of understanding acceptance.

In this kind of relationship, patients experience a reactivation of thwarted needs for compassionate understanding and families for intimate dialogue.

Empathy is often harder to achieve, yet even more important in family therapy. With only one person present—an individual patient—there is only one point of view. We may consider that point of view to be misguided or confused at times, but at least we can understand the feelings behind it. Family therapy introduces a number of complexities, not the least of which is that there are several points of view, often conflicting. When a parent and a child, or a wife and a husband, are quarrelling, we may find ourselves drawn into sympathy with one or the other of them. Most therapists know enough to resist taking sides, but in the process some suppress empathy altogether.

Integrating empathy into family therapy does not require any radical change of strategy. It means working a little harder to understand people before trying to change them, and it means demonstrating this understanding with empathic comments which help draw out individual family members. Simple empathic comments can express understanding, or be used to reach something unexpressed in the other. This helps break down the denial of feeling which often keeps family members apart. Denial is unnecessary if there is someone to share and accept feelings. The empathic therapist can be that someone.

The empathic therapist celebrates the naturalness of what is felt—"No wonder you were mad!"—against a person's need to deny a feeling. In individual therapy, there may be conflicting feelings to understand: "You hate what he did to you, but you're afraid to think about it." In family therapy you can count on conflicting feelings. The empathic therapist serves as an ally, first of one and then of other family members. Bringing out feelings in family members catalyzes more openness. This may intensify conflict, but it also creates the possibility for resolving that conflict. Empathic statements make it possible to acknowledge the conflict, which is the first step toward working it out or, at the very least, mutually accepting its existence.

Empathy is achieved by placing oneself attentively near the other and by being alert for expressions of feeling rather than concentrating exclusively on descriptions of behavior. It means listening without being in a hurry to take over.

LISTENING

Listening is a strenuous but silent activity, rare in our culture. Most of the time we are too busy waiting to get a word in edgewise to really hear what anyone else is saying. Foremost among the obstacles to listening are those that stem from our need to "do something" about what is being said: defend ourselves, disagree, or solve whatever problems are being described.

Curbing the usual problem-solving thinking releases our capacity to empathize. In order to listen well, therapists should begin with the purpose of achieving understanding, rather than rushing to cure, or help, or manipulate. Ultimately, of course, therapy must lead to change. But to achieve empathy—at the outset of treatment and periodically when individual family members need understanding—it is necessary to set aside the urge to change.

Nor is it possible to listen well if you are trying too hard to be "supportive." Empathy is not loving or sympathetic caring or gratification or praise; it is deep understanding. To illustrate these points, imagine how a therapist might respond in the following situation.

After several sessions of exhausting argument with her rebellious teenage son, a middle-aged woman says, "I can't stand it any more. I'm sick and tired of all this fighting." How might a therapist respond?

"I know how you feel" is an all too common alternative. This formula aims at both sympathy and understanding, but misses both. And it likely closes off further exploration.

Since family therapists are more concerned with what people do than with how they feel, a therapist might ask, "What are you doing about it?" "What are you doing?" questions have the advantage of uncovering interactional dynamics, making it possible to solve problems by changing relationships. Unhappy feelings often take care of themselves as soon as unhappy relationships are transformed. Early in therapy, this is precisely the kind of question that should be asked. But after several sessions, a therapist probably has a pretty clear idea of how family members interact to maintain problems. At this stage, it may be useful to inquire more carefully into what people are feeling. Therefore, a therapeutic response might be, "You really sound upset, but I'm not sure I understand what you're going through." This conveys both empathy and an invitation for the mother to elaborate her experience, much of which may lack clarity and differentiation until she has a chance to talk about it. Perhaps she feels sad, misunderstood, frustrated, inadequate, or lonely. I don't know, and neither does the family, as long as she shows only anger, and as long as no one inquires.

Because my example was deliberately sketchy, readers might object that they don't know enough about the context to formulate a response. Is the mother enmeshed with or disengaged from her son? And what about her husband? While it is true that therapeutic strategy should be tailored to fit the case, empathy—an appreciation of the inner psychological state of family members—should be a constant. An empathic response to the woman above helps her formulate her own experience and, therefore, enables her husband and son to understand her better. This is useful whether they are enmeshed or disengaged. Understanding brings people closer, but it also clarifies ego boundaries. Enmeshment reflects a loss of boundaries between oneself and others. It often means feeling at one with someone, thinking that both experience and feel the same feelings. An empathic response helps clarify the unique aspects of a person's experience and thus increases and sustains self-cohesion—a feeling of being a whole person, understandable and worthwhile.

Feeling With and Thinking About Others

Empathy begins with listening, but even when we listen, empathy is not a passive or automatic experience. Good therapy does not automatically result from natural warmth and acceptance the way spring flowers flourish in the sunshine. This is a Pollyannish and romantic notion. That which we feel automatically, passively, is colored by countertransference. When empathy is equated with "gut reaction," we confuse our reactions with the patient's meanings. In addition to passive receptivity, empathy requires active thinking, understanding, and eventually communicating. Truly respectful listening requires trying to fathom the experience implied by what people are saying. Empathy involves actively imagining what things look like from inside someone else's lifeworld.

Empathy requires two kinds of activity. The first is what Fliess refers to as "trial identification."[8] To feel what a patient is feeling requires receptivity and openness, like a theatergoer who allows herself to be stimulated and moved by the players. Secondarily, there is an oscillation between feeling and thinking. This requires a deliberate shift from thinking and feeling *with* the patient to thinking *about* the patient. Schafer refers to this as moving from the experiencing ego to the observing ego.[9]

Here is an example. Suppose an 11-year-old girl complains that she has no friends and is lonely. How does she feel and what does she want? Most of us can identify with the feeling of loneliness. Eleven years old or 35, man or woman, we all know what loneliness feels like. Feeling with this little girl initially requires little more than taking time and being receptive. But empathy, real empathy, also requires a second step: thinking about *her*. How does *her* loneliness feel and what does *she* think about. Our loneliness might be a dull ache and a longing for lost friends. The little girl's loneliness might be that, but also shaky fear, a profound sense of inadequacy, and a wish for her mother to make the loneliness go away. In other words, to feel only what we feel automatically may miss the boat. To us, lonely makes us think of friends. To her, lonely makes her want her mother more.

Sometimes we empathize too much. If we overidentify with one individual, we may begin to overlook that person's contributions to the family problems. Perhaps a better way to put it is that we take one person's side and don't get around to understanding the others. Empathy for the little girl might help us to express the child's needs to the mother—"She misses you; she wants your attention"—resulting in tears and hugs, and apparent closure. But if we stay too long or too much with the little girl's point of view, we may overlook the mother's needs and feelings. After all, she's human too. Maybe, by 11, it's time for the little girl to be sympathetic to the burdens of being a mother.

Trial identification is like wine tasting. You take a sip and consider; you don't merely swallow it down without consideration. Kohut calls this "vicarious introspection." But in the process of elevating empathy to the primary mode of therapeutic investigation, he makes it mystical and blurs the distinction between passive receptivity and active thinking, conjecturing, formulating, and communicating.

Reflecting on One's Own Experience

We have all had the experience of watching a grown-up and seeing a child. The fat man at his dinner reminds us of a lonely little boy soothing himself with an ice cream cone, the bickering couple reminds us of two children trading insults, and the nagging spouse reminds us of a bossy child who really wants to be liked. It's automatic. With a little practice, we can see a great deal of human behavior this way. And we don't have to be disdainful. We hear the voice of the child and know intuitively something of that person's lasting agenda. Seeing the childlike hurt behind the adult facade is an example of empathy without effort. Sometimes we have to work at it.

Several years ago I was treating a family with a severely depressed daughter. Early in her senior year in college, Gretchen began slipping into a depression. When it got so bad that she no longer attended classes and didn't even get out of bed, her family became alarmed and sought treatment. In our sessions, Gretchen's parents did what people do when a family member becomes depressed. They tried to figure out "what's wrong" and they discussed "what to do." "What to do"—try to finish out the year, take a leave of absence—was a sufficiently compelling question that I too was preoccupied with it. Fortunately I was still in supervision, for my supervisor saw what I did not. Neither I nor the family seemed to understand how Gretchen felt. Just the opposite. We were defensively avoiding empathy, attempting to control not only the situation but also ourselves.

If Gretchen had been more articulate and more forceful, she

might have told us how she felt. But then she might not have had to become depressed to get the point across.

The turning point in this case came when my supervisor suggested that I try to imagine—remember and construct—what it feels like to be Gretchen. I did not, could not, know what it feels like to be a young woman, but I did know what it feels like to be a college senior, to be lonely, to be uncertain about the future, and to want more understanding from my parents.

The supervisor's suggestion brought about a remarkable transformation in my frame of reference. Previously I had thought about Gretchen only as an object in relationship to myself. Why couldn't she allow herself to become dependent on me, I wondered. Why didn't she trust me? Why didn't she confide in me her guilty secrets? I am ashamed of these remarkably selfish concerns, but it took a deliberate shift to let go of them.

As I began to understand Gretchen more, I tried to let her know and her parents know what I thought she was feeling. When I came close to the mark, she took heart, felt less alone, and gradually began to tell her parents more of what was going on inside her. This could be described in systemic terms—"breaking the problem-maintaining sequence"—but it wasn't just a block or an interruption. It was a transformation, a release. The change was circular and progressive. As they listened more, she expressed more, and as she expressed more, she felt better about them and better about herself.

Gretchen did take a leave of absence from college. It was brief and constructive. She returned home for a few weeks during which she escaped temporarily from the social climate that had become so stressful to her, and she found refuge in the understanding of her parents.

The lesson from this experience is that we have a remarkable range of experience from which to identify with our clients. We can better understand why people resist change by reflecting on our own experience. This is easiest with people most like us, but with a little effort we can extrapolate from common experiences to understand people who are different. Search your experience for episodes that are similar in some way to the client's dilemma. Try to identify what you felt, what you wanted from those around you, what made it hard for you. Or imagine some situation in the future when you might be in a similar predicament. How might you feel? Of what might you be afraid?

To be empathic, a therapist must not only be capable of understanding people different from himself or herself, but be fascinated by such people. He or she must have sufficient self-esteem so as to not be threatened by difference, and enough warmth and sympathy and an ample concern for other people, not only to tolerate but even to celebrate a world of differences.

STUCK IN ONE'S OWN POINT OF VIEW

Some family members have little or no feeling for others. They walk through a lifelong mystery, wondering why their children won't behave or why those cruel monsters they married deny them the little sympathy they crave. Such people are not stupid or insensitive, though they appear to be. They are preoccupied with their own unhappy feelings. They want, before anything else, to talk about their hurts *and* to have someone listen. Here are some examples.

My first session with the Ogden family was dominated by Mrs. Ogden's complaining. Her three teenagers "never listen," "won't help out," and "don't have any respect." Her husband "doesn't care about anything but his work" and "leaves everything up to her." Meanwhile, children and husband stare off into space, glassy-eyed. They had heard this litany so often that the complaints were by now of no more interest than TV commercials.

I listened but with growing annoyance at them for letting her rattle on and at her for not shutting up. After a while, I prompted the others to speak up. "What do you think about what your mother is saying?" "How do you answer your wife's complaints?" They responded tentatively and, predictably, she recaptured the platform. The first session ended in stalemate: me pushing vainly against the family pattern, and the family members finding out that therapy may be no different from what happens at home.

That night I lay in bed going over the session in my mind. I understood the family structure—she was enmeshed, he was disengaged—and I thought I understood what they felt. The kids probably felt smothered, annoyed at their mother for nagging them, and disappointed in their father for his lack of involvement. Mr. Ogden must have given up arguing with her; maybe he forgot how. Mrs. Ogden, I supposed, must be feeling isolated and ignored. But what was that really like? I realized that I had only the vaguest idea of what her life was like and, moreover, that I hadn't cared. I was too annoyed by her lamentations to draw out how she felt.

Next session I began as usual, letting the family members say whatever was on their minds. What happened was a duplication of the first session. After a while I interrupted and asked Mr. Ogden what his wife was feeling. He replied with a cursory statement of her frustration, accurate as far as it went, but about as sincere as a car salesman's smile. Then I talked for a long time with his wife. Oh, I guess I also said something about it being hard to understand each other as long as none of them felt understood. But I don't know that pontificating does any good. We teach empathy by example.

I talked with Mrs. Ogden for about 40 minutes, making it my business to try to put myself in her position. When I had trouble doing so, I asked her more questions. What did she do during the day? Why hadn't she made friends in her community? How often did her husband invite her out for the evening? By the end of the session, I began to understand how unhappy she was, how she perpetuated it by nagging, and how the others had played a role in the status quo with their passivity and lack of sympathy. I think we all understood. This certainly wasn't the end of therapy, but it was a beginning.

Parents often polarize each other into complementary positions and become locked in impasse until they learn to understand each other. Commonly, a mother's leniency increases in direct response to her husband's call for more discipline, and vice versa. A wonderful example of this occurs in Salvador Minuchin's training tape, "Taming Monsters."[10]

In this session, Minuchin interviews a family of four, two little girls, age two and four, and their parents. The family came to the clinic because the four-year-old was described as a "monster," so uncontrollable that her parents locked her in her bedroom at night to keep her from getting into mischief. Two minutes into the session, family members act out their roles in this unhappy drama. While Minuchin tries to talk to the parents, the little girl runs around the room, singing and banging against the chairs: "Duck, duck, duck. . . . " When Minuchin asks the mother to quiet her down, she responds with feeble attempts. "Don't sit on the table, okay? You sit on chairs. Okay, honey?" The daughter pays as much attention as you would expect.

As the session unfolds, the problem-maintaining pattern is clarified. The father is a strict and effective disciplinarian. When he's around, he takes over as soon as his wife becomes frustrated trying to control their daughter. Here's how Minuchin puts it: "When the family enacts a controlling transaction, the three members activate each other in their usual role function. The mother enacts her helplessness, and this activates the father to take over control, to be effective in his authoritarian style, so that the definitions of each family member in the family are confirmed. The daughter is impossible; the mother is helpless; the father is authoritarian."[11]

Minuchin's most visible interventions are enactments, in which he pushes the mother into taking control while he restrains the father from interfering. What struck me about this session, though, was how Minuchin followed up the enactment by helping the parents understand each other's point of view. Minuchin himself does not mention his empathy in this sequence, but his effective use of empathy illustrates part of what makes him such a complete therapist. His purpose may be to "unbalance" the couple, but in the process he brings out how each of them feels and what each is afraid of.

Minuchin: How is it that she needs to be protective of your daughter from your short fuse?
Mother: I'm afraid of you really losing your temper, because I know how bad it is. They are little, and if you really hit them with a temper, you know you could really hurt them, and

you wouldn't want that, so that's why I go the other way to show them that everybody in the house doesn't have a short fuse."[12]

The mother's fears may—in fact, apparently do—turn out to be based on a family myth. Like the daughter, the father is not really a monster. But, right or wrong, this mother is unlikely to ever change her behavior, nor will husband or therapist comprehend that her position is motivated, until these fears are expressed and understood.

As therapists we too become stuck in our own points of view. We think and act not in direct relation to reality but to that part of reality that fits our models. If we see only systems and process, then we may neglect to see shyness, oversensitivity, holding back, fear, and longing.

The therapist's empathy creates an emotionally supportive climate in the artificial atmosphere of the consulting room. Feelings shared and problems solved in this contained setting may have a lasting effect even if the understanding and problem-solving are confined to this place and time. From my point of view, however, it is a needless waste to conduct family therapy without equipping family members with the same tools of understanding to take home with them. We should teach family members to empathize with each other. This suggestion evokes the familiar debate between those who think family therapy should be designed primarily for solving problems and those who advocate personal growth. Both approaches are valid.

However, regardless of what we teach, our families learn lessons from our intervention. If we manipulate them from a distance—"for their own good"—they will learn little more than people learn from physicians who write prescriptions for home remedies in Latin. If, on the other hand, we demonstrate that every person in the family has a point of view with three-dimensional subtleties, and that expressing these points of view can lead to mutual understanding and compromise, then they will be better able to solve their own problems in the future.

TEACHING EMPATHY

Therapists have tried to teach understanding in a variety of ways. When behaviorists teach "communication skills," they concentrate more on negotiation than on expressing feelings. The format includes instruction, modeling, roleplaying, structured exercises, behavioral rehearsal, and feedback,[13] while the content emphasizes being specific, phrasing requests in positive terms to avoid attacking, responding directly to criticism instead of cross-complaining, talking about the present and future rather than the past, listening without interruption, minimizing punitive statements, and eliminating questions that sound like declarations.[14]

In contrast, experiential therapists have concentrated on expressing and sharing feelings. One widely imitated example is Harvey Jackins' Re-Evaluation Counseling, in which he teaches "co-counseling."[15] Co-counselors are pairs who take turns listening while the other talks freely and tries to express pent-up feelings. While co-counseling was designed by Jackins to be used by nonrelated members of his self-help groups, the technique has been adapted for use with married partners. These devices may be useful, but they do not of themselves teach empathy. They teach taking turns. Taking turns is fine, but it is not empathy.

Empathy has less to do with dialogue than with understanding. Open conversation and empathy are related in circular fashion, one begets the other. But ordinarily we achieve empathy for the other people in our families when we think about them, not when we talk with them. Ironically, people often develop empathy by watching strangers. A woman sees male emotional reticence portrayed on the movie screen and begins to understand that her husband may be more shy than cold. A man sees a child in a playground searching in vain for someone to play with and realizes, perhaps for the first time, how much his children need him. I have at times been lacerated by my own neglect when listening to my women patients describe the frustration of being married to someone who doesn't feel—or show—concern for them.

In conversation, at home or in the therapist's office, we don't listen well as long as our own unspoken feelings and opinions are

on our minds. Family therapists teach communication with interaction, empathy by talking separately to family members. Wit-
nessing a family member talk to the therapist is a little like over-
hearing the conversation of a stranger. The common element is
being relieved of the obligation to respond.

Talking to the therapist one at a time relaxes protective defenses
against anxiety, in speaker and listeners. The process is circular. In
the absence of counterattacks and belligerant complaints, the person speaking begins to acknowledge his or her sense of defective-
ness, inadequacy, and insecurity. The warmth of the therapist's
understanding melts emotional reserve and the person may bring
out worries, unresolved grief, and feelings of abandonment. Idiosyncratic motivations and acute sensitivities often turn out to be
related to past experiences in the family of origin. One of the most
liberating aspects of these discussions is the discovery that not all
of one's unhappiness is caused by the marital partner or by the
children, in the present. Meanwhile, other family members, freed
of responding, are less likely to become anxious and defensive.
Watching a spouse being interviewed, the partner may begin to
understand for the first time long-standing complaints.

This form of interviewing, first recommended by Murray Bowen, is useful both at the beginning of therapy and at times of
misunderstanding or stalemate in the course of treatment. It is
worth noting that one of the major reasons that close to half the
people who apply for family treatment leave prematurely is that
they have not felt empathy from the therapist in the initial interview.[16] A good interviewer is a good listener.

In Bowenian therapy, the rationale for talking separately with
individual family members is that the individuals retain emotional
sensitivities until they work out unresolved problems with their
parents. That's fine. But these discussions also create an opportunity to enhance the contemporary family's empathy for one
another. As I have already said, it is more useful to give understanding than to preach it. However, once there has been a breakthrough of feeling and understanding, family members are in a
receptive frame of mind. Now the therapist can point out and
clarify the central and vital function members of a family play in

regulating each other's self-esteem and the family's cohesiveness by fulfilling each other's needs for understanding confirmation. The following clinical example will clarify this point.

Mrs. Polanski called about her son, Maxwell. "The problem, doctor, is masturbation." The boy was 15 years old and, according to his mother, "addicted to masturbation." She grumbled when I asked to see the whole family for a consultation, but grudgingly she agreed. Not, however, before giving me an earful of her version. Among the things I learned while I tried unsuccessfully to get off the phone were: The boy had been nothing but trouble since they adopted him as an infant; her husband was a lousy businessman and a lousy father; and they had consulted a psychiatrist last year, but "that fool told me not to worry about the masturbation, ease up on the boy—can you imagine!" (Forewarned is forearmed.)

I began the session by asking Mrs. Polanski to describe the problems she was having with her son. Her criticisms were interesting. She described him as willfull, stubborn, interested in girls from an early age—at 14 he wrote graphic love letters to a girl he met at summer camp—and inconsiderate. She alluded to the masturbation, but apparently felt it was too embarrassing to speak about openly in front of the whole family. Aside from the obvious fact that she worried too much about too little, what was interesting in her complaints was that she was describing a strong, precocious, and mature young man. He was doing well in private school, was on the wrestling and soccer teams, and was extremely bright. And even though she was complaining, there was a touch of pride in her voice. Then she turned on her husband.

In response to my asking him what he thought, Mr. Polanski said that he agreed with his wife but didn't think the problems were so serious. At which she launched into a scathing diatribe. He was never a father, couldn't run the family business without her doing his jobs, and so on and on. At that point, my plan to use the father as an ally to support his son and challenge his wife seemed futile. His wife's angry disavowal provoked his withdrawal into silence and self-pity.

There was plenty of self-pity in this family. Each of them manifested it differently. The presenting complaint, the boy's masturbating while reading "men's" magazines in his room, could be seen as an adolescent expression of growing sexuality. (Leaving them where they could be discovered might be a way of engaging his mother in conflict.) But it was also his way of soothing himself, sexualized to be sure, but primarily a way of making himself feel good. Mrs. Polanski soothed herself with Valium and Mr. Polanski retreated by staying out late, drinking beer, and watching television.

Each of them had complaints which, like a baby's cry, were intended to call forth a soothing response. But it didn't happen. The lack of a sympathetic response set a process in motion where they disengaged from each other and tried to set up a new form of empathy, that of taking the self as its own soothing partner. All three of them were mired in self-pity, with an element of self-righteousness that was a protest against the other's failure to understand. The self-pitying responses had become a chronic, distorted way of trying to achieve a connection with the needed source of emotional support.

I offered an interpretation, tried to explain this to them, but my remark only felt like another attack. It just hurt. So I switched gears and tried to empathize at length with each of them in turn. Even this wasn't easy, because my listening sympathetically to one aggravated the others. I started with Mrs. Polanski, who obviously had the most to get off her chest. Only then did I try to speak to her husband, deliberately avoiding subjects that might put him at odds with his wife, concentrating instead on his own problems and his past history. He spoke without sentiment as though he were merely giving evidence. They were all so used to being attacked that they had trouble opening up. Even Mrs. Polanski had trouble talking about the hurt behind her anger. But I offered a model of acceptance that they were gradually able to emulate. I gave each one of them a chance to talk without interruption, to express his or her point of view, *and* to be heard by the others.

Did empathy solve this family's problems? No, that only happens in grade B movies. Empathy does not extinguish conflict. Even after they had a chance to talk and be heard, Mrs. Polanski still insisted on more control over her son than he could tolerate, and Mr. Polanski was still unwilling to stand up to his wife, leaving a vacant role for his son to fill. But the fact that they

began to feel understood, at least a little, made them cooperative partners in trying to find a solution for these problems.
And, more important, when therapy was concluded, they retained the ability to discuss their disagreements a little longer
before retreating into defeatist self-pity.

Taking the time and trouble to empathize with one family member creates a dynamic tension in the room. While you are empathizing with one, the others may feel threatened. For this reason, simple empathic statements may be more useful than lengthy
speeches. Simple empathic statements often come out as exclama-
tions—short emotional utterances by which the other's feeling
state is shared and acknowledged. When we follow with empathy
we speak with exclamation. If a man tells us he lost a valued
promotion, we might automatically come out with, "How awful!"
Alternatively we distance ourselves with, "Don't worry, it'll work
out," or "Yeah, that happened to me once." Spontaneous reactions are hard to describe, but they are a *spontaneous* product of
caring and understanding. Empathic comments may seem unctu-
ous or patronizing when used deliberately, like the false mask of
concern we so often see on graduate students trying so hard to be
"understanding."
   Family members sometimes find it hard to empathize because
they don't understand each other's point of view—not just don't,
but can't. How, for example, can a man understand the depth of a
woman's concern for a baby? Suppose we as therapists find it
difficult to empathize—the way I felt toward Mrs. Polanski, for
example. If such a person does not feel understood, we can certainly comprehend it, since we ourselves do not understand. At
times like this, an honest empathic statement is, "No one understands, do they?" This also creates a tension state, implying that
the other family members do not understand either, while at the
same time challenging them to try.
   In this chapter I have tried to explain that empathy is a valuable
and neglected tool in family therapy, in fact in any form of human
helping. That it has been neglected is attributable not only to the
depersonalizing side effects of systems thinking but also to the

temptation to insulate ourselves from the emotional pain of our patients. Putting ourselves in our client's shoes and trying to understand what they suffer exposes us to the same gut-wrenching anxiety most people feel when they a hear a baby wailing.

Empathy takes work. It doesn't necessarily come automatically as some psychoanalysts imply. It may be easier for an insecure analyst to intuit the private feelings of insecure patients than for a middle-class family therapist to understand the plight of poor clients or ones from chaotic families. Still, empathy is worth the effort. It engages the persons in a family in the process of therapy and it opens honest feeling, potentiating a more elaborate view of the life of the person and uncovering repressed aspects of relationships so that they can be incorporated instead of repressed. It is not, however, an all-purpose remedy. It is an instrument of understanding, but it is only one such instrument. Empathy without informed and disciplined conceptualization leaves us with only a partial understanding of persons *and* it is of little use for understanding systems functioning.

5

Assessment and Reassessment

My aim in this chapter is to explain how to better understand the self in the system, and how to put this understanding to use in family therapy. I will not offer a comprehensive model but will limit my discussion to selective concepts, concepts that may be incorporated into a variety of treatment approaches.

Logically, this chapter might have preceded those on interaction and empathy. First we make an assessment, and then we begin treatment, yes? No. In practice, we build a working alliance and then stimulate dialogue in the process of beginning to understand family problems. We have to *see* patterns of interaction before we can analyze them.

In this regard, notice that I have avoided the terms "diagnosis" and "evaluation." "Diagnosis" suggests static conditions that fall into discrete categories, and is therefore more appropriate for medical diseases than for psychological problems. Once you arrive at a diagnosis you can stop thinking about the problem. That way leads to treating families according to a formula. "Evaluation" suggests a process that starts and ends before treatment. If one's first concern is with evaluation, one is likely to impose a pattern of question and answer which constrains the data. Instead, I recommend getting things started and then leaning back and letting family interaction flow. While they are talking, we are thinking.

Assessment, like family life, is not a static process. It is less like a still photograph than like a motion picture—we shape the action at the same time we are observing it. Conceptualizing a family's functioning involves testing their responsiveness to our efforts to help them solve their problems. In fact, although I will describe how to make preliminary assessments, the hard work of conceptualizing comes later, when we run up against problems and get bogged down. If our exploratory efforts worked without complication, there would be little need for additional insight into the psychology of the individual.

THE PROVISIONAL ASSESSMENT

The model of human action which says that behavior is influenced both by autonomous forces within the individual and by interactional forces suggests a particular approach to conceptualization. Since the external influences are more plastic, it is wise to work from the outside in. A young mother's phobic fears of leaving the house may reflect her own conflict over personal freedom as well as her husband's need to reassure himself by having a "helpless woman" for a wife. A therapist could help her by working on either her private conflict or the marital relationship—but the latter way is quicker.

Surely most family therapists know this. But, just as surely, many are tempted to overlook the context that extends beyond the nuclear family. Some therapists, for example, underestimate the difficulty of finding quality day care and the role that a woman's parents and friends play on whether or not she returns to work after having children. In many cases, influences external to the family are not critical; sometimes, however, they are. If ignored, extrafamilial complications can defeat the work before it gets started. An abbreviated example may help.

I was recently asked to supervise a case in which the parents requested an evaluation of their three children. The parents thought the children were "just fine," but the school said the children "seemed to have some problems." By the time I met with the therapist, she had already had two meetings of an agreed upon three-session evaluation. She began our consultation by showing me a videotape of the first session. As far as I could tell, the family seemed a normal family. The parents were on friendly and equal terms; the children appeared cheerful and respectful. The parents' only concern was that the school guidance counselor had complained. I asked the therapist what exactly had the counselor said. She didn't know. Moreover, it turned out that the mother had also consulted her pastor for advice, and he had urged her to take the children out of the public school and transfer them to a Christian school, which the mother had done.

By this time, it was a little late to do anything about changing schools, but at least there was still time to call the counselor at the public school to find out what problems she had noticed. The counselor said that all three children seemed to have emotional problems. They were often moody, sometimes withdrawn, while at other times quite rowdy, even rude to their teachers. In addition, she thought it odd that the children spoke so much about the supernatural and said that their mother was an "extremely strong caller," meaning someone who could summon spirits.

So. To quote Oliver Hardy of Laurel and Hardy fame: "This *was* a fine mess." The clinic therapist's ability to help had already been severely compromised by her failure to coordinate her efforts with those of the school and the family's pastor. Still, there was no use crying over spilt milk. I suggested to her that the only structural problem we could find was in the lack of communication between the real parents and the school *in loco parentis*. But since a "divorce" had already taken place, the only thing we could do was recommend not allowing that to happen again. Specifically, I suggested the therapist tell the parents that, although the children had not displayed emotional problems in the evaluation sessions, they may have done so in the public school. Now that the parents had taken steps to alleviate the problem by changing schools, the best thing to do was wait and see how things worked out in the new school. If there were no problems, fine; if problems arose, the parents could call the clinic. Meanwhile, she should recommend that the parents try to keep in contact with the new school to find out how the kids were doing.

Therapy is usually initiated by a phone call, most often from the person requesting help, occasionally from a referring agency. My approach to these calls is guided by my intention to establish direct contact with the whole family, minimize alliances with any single party to treatment, and avoid outside interference or working at cross-purposes with other helpers. If other professional agencies are involved with the family, I want to know about it right away. The fewer advisers the better.

For a similar reason I encourage people to try to resolve unhappy relationships with previous therapists before coming to see me. Often I will refuse to see a family or couple when one or more of them is involved in individual treatment. Not always, but often. The problem is competing influences.

Clients are the customers. Theirs is the right to enter and terminate professional relationships when they wish. If someone wishes to engage in two therapies at one time, that is his or her prerogative. Mine is to refuse to enter professional triangles. Therapy is hard enough without unnecessary complications.

When I do undertake treatment in a case where other helpers are involved, I strive to minimize competitiveness. If the interests of multiple agencies can be sorted out and their inputs coordinated, they can function as kitchen cabinet advisers. Achieving coordination among various agencies requires that each be aware of the others' involvement and goals. Often, it is wise to meet with other workers; sometimes a therapist may help the family negotiate with other agencies. "You don't understand why Sarah's teacher is always complaining about her? Let's call the school and set up a meeting."

Once you are satisfied that other professionals are either not involved or that their efforts are coordinated, the next step is to get the whole family in. (The "family" usually consists of all of those living under the same roof, as well as anyone, such as a divorced parent, who has frequent contact with the nuclear group.) Phone contact should be brief—just long enough to ascertain the problem and insure that everyone will attend, and no longer. The caller has a certain point of view; the longer the call, the more the therapist is put into the position of either accepting that point of view or arguing with it.

The most frequently asked question in introductory family therapy workshops—way ahead of any other—is, "How do you get them all to come in?" The question betrays a beginner's anxiety and uncertainty about the family approach. If you work with families and intend to see the whole group, and you are clear about this, the vast majority of families will come in. Occasionally a little diplomacy is required. If the caller refers to interactional aspects of a problem—"I'm having a problem with my daughter" or "I've been depressed lately and I can't talk to my wife about it"—mention this when asking to see the family. If the caller limits the problem to one person—"I'm depressed" or "My son isn't doing well at school"—it is helpful to broaden the focus by asking, "How has this been affecting other people in the family?" This recasts the problem in interactional terms and allows the therapist to find out about the other members of the family and how they may be involved.

Remember, systems aren't resistant, people are. If the caller is reluctant to participate or to invite a problem child's siblings, it is the caller you must convince. If the person on the phone seems willing, but says someone else is not, you must figure out who is the resistant one and consider whose job it is to get the resistant person to attend. If, for example, a grandparent doesn't see why it is necessary to make a long trip to participate in a therapy session, you may wish to call and explain the need. On the other hand, if a mother says her teenage son won't come, you may want to urge the mother to take charge of getting him to do so.

Initial hesitation or even apparent refusal to attend rarely proves intractable if met with an understanding but gently insistent response. "Why do you need to see my family?" "It's helpful for me to get as much information as possible." "Okay, but I doubt my husband will come." "Please tell your husband that I need to hear from everyone, at least for the first session." Any direct suggestion that others are part of the problem is likely to produce anxiety and resistance; saying that the therapist needs information and help is much more effective. Once in a while family members need a little coaching about how to invite a reluctant spouse or teenaged children. In these cases it may be useful to conclude by saying, "Okay. If there are any problems just have (that person) call me." It's harder to say no to an authority figure.

Incidentally, these preliminary contacts are not just something to get through; they also provide useful information. If a woman says that her husband probably won't attend, but then he gladly participates, this may indicate that she might not know how to get him involved in family life or may have her own reasons for wishing him to remain peripheral. On the other hand, if he steadfastly refuses to attend, she might need to learn how to manage the children (or other problems) without him. If the therapist can succeed in engaging only a subset of the family in treatment, it is critical to remember that the missing person represents an unresolved problem. Even though some persons may not be present, their influence is.

Sometimes the provisional assessment can be short and sweet. It is only necessary to delve deep enough to resolve the client's complaint. For all its potential complexity, successful family therapy boils down to this: Discover the pattern surrounding a problem and change it.

Sometimes these patterns are the product of ingrained personal habit or submerged conflict, sometimes not. With acute problems and with families stuck in transition, it may not be necessary to go beyond a fairly simple assessment in order to produce results. Before moving on to those instances where complex dynamics are involved, I will mention two of the most common situations that require only brief intervention: (1) simple problem-maintaining sequences, and (2) families stuck in transition.

SIMPLE PROBLEM-MAINTAINING SEQUENCES—
"MORE OF THE SAME"

It is now a familiar fact to family therapists that many problems are maintained by well-intentioned but ineffective efforts to solve them. Nagging a husband to get him to spend more time at home, or alternately threatening and then giving in to a child's temper tantrums, illustrates this process. The brief therapists of MRI are masters of understanding this dilemma and they have written the book on dealing with it (in fact, two books[1,2]).

Brief, problem-focused therapy is most effective with brief, focused problems. Those who specialize in this form of treatment begin by translating vague complaints—"We just don't get along" or "I'm not very happy"—into clear and concrete goals. Unfortunately, this sometimes results in fitting the problem to the treatment, rather than the other way around. While it is certainly possible to negotiate specific goals for diffuse complaints—for example, asking the family that "just doesn't get along" to spend one afternoon a week in some family activity—doing so may trivialize the complaint. Delineating manageable goals may be a useful ploy to motivate a negativistic family, but working hard to redefine a family's goals is taking too much responsibility away from them and risks distorting their aims.

The most appropriate problems for a behavioral approach are specific, behavioral problems, including temper tantrums, school refusal, misbehavior at home, poor school performance, lack of cooperation with household chores, sexual problems, a spouse's nagging, one spouse's avoidance of the other. The list is long but, as you can see, it includes behavioral problems with children and specific behavioral complaints about a spouse. Incidentally, the latter are most likely to be maintained by simple behavioral sequences if they are acute.

When a family does complain of a specific and focused problem, always ask them how they have already tried to solve it. "And what did you do about it?" is the family therapist's counterpart to the ubiquitous "And how did that make you feel?" of individual therapy. Inquiring about the response to a problem may reveal a simple problem-maintaining solution; it always conveys the message that family members' behavior is interrelated and that they are responsible for their own dilemmas. *If* the family's response to a problem seems to make it worse, or at least perpetuate it, intervening is simple: Block the attempted solution that only makes things worse. Or reverse it, or substitute a new response. In short, do anything that interrupts the problematic pattern. This is illustrated in the following example.

Mr. and Mrs. Braverman came to see me shortly after he confessed to having an affair and moved out "to think things over." In our first meeting, I asked them to decide whether to work on their relationship or work on a separation. This is a confrontive intervention, useful for pushing couples to face up to what they intend to do and for seeing how they negotiate competing interests. Like other pushy interventions, however, this one risks promoting the therapist's personal agenda. Nothing stirs up countertransference like extramarital affairs and discussions about separation. All the protestations of neutrality cannot alter the fact that most of us have very strong opinions on these subjects. Keep your opinions to yourself. Know what they are, but keep them to yourself.

The Bravermans' conversation about what to do was instructive. She wanted him to move back, and carefully avoided any criticism or demands, controlling her hurt and anger for fear of provoking him to flee. He was not at all sure he wanted to give up the marriage, but he was sure that he didn't want to be branded the guilty party or return and be forced to make amends. He made brave speeches about his unwillingness to give up too much freedom. His defiant attitude reminded me of an adolescent masking insecurity with bravado.

He stayed away for two more weeks, during which time he began to realize that he was in charge of his own life, but that living it without his wife was lonely. So he moved back. At first they were as tentative with each other as porcupines on a first date, voicing few complaints and tiptoing around to avoid irritation. Like most of us, they were resorting to the same strategy that got them into trouble in the first place. When things settled down a bit, they got to an issue which seemed to be related to why they separated in the first place. Sex. She was pregnant; he seemed to lose interest and often had trouble maintaining an erection. Impotence in a man with fragile self-esteem and unacknowledged guilt can become quite complicated. Before it does, however, it may be possible to find a simple solution.

Discussion of their sex life revealed a fairly common pattern. After a few painful disappointments, Mr. Braverman became anxious and tried to avoid sex. His wife told him "not to worry" and tried not to pressure him. After a while, though, insecurity and desire overcame her restraint and she tried to seduce him. The result was sadly predictable: Her approach aroused more insecurity than libido. The sexual impasse was now affectively supercharged. To her, his lack of interest made her doubt that he still loved and desired her. To him, his impotence meant that he could neither find satisfaction nor demonstrate his virility.

I decided to treat them with in vivo systematic desensitization, à la Masters and Johnson.[3] This approach, in which couples are taught to proceed so slowly with lovemaking that they learn to overcome anxiety, is thought to work by *reciprocal inhibition*—anxiety is "counterconditioned" by an incompatible response, in this case pleasure. The procedure involves an elaborate assessment and a complicated sequence of homework assignments proceeding very gradually toward coitus. The most powerful effect, however, may be contained in the preliminary instruction: *Do not attempt intercourse even if you feel like doing so.* This instruction is obviously a potent way to relieve performance anxiety. If there is to be no performance, what is the occasion for anxiety?

I told the Bravermans that I would explain the Masters and Johnson approach to them and give them a trial for a couple of weeks, but that most of the work would be delayed until after the birth of the baby. I first explained the theory and procedure to them, and then told them that they must agree not to even consider having intercourse. Instead, they were merely to practice lying peacefully in bed together and exchanging pleasurable caresses. They came to the next session with an embarrassed confession: "We're sorry, we didn't follow your instructions"—and they were beaming. In this case, solution came simply as a result of blocking the problem-maintaining sequence. Once they stopped trying to have sex—or trying to try not to have sex—they stopped worrying about it and simply did it.

Note, by the way, that the Bravermans overcame their sexual problem by *disobeying* my instructions. As Jay Haley once said, the trouble with giving advice is that psychiatric patients are notorious for not following advice.[4] Many, in fact, do the opposite of whatever we tell them. This observation has led to the conclusion that families fall into one of two types—defiant or compliant[5]— and that successful therapy can be done by giving compliant families good advice and by telling defiant families to do the opposite of what is good for them. When was life ever this simple?

The limitations of this analysis are inherent in the assumption that problems are behavioral and dyadic. Sometimes, of course, this is true. In the case of the Bravermans, for example, a simple behavioral intervention in the couple's (dyadic) interactions around sex was sufficient to break a negative cycle. In many cases, however, things are not so simple. Indeed, complications may exist even in the Braverman case. It is one thing to produce quick change in patients, quite another to sustain it. The best way to succeed with behavioral interventions may be to do only brief therapy: Get in and engineer a quick change, and then get out before relapse sets in.

Sudden and rapid shifts may and sometimes do occur with human problems, but complications, triadic or monadic, may block change or lead to relapse. The improvement in Mr. and Mrs. Braverman's relationship may be sustained or it may be complicated by his unresolved insecurity or by her relationship with the new baby. Only time will tell. The interactional context for this or any other couple is never static. Looking at simple problem-maintaining sequences is looking at context in only a very limited way. The next most obvious context is developmental.

FAMILIES STUCK IN TRANSITION

This is another situation that often requires only brief intervention.

Over the years I have listened to countless intake reports that take the following form: "The patient is a 23-year-old married, white female. Her presenting complaint is, 'I'm depressed; I just can't seem to cope.'" Then, after a brief inventory of her depressive symptoms, comes a lengthy description of her childhood, a veritable Rorschach in which even a beginning psychodynamicist can locate oodles of trauma and deprivation. I often start nodding off at this point. Not because the past isn't important, but because these obligatory summaries are little more than a bill of particulars, listing events, dislocations, grievances, and nostalgias. Facts, only facts. The important data—psychic experience—is incompletely understood, undisclosed, sometimes just plain fabricated. Then, lost somewhere in these trips down memory lane, is the information that the young woman is at home with her first infant. Somehow this fails to register as an event of note. Because it is "normal," I suppose.

Sometimes the depression of a young mother is a temporary problem of adjustment. She's stuck at home all day with her baby and the baby's insatiable demands, and, as often as not, she gets very little help or sympathy.

As therapists, our training and instincts tell us to look for something wrong. We can't help it. Sometimes this instinct serves us well. We find schizophrenia, a treatable affliction, where others see only disorganized behavior and shun it. But life itself can be disorganizing. No sooner do we learn to cope with a particular set of circumstances—say, married life and two careers—than we are faced with new demands that strain, even fracture, previous adjustments. The woman who stays home all day with an infant disrupts connections with her friends at work, loses some of the satisfaction (and income) of a career, may be less available to, and require more from, her husband, and probably changes her relationship with her parents and his parents. Thanks to some excellent writing on the family life cycle,[6,7] we now have a better understanding of the normative strains of development and their impact on the entire family. Here too, however, the myth of the system comes in.

The important benefit from the concept of a family life cycle is realizing that not only individuals but whole families progress through a series of developmental stages, each one requiring shifts in organization. Families do not stand still. When they do get stalled, however, it is not because a machine—the system—gets stuck, but because their individual members endeavor to avoid new and potentially painful experience.

A family's development is not only behavioral; it is also existential. Problems which perplex and disturb families, however practical, are set in the context of how family members perceive themselves and each other. The complexity of interdigitating experience is not fixed in the course of time, but the seasons of a family's life are made up of psychological moments.

At the same time that the family life cycle literature helps clarify the interpersonal context of many problems, it also contributes to a lack of appreciation for the growing autonomy of the self. Personal development and family structure are inextricably interrelated, but the nature of human beings is such that they become progressively less dependent on family relationships to determine their fate. Family relationships *never* become unimportant; nevertheless, as we grow toward maturity, we, ourselves, play an increasingly significant role in determining how we will respond to these relationships.

David Shapiro describes the nature of individual autonomy this way:

> We have no reason to find human self-directedness intrinsically puzzling or philosophically doubtful. We recognize self-regulation of various sorts not only in other living organisms and in biological processes but also in certain kinds of machines, organizations, and even political entities. The functions of the organism, for example—or the activity of the organism as a whole—are regulated by processes internal to it. These processes confer a certain degree of autonomy, of independence of circumstance and surroundings, and endow the organism with a range of adaptability.[8]

Moreover, as Shapiro points out, this "range of adaptability," the autonomy of the self, becomes greater over time:

> The more autonomous and independent of its immediate

surroundings and circumstances an organism is, however, and the greater its range of adaptability, the more difficult it is likely to be to predict its behavior.[9]

And the less that behavior is a simple function of family pressures. Thus, some of our clients—say, a tyrannical father or perhaps an alienated adolescent—may be less amenable to influence through family interactions than through individual interviews.

The child's increasing independence of the immediate impact of the environment is a general trend of human development. In psychodynamic theory, the advance of *internalization*—the process of internal representation of external reality—is regarded as central to this aspect of development. That theory emphasizes two dimensions of internal experience which, once established, operate more or less independently of external reality: (a) automatic internal signals of danger that inhibit certain behavior that might be punished, and (b) imagination and thought. Whether or not we choose to emphasize these particular dimensions of maturation, the fact remains that, although the life cycle means growth and change for families as well as individuals, the individual becomes progressively more autonomous. Regardless of whether we refer to the life cycle of individuals or of families, it is the individual who must grow and change.

Take the depressed young mother above, for example. Certainly she's depressed; having a baby is enormously stressful. It is one of those facts of life no one ever fully appreciates in advance. (Veteran parents must swear an oath of secrecy to insure the continuation of the species.) And, yes, it is true that family structure must undergo change to cope effectively with new stages of development. A sympathetic and helpful husband makes the mother's job easier—and his life richer—and a network of support from neighbors, friends, and kin helps ease the burden.

The concept of the family life cycle points to the rhythm of growth; everyone is unique, but similar. Families progress in stages, with plateaus of stability and developmental crises which demand change. This metaphor is popular because it clarifies, but also because it is simpler and hence more appealing than the truth. What seems to be illuminating is, in fact, an oversimplification. It portrays the self as a passive thing, pushed along by developmental forces that it is ignorant of and powerless to resist. And it ignores the presence of the past. The past, as such, may not require primary attention, except as it is present in the minds of family members. We all filter our experience of what is through the living memory of what was.

Families do have certain superordinate properties—roles, boundaries, and subsystems—but we must also be prepared to take into account that families are made up of individuals, whose total structured personalities change over time. The woman herself—her energy, her enthusiasm or ambivalence about being a mother, her ability to assert her need for support from her husband—plays a central role in what happens.

In reality, we do not completely pass and leave behind the conflicts of any stage. In developmental terms, the persons who make up families never completely work through critical conflicts. At times of stress, these earlier conflicts may be restimulated. New tasks emerge, but old ones may need to be reworked.

When we try to apply the concepts of fixation and regression to the family life cycle, we think of fixation as staying stuck at a particular stage. Then, under stress the family reverts—regresses—to an earlier mode of functioning. But the family is made up of individuals and individuals never fully graduate from any stage. Fixation is a more-or-less, not an all-or-none, process. Therefore, therapists should check how the family handled earlier transitions. If the family was unable to resolve the crisis of one stage—for example, establishing boundary around the married couple—then it will face increased difficulty in subsequent stages. Moreover, to fully understand developmental impasses, a therapist must take into account the experience of individuals as well as the pattern of their interactions.

To cite just two examples to illustrate that individuals have autonomous developmental issues, let us look briefly at "the terrible two's" and adolescence.

Conventional wisdom has it that two-year-olds and adolescents are engaged in different stages of a similar process, defining themselves by opposing their parents. This description, which emphasizes the interaction, may distort the child's experience by filtering it through an adult bias. The two-year-olds who drive their parents to distraction by saying "No!" to every other request are not willful; they are only exploring their autonomy. They aren't particularly interested in defying their parents, any more than they are interested in obeying them. They just want to do what they want to do. Why not, until they learn otherwise?

Similarly, the exaggerated willfulness of adolescents reflects relationships with authority, to be sure, but also internal processes: prideful, defensive sensitivity to condescension or disrespect, reflecting acute feelings of inferiority, denied by arrogance or covered by dogmatism. Family therapy says to the parents, "Let go," but that may not be enough.

Adults see the child's angry self-assertion stimulated by, and directed at, parents. Systemic thinkers believe that adolescent rage will disappear immediately the minute the relationship between parent and child shifts. But a psychological analysis suggests that the interaction may not change (and stay changed) unless the individuals are mobilized to think and act differently. Nor does the rage cease to exist the moment it stops being regenerated. Old hurts still fester.

General systems theory points to an expanding series of open systems, each one affecting and affected by others. Yet a typical systems analysis neglects levels other than the family. Not only does the concept of the family life cycle deemphasize the individual, it also ignores larger social forces operating on the nuclear family. Transitions affect whole societies as well as individual families, but although family therapy is "a therapy of context," this commitment is often reduced to an abstraction. Meanwhile, we pay attention only to what is going on *in* the family.

THE LARGER CONTEXT OF THE SELF

A full appreciation of any family's dilemma must include its cultural context. Changing sex roles, economic pressures, racial bias, and accelerating technology are but a few of the many social facts of life that impinge on the people we work with. Sometimes, these pressures have such an obvious impact that we cannot ignore them. A family with both parents working and attending school to upgrade their skills obviously suffers from an energy crisis. In such a family, the children's disruptive behavior, which gains attention, might reflect these added pressures as much as any fundamental selfishness in or conflict between the parents.

There are at least two practical reasons for considering the impact of contemporary social trends on our client families. First, even when they are the victims of added stress, families are as prone as therapists to blame themselves for pressures they cannot escape. Often it seems there isn't enough sympathy to go around. A little strain unites couples; they pitch in and fight as a team. But when the strain is great, it becomes divisive. When working parents come home at the end of the day, they are tired and often under a great deal of stress. What they want most is to relax. But it's hard to relax when other members of the family are eager for attention. The resulting family interactions are often brief and tense, and the favored activity (television) is passive.

Therapists may not be able to do much to alleviate economic and social pressures, but we can help family members see how much they are affected by stress, which in turn may lessen guilt and blaming. Reminding people that some of the strain is "out there" may enable them to unite against outside pressure rather than let it divide them.

A second reason for taking into account the cultural context is that we tend to measure events against our own values and experience. Seeing a wide range of families broadens our perspective, but even the most diverse client population is a biased sample. Enmeshment, for example, is so common among families who seek treatment that we may exaggerate its prevalence and begin to think of parental "overinvolvement" as a social problem. In fact, I question whether parents *can be* overinvolved with their children. It is the nature of the involvement that is the problem. Some parents dote endlessly on their small fry, but deprive them of the chance to discover life for themselves. Instead, their days are plotted out and structured—with ballet lessons, piano lessons, karate lessons, swimming lessons, Cub Scouts and Brownies, soccer,

Little League, and on and on—all in the service of self-improvement and getting a jump on the serious adult business to come. Children rarely get too much attention. They get attention that is selfish, intrusive, and controlling.

Even when we don't ignore the cultural context, we sometimes think of it as a cloud that falls equally over the entire family. Among the most widely reported contemporary stresses on the American family are an unstable economy, a rising divorce rate, and the increased participation of mothers in the work force. Although sociologists speak of the influence of these changes on "the family situation," the truth is that social pressures fall on individuals. Adolescents—those spoiled teenagers who haunt the shopping malls wearing loose-laced Reeboks and overly vivid make-up—live under terrific stress. Adolescence has always been a tough time; contemporary social changes only make it harder. The proportion of children under 18 with mothers in the labor force doubled from 1960 to 1980 (*U.S. Statistical Abstracts, 1984*). During the same period the annual proportion of children under 18 whose parents divorced increased 140% (from 7.2 to 17.3 per 1,000 children). Based on 1980 rates, it is estimated that more than half of all children born in this decade will spend part of their childhood living with a single parent. While there is much debate about the long-term effects of mothers who work and of divorce, it seems undeniable that working mothers and single parents have less time in which to interact with their children. Nor can they provide the same level of supervision.

These social pressures have resulted in a clearly measurable decline in the well-being of American adolescents. Consider that educational performance improved for many years until 1960, but has declined sharply ever since, while the rates of juvenile crime, unwed teenage mothers, drug and alcohol abuse, abortions, venereal disease, and death from violent causes have all increased. And the suicide rate among adolescents doubled from 1960 to 1980.

Not even children of the rich have an easy time. Although they may enjoy unprecedented material luxury, they are no more likely than their less advantaged counterparts to have much of their parents' attention. And they are subject to intense pressure to succeed, which begins early. Competition for admission to the best schools starts with preschool and doesn't let up. By the time they reach high school, most middle-class children are subject to enormous pressure to do well in school in order to get into the right colleges.

Since most family therapists are adults, most of them are more attuned to the stresses that fall upon the adult members of the families they treat. When clinicians think of the effects of stress on children, they may think about helping them by helping their parents. This is sound theory—the fate of the family does rest largely on the shoulders of the parents—but adolescent children may need individual understanding and attention as well. We may not need special techniques to deal with their private worries and concerns, but we can't deal with them at all unless we remember to talk to the younger individuals in the families we treat. Besides, adults have their own concerns.

Inflated expectations combined with inflated prices have had a profoundly depressing effect on nearly all American adults. Most respond to the pinch by cutting back on luxuries and entertainment—precisely what most middle-class Americans have learned to rely on for the relief of stress. As they are forced to stay home, many families are further stressed by unaccustomed proximity. Add to the already high cost of food and housing the monumental expense of putting children through college and you will see why financial worries dominate everyday existence, eroding energy and draining the spirit. People may want to think about other things when they come home at night, but money and career worries are a persistent daily source of irritation. Dulled by the effort to get through long days, many grownups drink too much and soothe themselves with shopping expeditions they know to be meaningless. Ironically, these diversions are part of a vicious spiral. As long as shopping remains the chief recreational activity of American families, accumulating money will be a never-ending fixation.

Family therapists should remember to consider these social pressures since families do not always bring them up. They may be too busy talking about the problem that brings them to treatment and their conflicts about resolving it. While this is the proper focus of effective treatment, it may be that some individuals are too preoccupied with other worries to effectively participate in solving the presenting problem or becoming involved with family life in general. A good assessment should include consideration of the family's cultural context. In practice, this means talking to family members about their special concerns—job, school, hobbies, and friends. Whether or not a therapist decides to point out that a lack of friends, say, or being stuck in a low-paying job, adds to the family's problems, it is important to know about these things.

Like ourselves, the people we work with have interior and exterior realities. Family therapists discovered hidden sources of behavior in the external reality of patterned interactions. But success in identifying dysfunctional family structures[10]—rigid patterns of interaction that constrain flexibility—led to a certain neglect and underestimation of other aspects of the person. Family structure is a product of personal action. To say that families are structured with boundaries and triangles means that family members have learned to relate to one another in certain routinized ways. Sometimes, to understand and change family structure it is necessary to take into account these personal rigidities.

THE STRUCTURED DYNAMICS OF FAMILIES

There are two common sticking points in family therapy. The first comes early. It might be called "the presenting dilemma," the therapist's problems as distinguished from the family's. The family's problem may be a depressed mother or a child who is failing in school; the therapist's problem is to figure out how the family members, individually and collectively, got themselves into a muddle, and then help them find their way out of it. This is sometimes simple, but rarely easy. That is, it may be obvious what's wrong and what needs to be done, yet the more obvious it is to an outsider, the more likely it is for the family to resist this solution. They have their reasons.

Most of the time our clients live their lives within the well-worn grooves of habit. They do not consciously reflect on what they are doing or consciously control it. They only start to think about what to do when they are uncertain of themselves. When they do reflect on their conduct, it is likely to be as individual actors, less likely as members of an interconnected family unit. The family therapist's first task is to discover interactional patterns—patterns of which family members are unaware—that keep them stuck in unproductive ruts. Even "brief" therapists and "problem-focused" therapists look for "underlying" problems in the form of repetitive interactions. It is also important to recognize that discrete patterns of interaction are usually embedded in family structure.

Imagine a case in which a man and a woman who have been divorced and remarried come in for couples therapy. Whatever the process of their dialogue, the problems in their relationship may be enmeshed with her children in such a way as to make it difficult for her to get close to her husband or permit him to develop a role in parenting.

Most of what is written about family assessment is addressed to this problem—discovering interactional patterns and structures that freeze maladaptive behavior in place. These patterns are often described as "the way the system maintains itself." This way of thinking brings the interactional patterns into sharper focus, and points toward solution of the presenting dilemma. But most of us are also familiar with a second problem: following an initial breakthrough, when the heat is off, therapy gets mired down. The interactional diagnosis may be refined, even modified, yet what may be needed is an altogether different level of analysis.

THE BOGGED-DOWN TREATMENT

Most clinicians are familiar with the second sticking point in therapy—what happens when treatment gets bogged down.[11] The same issues are discussed week after week. The therapist becomes impatient with family members' failure to follow through on plans for changing how they respond to one another. Meanwhile, family members feel misunderstood and let down, since their initial high expectations have been disappointed. Often we mask our irritation, leaving only an atmosphere of boredom. "Three o'clock? Time to see if the Joneses are here. Oh, well. . . ." Continuation is sufficiently tenuous at this point that any disruption—a vacation, say, or a cancelled appointment—may result in termination. Here is an example from my own practice.

Carl had first gone for treatment by himself to do something about his bad temper. Following a brief course of individual therapy, his therapist recommended that he and his wife be seen together. I was initially enthusiastic about the assignment because in my experience one person's "bad temper" usually turns out to be the result of fairly obvious difficulties in communication between married partners. I was sure I could help.

Sure enough, the first session with Carl and Peggy revealed a recurring sequence of interaction that seemed to explain the outbursts. Whenever Peggy talked about her worries, she tended to become critical. Moreover, because she was considerably more articulate than Carl, her criticism cowed him into submission. The louder she got, the quieter—and angrier—he became. Only after several minutes, when he got good and mad, did he finally start to shout at her. The result was that Peggy got exactly the opposite of what she was looking for. Instead of understanding her concern, Carl felt threatened and tried to withdraw—until her pursuit finally made him lose his temper. At home, when things got out of hand, he smacked her.

I concentrated first on interrupting this cycle and then helping the two of them see the pattern so that they could prevent its recurrence. We made such quick progress that I anticipated a successful conclusion within a month. Unfortunately, while they learned how to relate effectively in my office, they forgot at home. Week after week they returned with the same story: "We get along fine after we leave here, but then something happens and it all starts over again." I thought the problem required working through and consolidating what they had learned, and so I persisted. But progress was often interrupted by their missing one or two sessions. Peggy got sick; Carl had to work overtime.

If they missed or cancelled, I waited for them to call. As far as I was concerned I was leaving them with the responsibility. The truth is, I was glad when they didn't come. We were bogged down and their spotty attendance reassured me that it wasn't my fault.

This bogging down may result in long-term therapy that never really gets anywhere. Most therapists have several such cases. The most common solution, more and better techniques, may not work. The problem may be an inadequate understanding of the self in the system.

As actors, perhaps we take ourselves too seriously; as observers (professional or otherwise), we take other selves not seriously enough. We like to think of ourselves as independent agents of our own destiny, men and women of initiative and self-determination. But as family therapists, we see the actions of our clients as dictated by unseen patterns of social relationship. Yes, people are connected; but the fact of connectedness should not obscure the fact that the nature of their interactions is partly dictated by psychic organization of unsuspected depth and complexity.

Family therapists, champions of circular thinking, sometimes forget that while the individual is continually defined by family relationships, those relationships are continually defined by individuals. Moreover, unlike billiard balls, those individuals are quite complicated. We cannot hope to fully understand the nature of family dynamics without understanding the dynamics of the individuals who make up those families. We need no psychology of the self to see triangulation and disengagement, but we may not be able to alter these social patterns without understanding private conflict and self-absorption.

Consider again the case of Carl and Peggy, the combative couple who drifted away from treatment. Looking back, I think I missed the boat. The interactional pattern was absolutely clear, relatively simple, and completely impervious to my efforts to change it. Today I would take that as a sign not for more indirect techniques but for more attention to the individuals. Why couldn't (wouldn't) Carl stop hitting his wife? The fact that she provoked him doesn't really explain it. Not every husband who is provoked hits his wife.

I remember that Carl used to say with a concern that seemed somewhat affected, "I *must* control my temper." I also remember how dramatically he described his intimidating and uncontrollable outbursts and his wife's cowering. And I remember that when she talked about his brutality a smile played around the corners of his mouth. These hints of a willful, motivated quality to Carl's abuse could be described in the jargon of unconscious psychodynamics which, because it is alien, might lead a family therapist to dismiss the point as a relic of outmoded thinking. Psychodynamic language might imply that Carl's unconscious is responsible for his abusing his wife; he himself is innocent, and helpless.

Psychodynamic theory may be useful to more fully understand the self in the system, but it is unnecessary to be highly technical. We can begin to try to understand the full nature of our clients— not just the sanitized version they allow to the surface—by formulating our understanding in the same dramatic and human way we might formulate the theme of a play or novel, rather than the way we would write a textbook. This vision and its application is a subtler, more humanely alert kind. It depends on the therapist's being able to subordinate theory in order to attend to the personal experience of the persons in the family.

If we wrote a dramatic narrative about Carl, we could say that he was misrepresenting, even to himself, his feelings and intentions. He fooled his wife, he fooled himself, and he fooled me (perhaps because I have such a tight rein on my own wish to achieve self-respect through aggression). Carl, who thinks himself concerned with his "temper" (his version of nonhuman agency), is actually pleased with his power to intimidate his wife, and the manliness it implies. This explanation does not vitiate the interactional one, but only complicates it. His attacks were triggered by her, but they were propelled by his own unrecognized frame of mind. Knowing the motives behind his behavior enables us to help Carl understand that he hits his wife to make up for feeling weak or to help him find some other way to feel more powerful, or both. As long as I stayed at the simple behavioral level of interaction, we made little headway and probably never would have. No wonder they stopped coming.

Some techniques are so powerful—like an invariant prescription—that we may be tempted to employ them routinely, almost automatically. Similarly, some personalities—a Carl Whitaker, say, or a Maurizio Andolfi—are so forceful that they seem to intervene to good effect with little apparent exploration of the dynamics of a particular family. This is an illusion. Techniques only work when they fit, and Whitaker and Andolfi know what they are doing. You should always be able to say what is wrong with a family you are treating—what there is about this family that isn't working. That means looking at the group *and* its members.

In families, almost no extensive action is the simple result of group processes. Virtually all action is to some extent self-directed and planned. That this power of self-determination is denied or taken for granted doesn't make it less important. In fact, the opposite is true. This adds up to a prescription for the therapist to recognize clients' potential for interacting differently and to mobilize it. This may require delving into the experience, psychology, even psychopathology of the self. This leads us to the topic of psychodynamics.

6

Interactional Psychodynamics

I recently had lunch with a dear friend whom I hadn't seen for several years. My friend, Jerry, is an excellent therapist, very well trained in both structural and strategic family therapy. Since I had seen him last, Jerry had been dating a psychoanalyst. At first, he said, they took delight in jousting with each other. You know, the kind of teasing that friends from rival camps like to engage in. But after a while Jerry got interested in psychoanalytic theory and started reading from a list of books his friend gave him. Jerry was fascinated. He found much of what he read illuminating and thought it helped him better understand both himself and his patients. "But," said Jerry, "it hasn't really improved my clinical work. I know a lot more, but I don't know how to put it to work."

Jerry cited a couple of examples. "I now understand the symbiosis that underlies some cases of enmeshment, and I realize that obsessive people are preoccupied with control because deep down they feel weak and inadequate. But, so what?" I smiled. That's exactly the way I used to feel in graduate school. Psychoanalysts have produced a welter of confusing literature, some of it very interesting but not all of it very practical. What I discovered, and what I told Jerry, is that it all boils down to this. The essence of psychodynamic theory—the *practical* essence—is being able to recognize and interpret basic impulses and the defenses that obscure or distort them. These basic impulses are illuminated by two major sources: Freudian drive theory and Kohut's psychology of the self.

In this and the following chapter I will describe the essential elements of psychodynamic theory and show how they can be incorporated into family therapy. I will not present a complete exposition of psychoanalytic theory, nor will I describe how to do psychoanalytic family therapy. My aim is not to advocate a particular brand of therapy, but to add an additional dimension to whatever brand of family therapy you already practice.

Among the first to call attention to the hidden dynamics of family interactions was Jay Haley. His *Strategies of Psychotherapy*[1] was a brilliant exposition of the masked struggle for power that makes up so much of family life. Subsequently, Haley has concentrated his attention on the struggle for power that takes place between therapists and families, while others have often reduced the dynamic patterns in marital unions to simplistic formulas: aggressive/submissive, extroverted/introverted, pursuer/distancer, and so forth.

One notable exception to this affinity for the superficial was Henry Dicks, whose splendid *Marital Tensions*[2] deserves much wider attention than it has received. Dicks pointed out that there are three levels of interaction in a marital relationship: (1) cultural values and norms—race, religion, education, values; (2) central egos—personal norms, conscious judgments and expectations, habits, and tastes; and (3) unconscious forces that are repressed or split off, including drives and object-relationship needs.

Marital battles are usually fought over conflicts manifested on the second level, personal habits and expectations. Flexibility and tolerance affect the outcome, but perhaps not as much as do unconscious factors. A successful marriage is one in which the couple is compatible on at least two out of three levels. Dicks' analysis helps to explain why many couples seem to remain together despite constant fighting and why other couples who seem content suddenly split up. Presumably the battling couples who cleave together fit each other's unconscious needs, and their inner object relationships dovetail.

Unfortunately, Dicks' work had little impact on American family therapy, which has followed Haley to a fairly narrow concern with the struggle for power. With minimal appreciation of unconscious complexity, families have been treated as units ("systems") in conflict, not among themselves but with therapists.

One reason family therapists have neglected to study the depth dimension of personal psychology is that much of the richest material on personality dynamics is written in psychoanalytic-ese, a learned jargon that is formidable, canonical, or pretentious, depending upon whether the reader is uninitiated, indoctrinated, or scornful. One particularly salient example of the inaccessibility of psychoanalytic writing is the work of Heinz Kohut. In order to get to the pearls of Kohut's wisdom, readers have to wade through the wet sand of terms like "transmuting internalizations," "bipolarity of self," "genetic matrix of defeat," "mirroring selfobjects," and so on. The easiest thing is to give up and devalue as useless that which is difficult to comprehend.

I will explain (and define) some of the most useful psychoanalytic concepts, but I will do my best to recast this jargon in more familiar, more human, terms. My purpose is neither to provide a comprehensive course in psychoanalytic theory nor simply to retranslate familiar psychoanalytic concepts into ordinary language. Rather, I intend only to offer some selective ideas for understanding the self in the system.

Explaining psychoanalytic theory is a little like explaining family therapy; the problem is that there is not one but many psychoanalytic theories. The parallel is not quite perfect, however, because in psychoanalysis theories are many and complex, interventions are few and simple; in family therapy the situation is reversed. Since Freud's time significant innovations have either been incorporated into the mainstream of psychoanalytic theory—Heinz Hartmann, Melanie Klein—or expelled to the status of apostasy—Carl Jung, Alfred Adler.

An apparent exception to this rule (though it may be too soon to tell) is Kohut's psychology of the self. Even after Kohut's second major work, *The Restoration of the Self*,[3] established him as a major pioneer, his contribution seemed specialized (applicable primarily to narcissistic personality disorders) and tangential. Although his followers began to refer to his teaching as "self psychology" and to themselves as "self psychologists," most analysts continued to refer to "Kohut's ideas" and "the Kohutians," denying them the status of independent thinkers. Since then, however, self psychology has become firmly established as a significant movement within psychoanalysis, and today it stands as a major alternative to classical analytic drive theory. Like a powerful stepchild, it is strong enough to stand on its own, but valued enough to eventually be incorporated into the mainstream.

Let me illustrate these alternative viewpoints with a familiar example, the husband who assumes a submissive role with his wife. Self psychology would emphasize his narcissistic craving for attention and vulnerability to criticism; drive theory would hypothesize repressed aggression.

According to drive psychology, a submissive spouse is one in whom aggressive feelings and need for control are covered by excessive gentleness and avoidance of normal anger. Such people often use obsessive-compulsive defense mechanisms (intellectualization, rumination, doubting, isolation). The result is commonly a depressive picture. Dreams or waking fantasies may be of attack, sometimes on the partner but more often displaced onto someone else. One person I know who fit this pattern used to daydream of being accosted by a robber and "beating the shit out of him."

The submissive husband projects onto his wife the role of a powerful mother figure who cannot be attacked but only propitiated. He may have periodic explosions of anger and irritation, but these will likely be displaced to a safer target, perhaps his children. These outbursts are followed by abject guilt and attempts at restitution, and later by depressive withdrawal.

Even as a brief sketch, this picture is incomplete without some consideration of the partner's role. (It is not necessary to ignore interactions in order to pay attention to psychodynamics.) The wife caught in this pattern of a husband's passivity and withdraw-

al experiences frustration and rage, especially when she is increasingly loaded down with the burden of most of the parenting.
More often than not, the children become objects of her displaced
need for control. She identifies the children with herself, overva-
luing them and possessing them as bearers of her frustrated
hopes and aspirations, but also demanding much affection and
submission from them as compensation for her hard, long-suffer-
ing role. Where it is extreme, the resulting strain may lead to
phobic or hypochondriacal symptoms. These express hidden aggression and the guilt for it, the appeal to the husband and children (even to her parents) for succor, and the power-through-
weakness motive. Often such couples compete to prove who is
the most tired, sick, or overworked.

In the example above I mentioned several different psychoanalytic concepts—repression, displacement, intellectualization—and
alluded to several others. Although the concepts I chose to illustrate are simple, even self-explanatory, it is a great mistake to
reduce psychodynamic theory to a collection of discrete concepts.
Doing so makes it hard to see the forest for the trees. In explaining, first, drive theory, and then the psychology of the self, I will
strive for a succinct statement of basic principles. My emphasis
will be on understanding and intervening.

DRIVE PSYCHOLOGY

Freudian drive psychology is a theory of persons that says we
choke off realms of inner experience and avoid avenues of real-life
action out of fear and shame. We are still afraid, even as adults, of
what our childish minds learned and mislearned. And we are
ashamed of no less than our natural bodies and their impulses.
Accordingly, psychodynamic investigation aims, through understanding, to break down shame and break down fear. Family therapists may be more concerned with what people *do* than with
what they feel or dream about, but without some understanding
of these private agendas we often fail to affect what family members do.

At the heart of human nature are the drives. Sex and aggression are the motivating forces behind everything we do. However, since we learn early in life to fear punishment for unchecked expression of our animal nature, the human mind is ever in conflict. We are in perpetual struggle between sexual and aggressive impulses on the one hand and fear of retaliation on the other. Our resulting actions represent a compromise between our desires and the defenses we erect to inhibit them.

This is the "dynamic" of psychodynamic theory: The basis of all human conflict is the tension between drives and defenses. In a healthy person, the defenses are flexible enough to permit appropriate gratification of pleasurable and aggressive wishes. In neurosis, excessive fear of the life force, encoded in rigid defenses, results in a pinched compromise with life, a loss of energy drained off by repression, and symptoms of anxiety and depression.

Having reviewed the dynamics of drives, most summaries of psychodynamic theory would now move on to the other basic dimensions, including the *topographic* (conscious/preconscious/ unconscious) and *structural* (id, ego, superego). Regardless of how familiar or unfamiliar the reader is with psychoanalytic concepts, I believe that broadening my discussion would only obscure the main point. If the goal is to employ Freudian psychology to enrich our understanding of the persons in the families we treat clinically, rather than to master the theory as an intellectual discipline, then we must suspend our wish for completeness.

The reason psychodynamic theory is useful to family therapists is that it tells us where to look to sharpen our understanding of why people react consistently to others, especially others who live at the same address. Attributing consistency is something people do unto others more than to themselves. "My wife avoids sex because she is frigid." "My husband spends all his time in front of the television because he is aloof." Thus most people pin responsibility for their fate on someone else. When asked to explain their own behavior, they refer to the stimulus of others: "He doesn't want to make love, he just wants a quick fuck." "I watch TV because when I try to read she always interrupts; if I try to have a conversation, all she does is talk about the kids."

When they do look at themselves, most people see only a high-ly edited version. Psychodynamic theory helps supply missing dimensions of patients' accounts of themselves. Since there is much unsuspected that goes on in people's hearts and minds, it is prudent to select from the complexity of life certain aspects which are understood to lie at the center of human concerns. Drive theory serves admirably because it is simple: Unproductive behavior reflects inner conflict over having fun and getting mad. But if conflict is unconscious, how do we know it is there?

Inner conflict is signaled by unpleasant emotion, especially when it does not fit the circumstances. Anxiety and depression—these are signs that something is wrong beneath the surface. Though most clinicians have some workable theory to explain depression (usually oversimplified as a reaction to loss), it is astonishing how few have any useful idea about why people become anxious.

The Roots of Anxiety

According to drive psychology the roots of anxiety are in childhood, in four prototypic traumatic experiences.[4] The first of these is the absence of the mother, which to an infant seems as though she is gone forever. The second is when the parents scold the infant harshly, which at that moment feels like the loss of their love. Third is the so-called fear of castration, best understood as a Freudian metaphor for severe punishment that renders one powerless. The fourth situation of predictable anxiety is the harsh condemnation rendered by one's own conscience.

In each of these primal danger situations the child is overcome with anxiety. Ordinary events are distorted all out of proportion by the imagination of a child. As the child learns that his or her own behavior can bring about these unhappy occasions, an association is built up between the child's instinctual impulses and these fearful calamities. Most people manage to survive childhood, but many of us remain vulnerable to some combination of these four fears. Men are particularly vulnerable to fears of being smothered in relationships and of losing their powers; women are especially prone to fear that putting forward their own interests will result in the loss of love. The following vignette shows how this dynamic operates.

Ralph Dickson called for an appointment saying, "I think my wife is having some kind of midlife crisis. We need help." I was curious: "midlife crisis" usually refers to a man, worn out and discouraged by his job, now dreaming of shucking off duty and responsibility, and setting off with the wind of the world in his face. Calling these longings a midlife crisis often serves as an excuse for self-indulgence and irresponsibility, like trading in his family for a Porsche and a younger woman. Was this to be a 1980s version—the same thing, only with the roles reversed?

What first struck me about the Dicksons was that they seemed to be complementary images of each other. Ralph was about six foot five, dressed in blue jeans and a plaid shirt; he spoke with a booming voice. Gillian was quite small, wore a simple but elegant shirtwaist dress, silk with geometrical designs; her voice was soft and hesitant. He immediately dominated the conversation. "She's behaving very foolishly." "I don't understand." "She doesn't know what she wants, because she can't explain it to me." I felt sorry for him, but he was a bully.

Ralph seemed to have all the power in this relationship. Except for one thing, Gillian held the trump card: her threat to leave him.

No matter how much he argued and criticized and pleaded, Gillian just folded her arms and crossed her legs and said, "I don't wish to discuss it." My impression was that she was not unambivalent; she simply did not want to be overpowered by his arguments. The more he pressed, the more she hardened her resolve. Trying to avoid his intimidation, she was in danger of deciding in counterconformity to him. So I asked to see each of them alone.

Him I counseled not to push her. Her I asked what she really wanted. The answer was simple: freedom. Her life had become a dreary round of going to work, cooking meals, taking care of the baby, and cleaning the house. What bothered her most was that she never had any fun, never got to do things by herself, and never had any time with her friends.

Although we as therapists are prone to project our own ideas onto dilemmas like this one, it is rarely clear whether the barriers to a client's satisfaction are outside, in her marriage, or inside, in her own mind. I told Mrs. Dickson exactly that. And I encouraged her to try to negotiate more freedom and enjoyment for herself in the relationship. "Why don't you try to do more of what you want before leaving him? See if it's really him or primarily yourself that's holding you back. You can leave in a minute if it doesn't work out." It was to be a trial nonseparation.

Mr. Dickson proved to be surprisingly flexible. It was okay with him if his wife did more things for herself, and while he didn't really want to do much additional housework, he was perfectly willing to increase his time taking care of the baby. He was a little worried about Gillian spending more time with her friends—"What friends do you mean?"—but she convinced him that she was not interested in other men. Things went along fine for a few weeks, until she decided to go to the city for a weekend of shopping. Standing on the platform, watching the train pull into the station, she had an anxiety attack.

It wasn't hard to guess the source of Mrs. Dickson's anxiety. If much time elapses between the onset of anxiety and the person's seeking treatment, the difficulties are usually compounded by attempts to mask the symptom—medication, relaxation training, or self-medication—and by the building up of associations between the anxiety and the place the person happens to be at the time. Mrs. Dickson's problem was not a train phobia.

She was the oldest daughter in a large working-class family from West Virginia. Her parents were loving but hard. They had to be. There was always much to do, and having fun was seen as frivolous and self-indulgent. When I asked what her mother would think about her going shopping for a weekend, she just cried. Here, expressed in the language of feelings, was the root of Mrs. Dickson's anxiety: Having fun meant the loss of love. Her anxiety was a measure of the danger of an aroused instinct, the fear of displeasure that would ensue if she were to yield to her impulses. Such fears correspond to experience, often misinterpreted, and can be corrected by later experience.

I told Mr. Dickson, "She wants to change, but she can't do it alone. You have to help her." And I tried to make him realize that only if he actively reassured her and encouraged her to take care of herself would she feel free enough to stay with him. That this charge was consistent with his wish to feel strong made it easier for him to accept.

Depression—Remembrance of Things Past

Depression is widely believed to be the result of a contemporary event that restimulates an earlier loss. True, but depression can also occur when something in the present brings back earlier experiences of rejection, severe punishment, or moral condemnation. Family therapists rightly point out that the reaction of family members is often an impediment to the resolution of depression. Yes, but depression is also an intrapsychic event. Sadness may be the uncomplicated result of unhappy circumstances, and grief too, but clinical depression occurs only in fertile soil. The hopelessness and self-reproaches that are part of the defining picture of depression point to the predisposing condition—the feeling that old fears have come true, *and* as a result of one's own doing. The following example will illustrate these points.

Sid Girard came to see me because he was having an affair and didn't know how to end it. He had been married 15 years. He had a good job, two children, a house in the suburbs, a lawn full of crabgrass, and, to complete the picture, a station wagon. He had never even considered being unfaithful. He was far too conservative, he thought. "It just kind of happened." Away on a business trip, he had too much to drink and too little self-control when a friendly goodnight kiss turned into something else. He simply wasn't prepared to defend himself against a temptation that he had never consciously entertained.

The next morning he was overcome by remorse. They both agreed not to see each other again, but that resolve lasted only a few days. He had to see her again, "just to talk." But they had broken down a barrier to something even stronger than his self-control. Sex with Charlotte was delicious. Still, he felt obligated to break it off and return to the familiar security of his marriage. That seemed like a good idea. Rather impulsively, he told his wife that he had had an affair but it was over. That seemed less of a good idea.

Sid rationalized his decision to confess in the name of that overrated virtue, honesty. The effect of his "honesty" was to relieve his guilt by dumping the anguish onto his wife, Nancy. Now, instead of a man burdened by anxiety and self-recrimination for doing what he thought was wrong, he became, in effect if not in fact, a naughty child appealing to an all-forgiving mother. She did forgive him, but she was deeply hurt and very angry.

One way to infer unconscious motives is by examining the effects of behavior. Actions which produce "unwanted" effects may have been designed for precisely that purpose. I thought that might be so in this case, but I wasn't sure. In extramarital affairs, what appears to be purely sexual motivation can also be a form of aggressive acting out. Sometimes this is conscious— "I'll show her (or him)"—but often not. Sid's confession and its effect on his wife suggested a hidden wish to punish her.

She demanded that they have counseling. He wasn't sure what he wanted to do, but felt he should try to work things out. So, I agreed to see them together. Nancy insisted on knowing what was wrong with the marriage: "Why did you do this to me?" But she didn't really want to hear the answer. When Sid did try to talk about some of his dissatisfactions, she switched to the offense and attacked him for being unfaithful: "You and that whore!" She got angry, he got moody.

We met for about two months, during which time two things became apparent. One was that Sid's wife did not seem about to forgive him, and the second was that the marriage seemed to have very little but habit going for it. The affair may have been unpremeditated, but it did expose the poverty of the relationship. When Sid finally decided to leave, it seemed like a good idea. They both agreed. The marriage was probably a mistake in the first place and they both thought they would be happier apart. Sid's wife was worried about supporting herself, but she did fine. Sid was looking forward to his freedom; he got depressed.

Sometimes what appears to be depression is grieving. When couples break up, grief is usually time-limited, but it can be prolonged. What prolongs the suffering is that there is not a clean break. It takes some time to get over a loss, even one you chose, but the clock doesn't start until the loss is definite. Sometimes one partner appears to be depressed because he or she simply hasn't accepted the fact that the relationship is over. Sid was depressed. Not only was his suffering prolonged but, as happens in depression as opposed to grief, he felt guilt and self-reproach. Sid was not only unhappy, he was also convinced that he was a monster of depravity. In fact, he laid it on so thick that I was tempted to assume the complementary role— the all-forgiving mother—and reassure him that he wasn't so awful.

Sid's father had left his mother when Sid was a small boy. He was raised by his mother and his aunt, both of whom were cautious women who valued security over satisfaction. They taught this lesson by the example of their austere manner, by their sharp criticism of any sign of "foolishness," and by their disdainful disapproval of men and their "selfish ways." Sid learned well. He was obedient and compliant to win his mother's love. Even now at 35 he was cowed by her. She was too refined to condemn him openly for leaving his wife, but he could tell that she really disapproved. When he decided to move in with Charlotte, his mother stopped even the pretense of acceptance. "You're my son and you know I love you, but I won't approve of what you're doing."

Despite her censoriousness, she still expected a lot. Every Sunday when Sid went over for dinner, she had something for him to do. Mow the lawn, blacktop the driveway, something. He complied with every request, a little like a dog who endures frequent kicks in hopes of getting petted once in a while. Just as clearly, being obedient and acquiescent to his mother's wishes served a defensive function. It helped assuage his guilt, and it kept him from being aware of his rage at her and expressing it directly. While they continued to play out this relationship in the present, we continued to explore the past in our sessions.

Incidentally, I didn't direct him to talk about the past. His own spontaneous thoughts just led him there. This was, on the one hand, a measure of unresolved unhappy experience, and, on the other hand, part of his automatic tendency to comply with what he rightly intuited were my wishes. When I pointed this out to him, he started to cry. At first the crying was unconnected to any particular idea. Then, suddenly, he remembered something. A few weeks after his father had left the family, he had been sent to live with his uncle in Ohio. Amazing how he could have forgotten that! At the time he was terrified. He felt that his mother had sent him away, that she didn't love him anymore, and that it was because he wasn't a good boy. Oh, how he cried!

This forgotten incident had colored his whole life. Even though he continued to try to please his mother when he returned home, secretly he felt that he had already lost her love. His dramatic—and cathartic—memory of this event didn't suddenly make his feelings of insecurity disappear. Those had to be worked through gradually. However, it did clarify one source of his conflict over satisfying his natural desires. Moreover, his recollection, with feeling, of the past had an immediate impact on his relationships in the present. With the two women in his life, his mother and his lover, he was suddenly freer. Freer with Charlotte to express himself and freer in bed. And he was much less susceptible to his mother's guilt-tripping. He still helped her out quite a bit around the house, but now when she criticized his relationship with Charlotte he just got mad.

We all have personal problems and family problems. When anxiety or depression is acute, many people will seek out individual treatment. Although family therapists do encounter these symptoms, they are more likely to see the results of conflict manifested in chronic but mild anxiety and depression, loss of energy, or simply the absence of pleasure or anger. We know from the psychology of obsessive-compulsive personalities (if not from personal experience) that some people flee the vividness of the world of passionate experience into a monochromatic world of words and concepts—a form of defense in which warded-off instincts signal their presence by unpleasant affect (usually avoided).

Had we met Mrs. Dickson before she decided to leave her husband, we would have found her life dull, drab, and gray. Like most of us, she narrowed down the world to make her way in it, but eventually she got stuck. Her effort to cut the world down to size was stifling. Constricting her life-style too much prevented forward momentum, new choices, and growth. The crisis that reawakened Mrs. Dickson's conflict gave her a developmental second chance to recapture more of her full nature.

We see a similar dynamic played out in the conflict avoidance of disengaged couples. Beginners often think that moving disengaged spouses closer together means finding happy things for them to do together. Giving them tasks to have fun—"Go out to dinner and leave the kids a note"—naively assumes that their distance is unmotivated. In fact, what usually keeps couples apart is unresolved hostility. Part of the battle may be won by simply putting them together to fight it out. But if inner conflicts against anger keep them stymied, they may need a therapist's help. Step one is systemic: Strengthen the boundary around them so they have the opportunity to work through their conflicts. Step two, if necessary, is psychological: Help one or both understand why they may be afraid to get angry, where they learned that fear, and whether or not it is still valid in the present circumstances. "Do you really think she might leave you if you yelled at her?"

The complementary style of enmeshment may also be more than merely habit. A woman enmeshed with her children may become anxious if she tries to find adult satisfactions. Unless her fears are worked through, any change in the pattern of enmeshment might not last. But this does not mean she needs to be psychoanalyzed.

It is a mistake to imagine that a theory which says that the roots of anxiety and depression are in childhood also says that only a lengthy psychoanalytic exploration of childhood will serve. To put drive theory to use, all that is necessary is to remember that one way to look at human experience is in terms of drives and defenses: Look for anxiety or depressed affect, see if the person knows how to express anger and have fun, and, if not, consider what needs to change to help the person become more expressive. In Mrs. Dickson's case, for example, the critical facts were that she imagined she could not stay in her family and still have fun, and she became anxious when she tried to do something nice for herself. To have a therapeutic impact, one does not have to collect facts from her childhood and interpret her dreams. This is a parody of psychodynamic therapy. What is required is nothing more (or less) than a dynamic shift in the balance of instinctual conflict.

In the conflict between ego and id, there are two ways to strengthen the ego: Stiffen its defenses to push the drive further into submission, or relax the defenses to permit partial gratification of drive wishes. Repression might have worked. A counselor could have helped Mrs. Dickson shore up her defenses by pouring her unused life into some noble and selfless task. Instead of taking the part of her superego, however, I did little more than help her examine her fears and their obvious roots in her background, and then encourage her and her husband to work together to change the pattern.

To summarize:

Human behavior is propelled by basic drives, which fall into two broad groups, libidinal and aggressive.

Psychic conflict arises whenever one anticipates that the gratification of a drive will lead to punishment.

Conflict is signalled by unpleasant affect, either anxiety or depression.

Anxiety is unpleasure associated with the idea (often unconscious) that one will be punished for acting on a particular wish.

Depression is unpleasure plus the idea (often unconscious) that a calamity has already occurred.

The balance of conflict can be shifted in one of two ways: by strengthening the defenses against the expression of a wish, or by relaxing the defenses sufficiently to permit some gratification of the wish.

The utility of drive theory for family therapy derives from its ability to point to hidden dimensions of human motivation. As we shall see, however, there are also other dimensions, other dynamics, in psychodynamic theory. Freud understood the role of family relationships largely in relation to the discharge of drives: Family members may inhibit, facilitate, or serve as targets for libido and aggression.

Since Freud, several theorists have found limitations in the ability of drive theory to account adequately for the complexity of human motivation. These other theorists have argued that relations with others constitute the fundamental building blocks of mental life. The creation, or recreation, of specific modes of relatedness with others replaces drive discharge as the fundamental force motivating human behavior. Among the most influential of these interactional theories have been Harry Stack Sullivan's interpersonal psychiatry in the 1940s and, more recently, Heinz Kohut's psychology of the self.

The existence of alternative theoretical models raises large questions about human nature. Is the process of becoming human primarily a matter of taming and socializing inherently antisocial instinctual drives, or is it the establishment of loving human relationships? Here, my primary concern is not with choosing between models, but choosing from among them concepts that are useful to enrich the clinical practice of family therapy. The following introduction to self psychology will, therefore, emphasize practical applications rather than theoretical considerations.

SELF PSYCHOLOGY

Self psychology has emerged as a major systematic alternative to drive theory because it deals with a dilemma at the core of human experience: insecurity and longing for admiring attention.

Heinz Kohut began as an orthodox analyst firmly committed to the drive model. In his first book, *The Analysis of the Self*,[5] he described how patients with "narcissistic personality disorders" demonstrate one of two types of transference: (1) *mirroring*, in which the childhood need for acceptance and approval is reactivated, or (2) *idealizing*, in which the need for merger with a strong figure is revived. When these needs are not adequately met in childhood, the result is a weak and insecure self, with labile self-esteem and exquisite sensitivity to failures, disappointments, and slights. Instead of rejecting classical drive theory, Kohut argued that *both* instinctual and relational considerations are important, and he treated them as more or less independent lines of development.

But by 1977, in *The Restoration of the Self*,[3] Kohut claimed that self psychology dealt with more fundamental human needs than drive psychology—that the building of a cohesive and secure self is a more basic part of human development than the expression of drives. This claim to primacy has spawned Talmudic debates among contemporary psychoanalysts. Are drives and defenses more important than the regulation of self-esteem? Who has the last word, Freud or Kohut?

This is not the place to enter into or even describe these discussions. I will concentrate instead on providing a succinct statement of general principles from self psychology which may prove useful to family therapists. One point to remember, however, is that in drive psychology aggression is a primal human impulse, an inevitable fact of life, and that growing up is a process of taming this elemental force. In self psychology, on the other hand, aggression is derivative, not basic to human nature. It is not an instinct, but a reaction to frustration or rejection.

The differences between self psychology and drive theory are brought into focus by their response to the litmus test of psychoanalytic orthodoxy, the Oedipus complex. According to drive theory, the classic family love and hate triangle is an inevitable consequence of inexorable drives. According to self psychology, conflict at this stage is due to the parents' failure to accept with joy and pride the child's natural strivings.

Kohut believed that in well-adjusted children the oedipal period is a healthy stage of development, with intensified feelings of affection and assertiveness, rather than lust and destructiveness.[6] The parents' response is critical. Their pride in and acceptance of the child's libidinal and assertive strivings allow these to develop without undue conflict.

Freud believed that a boy's inevitable fear of castration by the father causes him to identify with the aggressor and to internalize the father's values. Kohut suggested that a father's pride in his son's emerging assertive efforts softens the boy's disappointment at having to share his mother. An Oedipus *conflict*, according to Kohut, is a perversion of normal development in which the parents respond with fear and criticism to their child's natural affection and competitiveness. Only then, when the child's self-esteem is impaired and his strivings are frustrated, does the child feel narcissistic rage toward his father, and only then does his healthy desire for his mother become exaggerated and sexualized.

To Kohut, parenting is more than a matter of taming inborn drives. Because he believed that the most basic human needs are expressed in relationships with other people and that people are more than convenient vehicles or "objects" for gratifying sexual and aggressive drives, Kohut's theory of normal development should be congenial to family therapists.

To the very young child, parents are not quite separate individuals; they are, in Kohut's words, "selfobjects," experienced as extensions of the self. As a selfobject, the mother transmits her fondness and acceptance with gentle words and soothing caresses, as though they were the child's own feelings. When she murmurs, "Mommy loves you," the baby learns that he or she is: (a) a person, and (b) lovable. Steady, loving parental validation in the early years nourishes a lifelong sense of security.

According to Kohut, a person's sense of self is developed out of early relationships with parents, especially the quality of *mirroring* and *idealization*. Mirroring is admiring acceptance of the child's healthy strivings. Every child (and the child in every adult) is a bit of an exhibitionist. "Look at me!" says the child. The parent's enthusiastic response conveys acceptance, not only of the performance but of the developing self. Disinterest or rejection, on the other hand, leaves the child feeling empty and worthless. Loving confirmation is the prerequisite to a stable and secure nuclear self.

The parents also offer a model for idealization. The little child who can believe, "My father (or mother) is terrific and I am part of him (her)," has an extra source of self-esteem. In the ideal case, the child, already basically secure from adequate mirroring, draws additional strength from identifying with the apparently enormous power and strength of the parents. In cases where parents have been deficient in the maternal function of mirroring, the availability of a suitable model for idealization helps compensate for the missing self-confidence. "Maybe they didn't tell me that

I'm fine just as I am, but I know that I will grow up to be just as big and smart and strong as they are."

The product of optimal development is a secure and healthy self. But what exactly is a "self?" "Self" is not quite the same as "personality." Personality is the sum of a person's typical and habitual ways of relating to other people; self is the core of the person, the heart of the personality. The distinction, in other words, is between inner nature and outward manifestations.

Under favorable circumstances, the child's exhibitionism and grandiosity are gradually modified until they become part of a secure sense of self-worth. The idealized parental image becomes integrated into the adult personality as guiding values and ideals. Thus, Kohut speaks of a *bipolar self*, consisting of ambitions and ideals. The individual is pushed from within by nuclear ambitions and pulled from without by an idealized vision of the parents. Kohut later distinguished a third pole of the self, "twinship," in which the child consolidates skills by sharing in the parents' competence. Thus, a little child working alongside Mommy or Daddy in the garden develops a sense of having talents and skills.

Problems arise when parents fail to provide adequate mirroring or a model for identification. If the childhood need to be admired and confirmed is frustrated, it is intensified into a lasting craving. The child grows to adulthood with a piece close to the heart left behind. People like this look like grownups, but the tenuous quality of their selfhood leaves them with childlike dependency on others for reassurance and praise. Failure of the selfobjects means that grandiose aspirations retain their archaic form and intensity. We see this in adults who seem to think it necessary to be Superman or Superwoman in order to prove their worth. Exhibitionism is not sublimated, it is repressed. The child who hungered in vain for praise becomes an adult who suppresses the craving for attention and then lets it break through in an all-or-nothing form in the presence of anyone who seems safe and receptive. "Look at me," cries the child. "See what I've accomplished"—"or endured"— echoes the adult.

Traumatic disappointment in the parents leads to a frustrated longing for someone to idealize. Figures of idealization are sought out for maintenance of self-esteem; they are not loved but needed. Only as long as the dependent person feels approved by various authorities does he or she experience self as whole and acceptable. At the first sign of disapproval, such persons may become depressed and angry, or withdraw into a cold, isolated and haughty facade of self-sufficiency.

Perhaps now we can better understand Mr. Templeton, the man in the first chapter who could not get close to his son. As a consequence of unmet needs for mirroring and idealization, his adult functioning and personality were impoverished because his self was deprived of the energy still invested in these unmet needs. Patients with self pathology, like Mr. Templeton, seek reassurance more than satisfaction. In all likelihood, they are too preoccupied with their own needs to be very receptive to what others in their families need from them. They crave praise, but it's never enough; they hunger for success, but the next achievement brings only transient good feelings. As with any drug, there must be another fix, and another.

Some people are "mirror-hungry" personalities. They crave admiration and praise and success, trying to counteract, however fleetingly, their inner sense of emptiness and worthlessness. Others are "ideal-hungry" personalities, forever in search of someone to respect and admire and borrow strength from. "Merger-hungry" personalities are pursuers, intolerant of independence, and extremely sensitive to separation. Such persons become enmeshed with others in the family and cannot easily separate.

The same inner insecurity, however, can lead to the opposite pattern. "Contact-shunning" personalities, distancers like Mr. Templeton, avoid social contact and become isolated. Their insecurity is so great that they are excessively sensitive to the slightest sign of rejection, which they avoid through isolation and withdrawal. In family therapy, we regularly see this pattern manifest as either disengagement or hypersensitivity to criticism, or both.

The Mr. Templetons of the world believe that if only they could banish the anxiety of being connected, of needing and being needed by other people, surely then they would be free. But there is a paradox. As long as they refuse to acknowledge their connection to others, they can never be fully reconciled to themselves. Mr. Templeton arrived at adulthood with a complex inhibition in the capacity to love and be loved. Unfortunately, his solution—avoiding intimacy—perpetuates his own unhappiness and passes it on to his son. In order to protect himself from rejection and further narcissistic wounding, he shuns intimacy. His avoidance is defensive, but not stubborn and not stupid. It is based on a correct assessment of his own vulnerability. Still, life kept at a distance and seen through a curtain is a pale substitute for the real thing.

Where is the way out of this predicament? As with many complex questions, this one lends itself to simple answers, most of which are more appealing than the truth. One simple answer is to send Mr. Templeton to individual therapy. While this might help, it also entails two clear problems. First, it deals with only one segment of the family. Second, therapists are ever prone to assume that functions are missing in the family. This happens in individual therapy when the therapist becomes a substitute friend and confidant, and it happens in family therapy when the therapist regularly takes over, solving problems, settling disputes, monitoring behavior, and soothing hurt feelings.

Another simple answer is to say that a rearrangement of family relationships will transform Mr. Templeton's protective isolation. Once we push him to engage with his wife and son, they will keep him involved. In fact, the opposite is true. The chances are that if the family draws him close he will come out of himself and enjoy their company, for a time. (This would be a good time to terminate therapy—before the rebound sets in.) But equally likely, the closeness will bring buried and forgotten emotions out of hiding. He will once again be exposed to criticisms, conflicts, and unsympathetic responses, inevitable and normal consequences of family living. Active participation in family life is part of a drive toward human wholeness. But given the fragile nature of this man's self-esteem, he prefers inauthentic living, and he will likely withdraw even further into himself.

If he is to become more involved with his family, Mr. Templeton must first find the motivation. The desire to help his son is a start, but it may not be enough. He may also need to discover for himself that life divorced from the family is lonely, that career success and safe but limited relationships leave something missing, and that he can learn to endure the occasional sting of criticism and disapproval that family life inevitably entails.

Once he decides that the rewards of increased involvement with his wife and son are worth working for, then therapy can help on two fronts. At the level of the self, Mr. Templeton can work introspectively to resolve his own conflicts. A therapist could help him repair his wounded ego by providing a supportive but restrained and nondirective atmosphere within which to explore his feelings, hopes and ambitions, present relationships, and memories of the past. The vehicle of change would be mirroring—*not* praise ("You're really a good person") or even reassurance ("I'm sure things will work out"), but letting him know you understand his longings and fears ("Oh, how you wanted her to notice!" or "You're afraid that if you speak up she will only criticize you more, is that it?")

Short of this, a more supportive relationship could provide him with understanding of his problem, if not resolution of his low self-esteem. Understanding something about the roots of his insecurity and self doubt will enable him to persist in the face of contemporary hurts. Criticism and rejection will, of course, still hurt, and he will still withdraw under attack, but if he understands that the magnitude of his hurt is a product of the past, then he will be able to cut short the withdrawal and reach out again.

Incidentally, this work can be done in the context of individual sessions or family sessions. Individual therapy has the advantage of providing the safest atmosphere for self-exploration, but individual therapy alone also has drawbacks. If Mr. Templeton changes, his wife and son may resist the change. Mrs. Templeton didn't just get used to her husband's distance; at some level it presumably met her needs. Moreover, an insecure self like Mr. Templeton is excessively vulnerable to the influence of others to sustain his narcissistic equilibrium. If he were in therapy by himself, any gain in his self-esteem is liable to be offset by unmodified interactions in the family. Mr. Templeton's wife and son must make room for him if he is to come closer, and they can learn to reach out to draw him closer, rather than wish for it in silence or criticize his remoteness. They may continue to be critical—people rarely stop altogether doing what they do—but they can be helped to see that criticism drives him away.

Self psychology not only helps explain the withdrawal we see in disengagement but also prepares us to understand what goes on in the hearts and minds of the disengaged. Remember that the nuclear self consists of ideals and ambitions laid down early in life. If childhood selfobjects are responsive, if they confirm and mirror the child's value and worth, and if they serve as models to whom the child can look up and with whom the child can merge, then the person will develop a cohesive and well-functioning self, with a built-in capacity for internal regulation that makes self-esteem relatively stable in the face of life's vagaries. When early experience confirms that we are lovable and that others are loving, we can approach life with confidence. But if the shadow of nonacceptance falls over the early years, we carry it inside, where it casts a chill over adult relationships.

No matter how big and successful they are, most people continue to be haunted by childhood fears of inadequacy and continue to long for relationships with people who accept and admire them. Lying, bragging, and name-dropping are blatant signs of flawed self-respect. A more subtle version of the same dynamic is the person who avoids asking directions in a strange city because he or she cannot tolerate not knowing everything. Emotionally undernourished as children, as adults they remain always hungry—hungry for praise, and hungry for attention. The unfulfilled may always be reaching for a special connection, one with the magic to heal emptiness. When someone looks for the "ideal relationship," he or she is looking for someone who allows for complete self-expression, without opposition or criticism. The only place on this planet that anyone is likely to find such a perfect selfobject is in the infatuation of an affair.

In a culture that conveys its highest prizes for competitive dominance, women and men seek rank and status as a defense against feelings of inadequacy. Despite this, however, we remain most vulnerable to rejection from the families we sometimes take for granted. The mortification comes from reexposure to the narcissistic injuries of childhood, and the hurt goes to the heart of the self. Narcissism—normal or overdeveloped—makes people long for admiration and eager for success. Dreams of majesty and power are born of fear of crushing rejection. Disappointments in these strivings cause sensitive people to react with withdrawal or rage. Narcissistic rage comes from disappointment in one's expectations from selfobjects. We see this in family members who cannot tolerate criticism and react with feelings of humiliation. This mechanism also helps us understand the rage of a wounded spouse who remains bitter for years, apparently unable to forgive or forget.

What makes self psychology so important is that it offers a fundamentally different view of human nature. At the core of human nature is not a raging id but a more or less insecure self, striving for fulfillment and longing for acceptance and admiration. Unhappy people seek reassurance more than satisfaction. For family therapists, there is another critical distinction. Kohut's basic disagreement with traditional ego psychology is in its Freudian vision that maturation proceeds to independence. Psychoanalysis has done much to foster the view that mature development means separation from the family and its influence. Margaret Mahler, for example, describes "the psychological birth of the human infant" as a long process of separation and individuation, and thus equates growth with separation.[7] The mature adult, according to this view, is one who can stand alone.

This theme of separation as the model and measure of growth is echoed in mythology and fiction. Heroes like Hercules and Jason were often forced to undertake quests of adventure by mortal conflict with their families. Cassandra and Diana were powerful, but alone. Even Zeus, father of the gods, achieved his stature only by defeating his parents. Great novelists often portray creativity and success as hard-won accomplishments, achieved only by rejecting the values and claims of the family (James Joyce, in *Portrait of the Artist as a Young Man*; Doris Lessing in *The Golden*

Notebook; Ann Beattie in *Falling in Place*). At other times, the family is portrayed as a deadening influence that either destroys its off-spring or cripples them (Waugh's *Brideshead Revisited*; Didion's *Democracy*). The greatest artists, like Dostoevsky, recognize that even saints and parricides never really separate themselves from their families, no matter how hard they try.

Kohut, too, rejects the myth of the separate self and adds that we never outgrow our need for self-affirmation. A network of loving and supportive relationships is crucial throughout life. When we sense our continuing dependency on other people and their opinion of us, we are tempted to believe that this is a weakness we should outgrow. Not so. The self always requires a milieu of empathic relationships. As Chessick observed, this may explain many cases of so-called pseudodementia in lonely and isolated elderly people.[8] It also explains why the self in the system is often a reluctant participant.

We cannot escape the fact that we are creatures of systems larger than ourselves. Still, those who minimize their participation in family life do so for what they consider good reasons. Some people spend most of their time at work, others use up their energy pursuing self-improvement or health-inducing exercise, and many people give up as a lost cause trying to maintain personal relationships with their parents. Isolated people may not even feel lonely. Loneliness means active longing for people. The feeling hurts, but it is a feeling of life. Sadder by far are those whose inner world is empty. Such people are alone, but do not feel it.

Those who resist intimacy the most are fragile selves afraid of getting hurt in relationships. The vulnerable and conflicted person may be in urgent need of a network of loving relationships, but being conflicted, being vulnerable, hangs back, afraid of love, afraid of demands, afraid of impingement.

Self-sufficient introverts, like Mr. Templeton, only loosely connected to family and friends, had the capacity to love frozen by early experiences of rejection, frustration, and disregard. These traumas, rarely remembered, are restimulated by countless rebuffs of everyday living. The result is a diffuse sensitivity to anything that wounds the ego. This is a different view of human nature than Freud's version.

Freudian drive psychology is a psychology of conflict; people suffer because they are at war within. We are anxious and guilty because, despite our efforts to repress the truth, we sense that our basic nature is dangerous and bad. According to Kohut, we spend our lives trying to feel secure in our own self-esteem. Weakness and dependency haunt us always. We find our littleness hard to endure, so we mask it with bluff and bluster. Others show their self-doubt more openly. We all need reassurance.

The fact that Kohut's writing touches a responsive chord in those who take the time to read carefully has led some to criticize self psychology for moving away from depth psychology toward the shallows of "humanism," which tends to abrogate the importance of unconscious drives and conflicts. Instead of choosing, perhaps we can have both. There are two major human tendencies: searching for pleasure and striving for self-fulfillment. While psychoanalytic scholars debate whether self psychology complements or competes with drive theory, we can use both as tools to a richer understanding of the self in the system.

Earlier, I described a case of depression where drive theory seemed relevant. Now I will illustrate how depression is sometimes better understood with the framework of self psychology.

Ned Oster came to see me because he was depressed, very depressed. Each morning he woke early, long before he wanted to, and lay in bed thinking of all the hours that stretched before him. When he finally did get up, there was nothing to do, or at least nothing he felt like doing. He had no energy, no ambition, and, worse, no hope that he would. This is the kind of disabling depression that might respond to antidepressant medication, yet it was somehow different. For one thing, although Mr. Oster was too depressed to function, he didn't look it. He didn't cry, and when he spoke about himself he seemed to perk up a bit. Also, there was an absence of any sign of guilt. He didn't condemn himself for being depressed, as most guilt-ridden people do. In fact, he didn't say anything negative about himself. Instead of guilty he seemed to be empty.

Mr. Oster had been retired for about a year. He spoke fondly of his work in the state education department. His job involved accreditation of minority assistance programs in colleges, which meant frequent trips all over the state to meet with deans and professors and students. He loved it. But about a year and a half ago things turned sour. His old boss, a woman who valued him and gave him tremendous support, resigned to take a high-paying position. The new boss was more concerned with the budget than with the minority assistance program. He didn't think of Ned as special and he cut way back on the number of trips to colleges. Ned hated being stuck in central office. Most of what he was asked to do was transmit memos, rewrite policy statements, attend meetings, and trim costs. He used to love work and never considered stopping, but now at 58 he decided to take early retirement.

At first, retirement seemed attractive. He envisioned doing all the things he never seemed to have enough time for: relaxing, reading, fishing, and traveling around the country. Later he might like to do some teaching. As he told me this, he interspersed comments about his wife's lack of sympathy. "I'd love to travel out west. That's one thing my wife would never understand. Her idea of heaven is reading a book in the backyard." But these remarks were usually tossed off as asides, and it took me a while to notice how many there were. After three sessions, though, I asked him to bring his wife in to see if she could offer any help.

Mrs. Oster was willing to come—"If *you* think it might help"—but not very enthusiastic. We had only one joint session. Initially she said little. Yes, he had been depressed. No, she didn't know why. She was pleasant but tight-lipped. Her brief answers offered little information. She was holding back, on unfamiliar ground. I chose not to push or challenge.

Mr. Oster spoke more about his own symptoms, complained of feeling hopeless, lethargic, empty—"things she doesn't understand." Directly challenged, Mrs. Oster said what she thought: "I'm sorry you're so unhappy but you have to get over feeling sorry for yourself. Find something to do and get busy. What about all those things you wanted to do? Even if *you* don't have any plans, there's plenty to do around the house." He looked pained as she spoke, not like someone who is angry and suppressing it, but like a child, disappointed, wounded, and deprived.

Mr. Oster's wife's lack of sympathy for his depression raises the familiar question: Is the problem in the person or in the system? The familiar answer, "Both," leaves us up in the air about how to proceed. Since the wife is unsympathetic and critical, should we work with the couple? We could try, but considering that the two of them have been married for 35 years and that Mr. Oster did not become depressed until shortly after he retired suggests a long history of getting satisfaction from his work, not his marriage.

When a man or woman retires, he or she does need to readjust relationships that were stabilized by years of working. The same thing is true when children leave home. In both cases, this means renegotiating the boundary between the couple. They may want to find ways to spend more time together, or they may want to find new rituals to preserve the distance between them. In the case of Mr. Oster, the problem was not conflict and it was not differences about how much time to spend together; his wife might be unsympathetic and that might hurt his feelings, but she couldn't supply what was missing.

Ned Oster's career had supplied his narcissistic needs so long and so well that it had not been apparent how dependent he was. What appeared to be a cohesive and well-functioning personality was sustained, almost like a diabetic taking insulin, by a network of professional relationships that provided him with admiration and respect. He felt alive and worthwhile, but only as long as his achievements brought him the lavish praise of his boss, and his college visits brought him into contact with people who were receptive and eager to please. The very pursuit of specialness cut him off from the real love—"object love"—that was available at home. His deep insecurity created too much pressure to succeed and stand out to allow him to respond to his family's needs or to let them respond to him. He wanted something more than everyday love. He wanted the glow he got from success.

Retirement separated him from his selfobjects and deprived him of his fix—achievement. The resulting narcissistic rage had no place to go. In the past, whenever even small setbacks wounded his vanity, he had what most people have, a circle of friends who go out to lunch or for a drink after work to bitch about the boss, the system, how unfair it all is, and how we "don't get no respect." A different wife might have tried to compensate for the worshipful attention he craved, but he wasn't married to a different wife. So he was disappointed and hurt. She wasn't really the problem and she really wasn't the solution. She had little patience with his need for reassurance, but she could help by not criticizing him.

I met with her privately and explained this to her. She agreed with the assessment that he had trouble giving up all the attention he got at work and was relieved by my absolving her of any responsibility for his problems. And she agreed that it would be a good idea to stop criticizing him or "encouraging" him to get busy, though I could see she would have trouble being more actively supportive.

Most of the subsequent work was with him. It wasn't psychotherapy really—not in the sense of resolving some underlying difficulty. It was more like supportive counseling. My interpretations had far less effect than my approval. It was astonishing that a man of his intellect could depend so much on other people's praise.

Mr. Oster's relationship with me, a sympathetic and attentive listener, sustained his need for "mirroring" enough to begin to restore his self-esteem, enough to interrupt the negative spiral. This is an important point. Although it is usually wise to find resources within the family, sometimes the family's resources are simply not adequate. Mr. Oster needed more attention than his wife (or almost anyone) could give him; he needed the special relationship with a therapist.

As he began to feel better, stronger, Ned was more willing and able to look around for things to do with himself. Even doing some of the chores around the house paid off by winning his wife's thanks. Gradually he did what many retired people do. He took more of a part in community affairs and he became an active member of two volunteer organizations. These activities are sometimes thought necessary to keep a person busy, or even to fulfill what Erikson calls "generativity," but for a man like Ned Oster the real value of these services was to create a context within which he could sustain a network of selfobject relationships.

Kohut's psychology of the self is a bridge between a one-person psychology and an interactional psychology. In fact, his position is somewhat ambiguous. His model can be considered either an object relations theory or as intrapsychic entirely—because the selfobject is not a real person. I don't see that the distinction matters.

For all its elegance, Freud's drive theory is a one-sided approach to human relations. As long as other people are considered interchangeable targets of our instincts, we underestimate the value of a wide and varied network of relationships. Modern analysts have come to terms with the human environment, giving relationships with others a more central explanatory role.

Freud was right in saying we are propelled by unconscious forces buried deep in the psyche. He cannot be discarded but he must be amended. We *are* driven by limitless desire, but from the start that desire is directed toward other people. Moreover, the creature at the source of desire is not a savage beast but a helpless infant. We are born small and weak; utterly fragile, we need other people for life itself. But family therapy is also one-sided. It treats relationships as central, but trivializes the nature of the self. The self that relates to others is more complex than usually assumed, and contemporary relationships with others that relate to the self are themselves shaped by the residue of earliest relationships.

7

Object Relations and Psychopathology

For all the insight we may gain from exploring the psychodynamics of the family members we treat, there is a hazard—the hazard of reverting to a one-sided emphasis on individual psychology. My aim is to integrate, not substitute psychology for systems theory. We must be careful that a correction does not become an overcorrection. For example, saying that unresolved narcissism underlies Mr. Templeton's disengagement does not mean that narcissism is the *real* problem in his family. Extreme conceptual positions—either psychological or family systems—falsify the essential interactional quality of the self and the system.

In this chapter, I will discuss two topics, object relations theory and psychopathology, both of which have been subject to polarized accounts. Among family therapists, the first is considered arcane and therefore often ignored. The latter is more mundane, and although psychopathology cannot easily be ignored it has sometimes been reduced to a mere artifact of family dynamics. In the short space of one chapter, I cannot explore either one of these complicated subjects thoroughly. Instead, I will discuss both topics briefly, using them as examples to illustrate my thesis: Thorough understanding of human problems requires recognition of the dual influences of personal psychology and the network of relationships.

The self cannot be conceptualized except as an open system developing and maintaining its identity through the social relatedness essential to it from the start of life. The formative nature of these earliest relationships is such that their influence is prepotent. As a result, though we are always influenced by our families, we are to some extent also independent of them. Human relatedness to the environment depends on a unique capacity to transcend it by making a reproduction of it inside the mind, where a person can then manipulate the possibilities. This mental structuralization of experience can be the source of creative alterations of circumstances or of deadening inflexibility that sets some people at odds with the world around them. This separateness and partial independence make possible intentionality and freedom on the one hand, repetitive problems and psychopathology on the other.

OBJECT RELATIONS THEORY

Freud taught us that human nature is propelled by unconscious forces buried deep in the psyche. What Freud did not fully appreciate is that we do not discharge instincts in a vacuum. From the start the human infant is helpless and absolutely dependent on other people. The residue of these relationships leaves internal images of the self and the other, and of the self in relation to others. As adults we react not only to the actual other, but also to an internal other. Object relations theory focuses on this internal other—the mental images we have of other people, built up from experience and expectation. These "inner objects" are often quite different from the real people of the external world.

R. D. Laing introduced the ideas of object relations theory to the field of family therapy in 1960 in *The Divided Self*.[1] In this provocative and influential book, he fused object relations concepts from Winnicott, Fairbairn, and Balint with existential ideas from Kierkegaard and Sartre. The result was a popular account of how the repressive "politics of the family" exert a deadening ef-

fect on the natural child, who learns to present a compliant facade, the "false self," while burying the "real self" further and
further inside. In extreme cases, this split becomes more pro-
nounced and leads to "ontological insecurity"—a profound fear of
the annihilation of the self. In such people, a schizophrenic epi-
sode can be, said Laing, a creative breakthrough in which the
hidden self finally emerges into expression. This radical aspect of
Laing's thought led him and his readers away from a thoughtful
analysis of early object relationships to a polemical attack on parental authority, a perenially popular stance.

Laing's influence fell off as the 1960s came to an end, and today
many regard him as a product of the excesses of that decade.
Subsequently, a handful of writers have reversed Laing's journey
and gone from family therapy to a study of the original object
relations theorists. Among these are: Pearce & Friedman (eds.)
*Family Therapy: Combining Psychodynamic and Family Systems Ap-
proaches;*[2] Sander *Individual and Family Therapy: Toward an Integration;*[3] Slipp *Object Relations: A Dynamic Bridge Between Individual
and Family Treatment;*[4] and Scharff & Scharff *Object Relations Family
Therapy.*[5] Unlike earlier attempts by Murray Bowen, Ivan Boszormenyi-Nagy, James Framo, Robin Skynner, and Helm Stierlin to
incorporate a diluted version of psychoanalytic thinking into family therapy, these more recent works have often gone back to the
complexity of the original sources. While this material introduces
family therapists to the rich insights of object relations theorists, it
also makes it easy to get confused.

The essence of object relations theory is quite simple: We relate
to people in the present partly on the basis of expectations formed
by early experience. Your grandmother could have told you that.
Actual, detailed accounts of those expectations, however, are enormously complicated. Each theorist has many competing versions
of this story and, because interpersonal expectations are formed
early in life, they are primitive and unconscious.

Just a partial list of the major object relations theorists includes:
Melanie Klein, Ronald Fairbairn, Donald Winnicott, Harry Guntrip, Edith Jacobson, Michael Balint, Margaret Mahler, and probably Roy Schafer, Otto Kernberg, and Heinz Kohut. Among these

thinkers there are two opposing poles. There are those closest to the Freudian model who consider other persons as objects of biological drives—"objects" because it is the mental image, or fantasy, of the other, not the actual other. Melanie Klein exemplifies this end of the continuum. At the other extreme, Fairbairn and Winnicott believe that object relations, not drives, are the determining factor in development. Interpersonal relatedness replaces the pleasure principle as the driving force in human personality. The experience of the object in reality determines psychic structure (rather than the other way around); internal objects are reflections of experience with real persons.

The two positions divide sharply in their understanding of anger. Those closest to drive theory consider aggression an inborn organic appetite; those who departed from drive theory consider aggression as a reaction to "bad" object relations.

Melanie Klein, considered the first of the object relations theorists, put forward the most hermetic view of mental life. Even the child's earliest relationships, she believed, were governed by the vicissitudes of drives, especially aggression, and primitive defense mechanisms, especially projection, introjection, and splitting. The infant projects his or her own innate aggression onto the mother who is then experienced as potentially hostile and malevolent. These projected fantasies of aggression are then reintrojected and form the basis of an inner "bad object."

The infant's first internalized objects are fragmented; that is they are experienced as "part objects," and as either all good or all bad depending upon whether interactions with mother are pleasant or unpleasant. The primitive ego utilizes *splitting* to keep these positive and negative images separate in order to avoid anxiety. What is important about all this is that the sense of the self as either good or bad is related to the relative predominance of good and bad objects in the internal world.

The concept of splitting and the failure to integrate good and bad early experiences, which results in a pattern of alternating between extremes of perceiving others and the self as all good or all bad, are central to Kernberg's explanation of borderline personalities.[6] The borderline's striking instability—intensity of feeling

and unpredictability of action—is seen as a product of a dissocia-
tion of contradictory ego states reflecting what Kernberg calls a
"nonmetabolized" persistence of early, pathological internalized
object relationships.

This brings up an important point. Primitive mechanisms of
object relations are most readily observed in primitive minds, notably infants and severely disturbed adults. Detailed examination
of the specifics of object relations theory is most useful in the
analysis of pathological character structure. One of the best ways
to discover the value of these theories is to study them at the same
time you are treating a family that contains a very disturbed member.

I do not have the space here to provide a detailed analysis of the
various object relations theorists or even of the major concepts.
What's more, trying to summarize what Winnicott said and what
Mahler said and so on would result in two problems. First is the
tendency common to textbook writers to reduce a mass of complex material to a pedantic list of concepts, mentioned and defined but reduced to a lifeless set of terms. The second problem is
even more significant. Getting lost in the details of the psychodynamic theories accentuates the false dichotomy between inner
and outer space. Family therapy came into being in the first place
when people like Don Jackson realized that human relations depend as much on what goes on between people as what goes on
inside them. The whole point of this book is to correct an overemphasis on that concept—paying so much attention to what goes on
between people that we forget altogether what goes on inside. But
the solution is not to say, as some have, that present family relationships *really* depend upon inner object relations. This is not
progress. It is regress, and it is linear.

Even when we recognize that individual family members are
motivated to behave the way they do, we must continue to work
primarily with real life family interactions if we are to use the
power of family therapy. Attention to the individual—analysis and
intervention—is still done in the context of the family. To think
first, or even primarily, of the individual is to step outside the

paradigm of family therapy. *Putting the self back into the system does not mean forgetting the system.*

When people write about object relations, they tend to make a sharp distinction between the "internal world" and the external one, the former conceived as either more primitive or more genuine depending upon whether the author is psychoanalytic or existential. But notice the linear thinking inherent in this logic: Inner experience *causes* interpersonal responses. "Why is Mrs. Jones enmeshed with her children?" "Because of her own unresolved *separation-individuation.*" Not only does the past cause the present in this version, but the problem resides in one person.

A more accurate—and useful—version of the truth is that contemporary relationships and early experience (encoded in the inner world of objects) interact in circular fashion. Life circumstances maintain internal expectations and are chosen because of them and are interpreted in light of them. "Why is Mrs. Jones enmeshed with her children?" Because her husband's distance from her and them leaves an emotional void that their closeness helps to fill, just as she expected it would; and she chose this particular man partly because he seemed to offer her the intimacy she craved, at least during courtship; and she interprets the children's demands for her attention as natural and imperative.

The way to make object relations theory useful in family therapy is to recognize that past experience and expectations still play a role—and then to look for them. When a family member distorts the implications of what someone else does, or is overly sensitive, or thoughtlessly overreacts—in other words, if the response does not fit the circumstances—talk with that person about what he or she learned about such things. The essence of this inquiry is historical and biographical, not technical or theoretical. Instead of looking for "separation-individuation" problems or "antilibidinal egos" or "incorporation fantasies," simply talk with family members and try to understand their experience in human terms.

Object relations theory says that the past is alive—in memory— and it runs people's lives more than they know. We can apply this basic idea simply by interrupting self-defeating family quarrels to discuss with family members how they learned to be so angry, sensitive, and defensive. Here is an example.

The DeLeos were one of those couples who had been living together unhappily for years. They quarrelled frequently, rarely went out together despite comfortable means, and neither one could remember the last time they had any fun. Their complaints were familiar—she wanted him to "Stop ignoring me and treating me like a servant," and he wanted her "Just to be happy and stop accusing me all the time"—but their animosity was uncommonly bitter. What keeps people like that together?

I wasn't optimistic. They had been in treatment with several excellent therapists, and they were still venomously disputing an incident that occurred 12 years ago. Or didn't occur. She accused him of having an affair; he denied it. The first thing I did was explore with each of them their separate sides of the dilemma. I tried to help her realize that she was allowing him to control her life and make her miserable. Whether or not he confessed, whether or not he had done it, she was living as if what a man said and did was the only thing that had meaning in her life. She had to learn to accept responsibility for, and take control of, her own life. His contribution was his rage and his fear of showing it. He was too angry at her to include her in his life, and too fearful to tell her off when she tried to control him by nagging.

Several object relations concepts come to mind: Klein's "paranoid position" and "bad object," Fairbairn's "antilibidinal ego," Sullivan's "bad mother," Winnicott's "false-self," and so on. However, it is impossible to reduce the complexities of real family life to any of the simple basic formulas proposed by the various proponents of object relations theory. Instead, I tried to understand the DeLeos' experience and help them to do the same by talking with each of them about their relationship and their own families.

They met at a dance. He thought she was pretty, honest, open, expressive. She did not feel strongly attracted at first. Her description of him as "different, quiet, educated" suggests that she was looking for a safe harbor, not passion. I pointed this out and asked how she thought security had become so important to her. There was, as you might guess, plenty of material in her family history to explain her unresolved attachment and need for mothering. Her mother was a narcissistic woman, too preoccupied with herself to pay much attention to her daughter. Her father was a successful and charming man, with whom she had a close and special relationship as a little girl. When she got to be a teenager, however, her father became aloof and distant. As an explanation for her insecurity, these early object relations were certainly pertinent, but not necessarily decisive.

Mr. DeLeo contributed more than his share to the couple's problems. He was drawn to his wife's emotional vitality, all the more because this was the most sadly lacking aspect of his own growing up. Yet he was too insecure to tolerate her anger or demands, and so he withdrew from her and sought reassurance of his worth in work and political activity. The marriage grew progressively more empty and bitter. What kept him from leaving was that he was afraid to stand up to her—if he *could* leave, he wouldn't have to. What kept her with him was her own frightened sense of inadequacy. As with him, if she could leave, she wouldn't have to.

Theoretically, either individual therapy or family therapy could help the DeLeos. Family therapy could help break the cycle of her clinging dependence and angry accusation, provoking his alternating retreat and passive attacks on her. But any focus on the contemporary pattern would have a lot of history to go against. Long-term individual therapy could help repair the developmental deficits that left them with raw wounds for the relationship to rub. Either of these approaches might succeed, but work on either the personal equation or the relationship alone would be handicapped by the effect of the other.

I was able to treat the DeLeos by helping each one of them understand how their own family experience had made them oversensitive and inflexible in certain ways, and how they could nevertheless begin to behave differently now. I saw them together, but talked with them separately a good deal of the time—call it boundary-making, in the sense of clarifying their separate experiences. Therapy didn't "cure" them; I didn't make up for their developmental deficits, but neither did I become a substitute for what they had missed growing up and hadn't achieved with each other. Therapy helped them change slightly, in spite of their early object relationships, and it was enough to make a difference.

I have stressed the value of exploring the personal past without overemphasizing specific formulas, not because the theories are not useful but because it is important not to get lost in them. For those who wish to refine their own understanding of how early experience shapes current relating and relationships, I recommend reading some of the excellent writing on object relations by Balint,[7] Bowlby,[8] Fairbairn,[9] Greenberg & Mitchell,[10] Guntrip,[11] Jacobson,[12] Kernberg,[13] Mahler, Pine, & Bergman,[14] Modell,[15] Schafer,[16] Segal,[17] Stolorow & Lachmann,[18] Winnicott.[19]

Among the most useful object relations concepts for integrating psychology and systems thinking are idealization and projective identification.

Idealization

Love, as everyone but lovers knows, is blind. We see what we want to see. Love is like a blanket of snow that covers sooty streets, leaving only soft white contours. It's a wonderful feeling, something young girls dream of and middle-aged men pine for. But if it is illegal to drive while intoxicated, shouldn't there be a law against choosing a partner for life under the influence of infatuation?

After the honeymoon, when reality sets in, two people who thought they knew each other often find out otherwise. He looks at the sexy wench he thought he married and sees his mother standing there. She looks at the serious man she fell in love with and discovers him to be a moody, self-centered adolescent.

So. What's all this got to do with family therapy? Everybody knows that love is blind and that marital choice is one of the least rational decisions people ever make. You might think we could help people who come for "premarital counseling" think through their plans and weigh their decisions wisely. Perhaps, but in my experience 99 out of a hundred people who seek premarital counseling have already made up their minds. They don't get along well but intend to marry anyway. They don't want us to change their minds; they want us to fix the fiancé(e). Once in a while you get a couple in which one of them wants out but doesn't want to say so directly, or at least wants to leave the rejected lover in the hands of someone who will take care of him or her.

Family therapists can make use of the concept of idealization by knowing not only that it exists but why it exists—what function it serves in the psychic economy—and then by using this information to help family members understand and modify their pattern of first idealizing and then devaluing each other.

Various theorists describe the function of idealization in different ways. Freud related it to reaction-formation. Idealizing someone is one way to defend oneself against recognizing dangerous aggressive feelings. The man who always makes a point of saying how "wonderful" his wife is may be protecting himself from facing his anger and resentment. Melanie Klein elaborated the Freudian position, saying that idealization is a defense against sadism and destruction in fantasy. Idealized "good objects" are internalized, setting up unrealistically high standards to strive for. Thus, idealization is part of what makes the superego so inflexible.

Winnicott spoke of idealization and with it infantile omnipotence as ways of combating feelings of helplessness. And, as I have already mentioned, Kohut described how the child draws strength from identifying with idealized parents. In the normal course of events, incremental disappointment in the parents results in the child's gradually becoming his own center of worth and initiative. Traumatic failure of the parents to behave as ideals, on the other hand, leaves the child forever insecure and with a lasting longing for people to idealize.

What all of these accounts boil down to is a statement that idealization is a means of compensating for one's own shortcomings. The object of idealization may be flattered and put on a pedestal until the inevitable disillusion sets in. People marry (and choose therapists) in order to make up for something missing and to protect themselves from unhappy feelings. Since it is asking too much of any relationship to sustain these needs, disappointment inevitably sets in. It isn't so much the disappointment that is the problem. Rather it is the person's blindness to the process of idealization and devaluation. Instead of reflecting: "Why did I need to exaggerate his (or her) good points?," the disappointed person blames the other one unfairly and turns elsewhere for the missing satisfaction. Here is an example of how an awareness of idealization can help.

Early in my career, a young couple came to see me after an unsuccessful course of treatment with another therapist. Mr. Cody told me that the other therapist had turned out to be an incompetent fool, but he *knew* I could help because he had heard what a *wonderful* therapist I was. I was pleased by his good judgment.

Married only three years, their problem was: "We argue all the time." They were so contentious that even when they tried to explain how the arguments went, their discussion was too destructive to clarify anything. These two had built up a lot of poison in three years.

The compulsive quality of their quarrelling might be taken as evidence for a "systemic need to avoid change"—that is, they *couldn't* stop fighting because it stabilized the system. Perhaps, but these personalities were pretty well formed before Mr. and Mrs. Cody met. The compulsive nature of their reactions can also be taken as evidence of the fixed nature of their identification with inner objects. This is an important point to understand. Object relations are not perceptions, nor even cognitive constructions, but internalized images—unconscious, affect-laden beliefs. They are structured in the mind and cannot be changed at will.

In order to get some room to maneuver I asked a question I routinely ask: "What did you think of her (him) when you first met?" Mr. Cody said, "She was so sophisticated, so smart. I come from a working-class background; she was everything I wasn't. I fell in love with her the first night we met." In short, he endowed her with idealized qualities he felt he could never attain himself. Through proximity to the possessor of these qualities, he could be included in their glow (gilt by association).

During most of their brief courtship, he saw her only on

weekends. In her presence he came alive. They were so in love. Everything they did was imbued with a romantic haze. The rest of the week he was immersed in his work, socially isolated and detached.

Mrs. Cody remembered how gentle her husband was. "He was so courteous and respectful. Unlike so many boys I knew, he really respected me." In fact, what she fell in love with was a defensive shadow. In his romanticized version of her, she was "so wonderful and special" that he curried favor, voicing feigned agreement with her to remain in her good graces. She declined sexual relations, but he took this as a sign of her values and self-respect, never considering that she might be frightened or conflicted. Since his aim was winning her respect, he didn't push. There were also unmistakable signs of hysterical rage, but he mistook them. "Her family was crazy," was his explanation of why there were so many screaming matches.

After the wedding, things deteriorated fast. They had fallen in love with each other's projected illusions—but married a stranger. Two things were different. In marriage, unlike dating, the partners no longer put their best foot forward. Moreover, once you get to know someone you have idealized and discover that that someone isn't perfect, you tend to devalue that person. That's certainly what Mr. Cody did. At home he began to see his wife as a source of frustration. She seemed "selfish" and "demanding," and "she dressed like a slob." When he did see her looking good, dressed for work in the morning, he was intensely jealous.

In their first two sessions with me, whenever they argued I intervened forcefully and directed them to take turns. Since this was the first time in a long time that either one of them had a chance to say much without being interrupted, they were encouraged and seemed to be on the road to improvement. Mr. Cody praised me profusely, and I was flattered. Soon, however, they reverted to quarrelling and before I could do much about it they dropped out. Later I heard that he divorced her and remarried within the space of two months.

Notice how Mr. Cody's idealization affected his relationship to the therapist as well as his relationship to his wife. Whenever a patient describes (or reveals) a history of repetitive problems with people, the therapist should be on the lookout for those problems to crop up in the therapeutic relationship. Recently, someone came for treatment, saying he had read one of my books and "It was wonderful!" Everyone else in his life had let him down. So I said: "You've had a lot of bad luck in relationships. Many people have let you down. Eventually you may begin to feel that way about me. If so, let's talk about it."

Internal images of others determine what we expect and how we interpret what happens. They can leave us with healthy positive expectations, and therefore open and flexible, or with unrealistically positive or negative expectations, and therefore stereotyped, rigid habits of relating that are relatively unchanged by new information. Not all conflicts and not all inner objects require attention in family therapy, of course, only those where there is interlocking conflict. When dysfunctional transactions seem impervious to our efforts to introduce change, that is the time to look more closely at the individuals, especially their past experience and expectations.

Not only does the past produce expectations and shape what we see, we actively create it. We shape our partners to fit our inner models, projecting onto them our repudiated feelings and then inducing the spouse to live them out.

Projective Identification

What keeps some couples together despite obvious suffering and mutual destructiveness? Adult responsibility, yes, and parental commitments, too. But in addition, when apparently ill-matched couples stay together, it is reasonable to assume that on some deep level they must be meeting each other's needs. In psychodynamic terms, this is "unconscious complementarity." Each partner supplies a set of qualities the sum of which creates a complete dyadic unit. This joint personality enables each half to reclaim lost aspects of their primary object relationships which they had split off or repressed and which they reexperience by living out in the relationship.

In courtship, most couples are extraordinarily close and their needs fit together like interlocking pieces of a puzzle. This makes it possible to establish contact with missing or repudiated parts of the self. He is delighted to find a woman who enjoys the luxury of expensive meals, good clothes, and having fun. All this was considered self-indulgent in his family. She is pleased to find a man willing to follow success even though it leads him away from the ethnic enclave he was born into.

Inevitably, these differences that delight give way to conflict. He begins to think of her as spoiled, wasteful; she is threatened and angry because he insists on moving across the country. The intensity of their reactions to each other arises from a deeper level where there are perceptions and, consequently, attitudes toward the other *as if he or she were part of oneself.* The partner is then treated according to how this aspect of self was valued: spoiled and cherished, or denigrated and persecuted. The same dynamic applies to parents and children.

The tenacity of the struggle between mothers and their teenaged sons reflects unconscious personal dimensions as well as family developmental ones. The son's hypermasculinity is a defense against feelings of helplessness and dependence. However, he oscillates between being a big man and coming home to "refuel" himself with his mother's concern. These oscillations interact with her needs as well. She wants him to grow up. Unconsciously, she may also want him to act out an adventurousness missing from her own life. And still she may not be ready to give up "her baby." The regressive pull of her need for him is felt and resisted. It propels him toward the world outside, toward his friends and swaggering bravado. But the inevitable bruising and disappointment here sends him, once again, back home, licking his wounds and looking for comfort. Yet he will not confess it, for fear of announcing his pitiful and humiliating weakness. This is enactment of a subtler sort.

Projective identification is a particular version of this mysterious interplay of two psyches. It describes an enactment in which split-off aspects of the self are induced in the other. The processes involved in projective identification include: (1) projection of the split-off part and (2) introjection by the recipient. It functions as a defense and blurs the boundary between self and other. In the process the self is changed. So is the relationship, for the other person is enmeshed in the role relationship being acted out. Let me illustrate this with a brief example.

As any of their friends could tell you, Camille and George had a terrible marriage. They always seemed to be arguing, and when they were apart each complained about the other one to whoever would listen. I saw them only once when I consulted to an agency where they were in therapy with their third student therapist. The therapist was helping them work on communication.

The session began, as most of their sessions did, with neither spouse having much to say. Eventually, with the therapist's prompting, Camille complained that George was totally unsympathetic about her chronic headaches. "He doesn't care about anything but sex." George snapped back like a spring: "That's not true! You're always criticizing me; nothing I do is any good." The therapist interrupted this squabbling to point out that they were cross-complaining, and they should take turns discussing one thing at a time.

From behind the mirror, I was interested not just in their way of expressing themselves but in the nature of the things they had to say. Her complaints were about headaches and sex, his were about anger and self-esteem. But because they dumped their feelings onto each other, it wasn't clear who felt what. The boundary between them was so blurred that it was difficult to determine what caused Camille's headaches or why she was unhappy about sex, and hard to tell why George thought that she was the only one who was angry.

Since I did not follow up on this case, I cannot say how useful any of my observations proved, but here is the gist of what I said to the therapist: "These two are so entangled that clarifying their communication is premature. They project so much blame onto each other that you should delay having them talk to each other. They are enmeshed not only by habit and mutual absorption, but by being bound together by a reciprocal process of projecting their own conflicts. Camille, for example, not only somatizes her unhappiness but also makes George responsible. Why she is so unhappy or what she feels about sex is unclear because she focuses only on his demands. George apparently prefers to think of her as the one with all the anger in the family. Why is that?

"Neither one of them contains painful feelings long enough to understand much about their conflicts. He lures her into his web of helplessness and self-pity by inducing her to actualize his split-off anger and ruthless self-reproaches. Perhaps he feels guilty for wanting sex, but who knows as long as the boundary between them is so blurred.

"The therapist's task with this unhappy but stable couple is to unravel the enactment, to help George and Camille differentiate between self and object, between expectation and reality. In my view, much of his work should be to help them learn about their own feelings and intrapsychic conflicts. Asking George, 'How do you think she is reacting to you?' gives him a chance to think about transmitted feelings. Asking Camille to talk not only about her headaches but also about her life in general gives her a chance to think about her own problems. Until they experience and recognize their own individual conflicts, they cannot understand, much less begin to resolve the conflicts between them. Help them extricate themselves from their web of blurry projection and establish more distinct self-definition by talking to them one at a time. They can talk together later."

Projective identification is communicative and defensive at the same time. The main defensive function of projective identification is to communicate one's own inner state by passing it on to someone else who then acts it out. In the example above, Camille acts out *George's* anxiety about separation and he acts out *her* anger and wounded narcissism. What makes this interpersonal projection so sticky is that the process is unconscious so that *neither one of them understands what they are doing.* Family therapy is usually the best way to help couples work out their problems, but without some understanding and clarification of the blurring of their internal states, it would be difficult to help *this* couple.

The concept of projective identification is a useful way for the therapist to understand how unconscious fantasy is acted out via verbal and nonverbal communications designed to evoke another person's reactions. Is there *really* such a thing as projective identification? Can you prove it? No, not in a scientific sense. Like many psychodynamic concepts, its validity rests not on empirical evidence but on clinical utility. Using the same criterion, clinical utility, some family therapists have treated individual psychopathology as though it were nothing but a family problem.

PSYCHOPATHOLOGY

Psychopathology has proven a fertile area for extremists on both sides of the individual versus systems debate. At one extreme are biological psychiatrists who believe that certain conditions—schizophrenia and bipolar disorder—are medical problems, period. Remarkably, they also believe that other more clearly psychological problems, including panic disorder and borderline personality, are best treated medically. At the other extreme, some systems theorists say not only is the pathology not in the person, *there is no such thing as pathology.* That is, they have followed Humberto Maturana in claiming that there are no malfunctioning systems—a system functions the way it functions.[20] How can conscientious people hold such contradictory views, and what is the result of this factionalism on practice?

General psychiatrists and family therapists hold such divergent views because they are isolated. By and large family therapists responded to the disappointing results of family treatment of schizophrenia by moving to other problems that seem more amenable to family therapy and away from the medical settings where most serious pathology is treated. Family therapy grew enormously in the 1970s and 1980s, but in directions that isolated it from the mainstream of psychiatry and inpatient institutional settings. There are exceptions, of course, but for the most part family therapists practice in settings where they have not been exposed to the tremendous advances that have made psychopharmacological treatment effective with many psychotic disorders. Here for example is Jay Haley:

"Because of a supposed physical problem, massive doses of medications have been used in ways which civil libertarians would not have allowed with any other deviant population, such as criminals. These medications have proved not only incapacitating in many ways, because of their side effects, but actually dangerous."[21] He goes on to recommend: "The wisest strategy for a therapist is to assume that there is no organic basis for mad behavior and to proceed as if the problem is a social one."[22]

Meanwhile, general psychiatrists have moved in exactly the opposite direction, taking the evidence that medication works with psychosis as proof that other treatments don't work, or at most play a subsidiary role. Psychiatry has moved a long way back toward the medical model. In contrast, the family therapy movement has grown in a different direction, focusing on systems factors to the virtual exclusion of all others. Family therapists pay little, if any, attention to individual assessment and diagnosis or to the specific phenomenology of mental illness. Clinicians so wedded to an etiological point of view—everything is due *either* to family problems, *or* to biology—may trivialize or ignore or explain away what's wrong. The effect of this polarization on practice is to neglect each other's expertise.

Family therapy concentrates on here-and-now interactions that perpetuate serious problems. A therapy that can stop a teenager's parents from escalating their efforts to control him can resolve his need for rebellious acting out without necessarily delving into his psyche or tranquilizing him into passivity. Even a serious case of anorexia nervosa may be resolved by a realignment of family relationships. In many cases, however, releasing a patient from the grip of pathological family relationships is only the beginning. What remains are problems ingrained in the person.

Family therapy says that the statement, "Joe is sick," is linear, and that we should expand the context until we see circularity. Maybe Joe acts sick when Sally criticizes him. But the circularity should also take into consideration the past; as object relations theory tells us, in Joe's head, the past is now. Family therapists are too prone to dismiss psychopathology as a side effect of family problems. We tend to equate psychopathology with the unpopular medical model and individual approach to human problems. Most of us are quick to seek psychiatric backup when one of our patients becomes actively suicidal or acutely psychotic, but short of these emergencies, many family therapists lump various signs of psychopathology into the general category of family problems. The harm of this is failing to support and relieve the suffering of the individual and dumping onto the family problems they cannot handle.

Another result of the narrow focus of family therapists is the limitation it places on the problems they can address. This is particularly unfortunate when insularity promotes a reactive neglect of family therapy in the treatment of patients with major psychiatric disorders.

Biology, psychology, and family context are interdependent and should all be considered in the treatment of major pathology. A knowledge of family systems is necessary, not only for individual psychotherapy but also for competent medical psychiatric treatment. Major forces that oppose both forms of treatment come from unrecognized and unresolved difficulties in the family. Drug treatment may unwittingly recapitulate family processes that the patient sees as dominating, controlling, rejecting, or humiliating. Furthermore, drug lapses may be related to the family's need to label the patient as a crazy, dysfunctional member. The family may, in fact, engage in maneuvers that ultimately sabotage drug treatment. Then, too, the patient's remission on medication may come at the cost of losing a sort of power that symptoms granted. If so, the patient may invite interference by the family or may refuse or confound treatment in ways that require dynamic understanding in order to minimize medication lapse, treatment refusal, and repeated hospitalizations.[23]

One reason general psychiatrists have not given family therapy full recognition is that family therapists claim too much. The pioneers of family therapy were expansionists, eager to stake out their claim to the widest possible domain. Even now, as long as family therapists denigrate the claims of psychiatry, they doom themselves to a peripheral role. It is time for family therapists— as well as for general psychiatrists—to get beyond parochial purism.

One of the axioms of family therapy is: Psychopathology serves a family function. The existence of a symptomatic family member may serve a purpose. A disobedient child may exact a father's revenge on a wife he secretly hates but fears; a woman's phobias may keep her at home, away from sexual temptation or out of professional competition with her husband. Understanding how symptoms operate to mask conflict opens a variety of therapeutic possibilities such as solving the conflict (or at least bringing it out into the open) to make the symptom unnecessary, attacking the symptom directly but predicting that the family will sabotage progress to avoid dealing with conflict, or assigning a ritual to break up a pathological coalition.

It is useful to consider the possibility that psychopathology serves a family function, but it is a mistake to assume it. Here is where family therapists replicate the thinking of the psychoanalysts they defined themselves in opposition to. Assuming that symptoms are functional implies that symptoms have an underlying meaning *and* that the meaning is in the family rather than in the person. This is causal determinism. Sometimes it unnecessarily complicates problems; sometimes it oversimplifies them.

The family is always an important context for human problems, but it is important for us to remember that context is descriptive not causal. Saying that a symptom fits in the family is different from saying that the family *causes* the symptom or even that the family *necessarily* plays an important role in maintaining the problem.

Another of the axioms of family therapy is: Disorders of childhood are family problems. Nowhere is it more essential to consider the family than with the treatment of young children. Children are so malleable that the greatest benefit can often be achieved by influencing their family environment. Since the child's behavior is shaped by parental attitudes and responses, symptoms are more likely to be products of experience than of biology. With rare exceptions, psychological symptoms of childhood are an indication for family therapy. "Hyperactivity," for example, often turns out to result from parental laxity and inconsistency, rather than from some neurological problem. Even in cases like diabetes where there is a clear-cut medical problem, the fate of the illness depends to a large extent on the family's way of handling it.[24]

Recognition that disorders of childhood are family problems had an immediate practical payoff. Instead of isolating children from the setting that was shaping their development, the family environment itself was brought into treatment. This shift made it possible to reverse unfavorable developmental influences and to quickly solve many otherwise vexing problems. Ironically, however, shifting the focus from the child to the parents sometimes resulted in neglecting children and their experience. Consider the following incident.

Mrs. Ghotti, a recent immigrant from Bangladesh, called the clinic about her son Arun, age eight. He was frightened of his new surroundings and so his parents had permitted him to stay at home "until he felt better." After 10 days he still refused to go to school and his parents were worried. In the first family interview, Mr. and Mrs. Ghotti quarrelled openly while Arun sat with his head down in the corner. "It's all your fault; you've spoiled the boy!" "You're so mean, no wonder he's scared!" With the therapist's encouragement, the parents readily shifted the argument to their marital relationship. "You never. . . !" "You always. . . !" The therapist, trained to work with adults, felt he had uncovered the root problem, and so scheduled the next few meetings to work on the couple's relationship.

The couples treatment went well. There was plenty to work on, and the couple was willing to work. Meanwhile, the boy had returned to school. Everything seemed to be going as planned. Five weeks later, however, the boy's teacher called to say she was worried. Arun spent his days moping. He wasn't doing his homework, he wasn't paying attention, and he wasn't "socializing." At recess, he sat alone. And the other kids teased him unmercifully. They called him a wimp, and they chanted: "Arun the baboon went into a cocoon." His parents' conflict certainly had affected Arun, making him afraid to leave home. But he also had fears of his own and after a few days of avoiding school he was even more frightened. Once the therapist recognized this and spent some time talking with Arun, the boy was comforted and better able to adjust to school. Even more important, the therapist helped the parents understand that Arun needed some special encouragement from them.

Neglecting small children in therapy may cheat them out of understanding and nurturance, while neglecting adolescents may result in failing to encourage their personal abilities and motivation. Moreover, when teenagers are ignored, they can get into more serious difficulties, as the following example demonstrates.

Bob and Carol Amacher were worried about their teenagers. The older two boys were "wild, disrespectful, and always getting into trouble." Their third child, Cheri, was "no problem." The therapist zeroed in right away on the disorganization in the family, helping the parents take charge and work out their differences so that they could work as a team. Sessions with the whole family tended to be so chaotic, however, that a pattern emerged where only the parents and therapist met. Still, things seemed to go well. The boys were less trouble, and a new problem emerged: Mrs. Amacher was afraid to leave the house without her husband. She had been this way for three or four years, only she'd been ashamed to say so.

Since the parents no longer complained about their children and there was ample to work on between the two of them, the therapist continued meeting with the couple alone. When, several weeks later, he did inquire about the children, the news was not so good. The oldest boy was working, but the middle one had dropped out of school, and Cheri was failing most of her subjects. Worse still, she had been acting more and more withdrawn and distant, and frequently stole money from her parents. The parents may be the architects of the family, but once problems develop it is a serious mistake to pay insufficient attention to the children.

Parents, too, need understanding. Treating the child's problem as the family's problem often carries an unnecessary and burdensome implication of blame. Regardless of what we as therapists say, when we act as though the child is a *tabula rasa*, with no special predispositions, we play upon the fears of guilt-prone parents. Recently, I met with the parents of an 18-year-old girl who had, not for the first time, cut her wrists following a setback at

school. The daughter was a seriously disturbed borderline adolescent whom the parents had adopted only the year before; nevertheless, they blamed themselves for her behavior. *"If only we had
been better parents* this would not have happened. What did we do
wrong?" Not much, in my opinion. Helping in this, as in many
cases, means helping the parents realize what they cannot do, as
well as what they can do, as may be seen in the following example.

Not long ago a woman called the child psychiatry clinic about
her 17-year-old son. Her major complaint was that he was disrespectful toward her, wouldn't do what she asked, slapped
her when he got angry, and even made sexual innuendos. Since
he was doing reasonably well at school, it seemed likely that
this boy had grown up without adequate discipline and control,
overindulged by a mother who could not—would not—set limits. She expressed the usual hesitancy about bringing her husband and son to the first meeting, but finally agreed. At least
she agreed verbally. She showed up by herself and said that she
thought it best to proceed slowly. "Maybe if I explain a little
about what's going on, next time I can get my son to come.
Then maybe after you get to know him, my husband might also
come." It was a short meeting.

The therapist was annoyed that she had, apparently willfully,
ignored his request to bring the family, and he had no intention
of allowing this woman a private audience for her grievances.
He decided, however, to meet with her long enough to learn
why the others hadn't come and to avoid alienating her with a
brusque dismissal. She volunteered nothing more about why
she had come alone and talked instead about her problems
with her son. "He doesn't respect me. I've never been strict
enough; I guess I don't know how. Now things have gotten out
of hand." "Well, I can see that you have a lot of concerns about
what's going on between you but, as I told you over the phone,
it's important that we all meet together." "Yes, yes, I understand. I'll bring them next time."

Next time she brought her son, saying only, "My husband
couldn't make it." By this time the therapist was convinced that
the problem was the mother's overinvolvement with her son

and exclusion of her husband. His plan for the session was to speak briefly with the son, then elicit the mother's complaints and encourage the two of them to talk. This, he felt certain, would reveal the familiar pattern of a willful child and an over-involved but lax parent. The therapist spoke briefly with both of them. The mother talked, mostly about an incident in which the son had lost his temper and slapped her. The son mumbled, mostly about school and not having any friends. Then the therapist said, "Can you talk with your son about why he disobeys you and what you intend to do about it?"

To the therapist's surprise, she spoke directly and to the point: "I don't understand what gets into you. That time when we were leaving the parking lot, all I said was we have to get home, and you started choking me. What makes you so upset?" In response he became extremely anxious; he was pale and obviously hyperventilating. "I don't want to talk about this stuff! This isn't the point; I thought we were going to talk about my problems at school. Stop prying into my mind!" The sheer concentrated intensity of the boy's panic was eerie. It was a dramatic moment, all the more so for being unsuspected. Was this a temper tantrum or an anxiety attack? In either case, the interaction revealed an ominous sign of serious psychopathology.

Does that mean that the problem is in the child rather than in the family relationships? No. What's the difference if we say that the child is disturbed? Even if the disturbance serves a function in the family, and even if his parents have not responded well to it, the child still suffers. So does his mother. And if we can relieve the suffering (with individual counseling, perhaps even medication) at the same time we are working with the family, shouldn't we?

Despite occasional esoteric debates,[25] no one serious doubts that there is such a thing as psychopathology—severe psychological problems that persist partly independently of what the family does or doesn't do. Moreover, even most partisans would agree that effective treatment can be approached *either* through the individual or through the family. But there are two points I wish to emphasize to family therapists. The first is to be aware that a strong belief in interactional causality does not lead you to ignore or underestimate the existence of serious disorders. The second is to consider, given multiple contributing factors, that serious problems may need multiple treatments. Consider alcoholism—admittedly a special case, but one that is relevant to other pernicious human problems.

A man comes home and quarrels with his wife. He withdraws behind the newspaper; she tells him he's a no good so-and-so. Then he retreats to his room where he drinks himself into a stupor. Does the man drink because he has family problems, or does he have family problems because he drinks? Regardless of whether we adopt the disease model or the psychological model, we must recognize that alcoholism is a serious problem in itself. Any therapist who thinks he or she can treat alcoholism by reducing psychological conflict is playing with fire. The alcoholic needs all the help he can get: detoxification, outpatient follow-up, group therapy, psychotherapy, and family therapy.

Other problems that may require a multimodal attack include severe eating disorders, drug abuse, sexual molestation of children, and schizophrenia.

Schizophrenic madness has long fascinated and baffled mental healers. The fascination comes from the bizarre symptoms, which make sufferers appear possessed or enchanted—human, but not quite human. Each era has had its accepted explanation for schizophrenia, ranging from demonology to biology, but none of these doctrines has led to anything like a cure. In the 1950s various family therapists thought they might have found the solution to this apparently hopeless problem. Their enthusiasm was short-lived, however, and today, with few exceptions, systems-oriented therapists have left the field to biological psychiatrists. This is unfortunate in light of recent research that offers convincing evidence that family interaction is directly relevant to the course of schizophrenia—if not its onset—and that family intervention helps to prevent relapse.[26]

Michael Rohrbaugh summed up current state of research as follows:

"The most influential studies of schizophrenics and their families have been those on *expressed emotion* (EE). An English research group, including George Brown, John Wing, Ruth Berkoritz, Julian Leff, and Christine Vaughn,[27] found that overinvolvement, hostility and critical comments by relatives (usually parents), measured in an interview while the patient was hospitalized, predicted relapse in a nine-month period after discharge. In one study, over half of 128 schizophrenic patients who returned to 'high-EE' environments (where relatives were critical or overinvolved) were rehospitalized during the follow-up period, compared to only 13 percent of those in low-EE homes. Relapse also depended on how much face-to-face contact patients had with high-EE relatives (over 35 hours per week was bad) and on whether or not they took medication regularly (drug compliance added some protection when EE was high but made little difference when EE was low until after the first year).

"The expressed emotion researchers believe that schizophrenia involves a core, biological deficit which makes the patient vulnerable to stressful stimulation from the environment. This assumption appears to be shared by a number of research groups investigating family factors in schizophrenia.[28] To a greater or lesser degree, all subscribe to what might be called a 'stress/vulnerability' model of the disorder. They hypothesize that schizophrenic symptoms appear, or are exacerbated, when the patient is overstimulated or aroused, as happens around critical or intrusive relatives."[29]

But before family therapists begin to feel too smug about these findings, an important distinction must be drawn. These findings *do not* support the systemic views of Palazzoli, the MRI group, or Haley and Madanes. The stress/vulnerability paradigm locates the disorder in a diagnosed patient and views the family as a source of stress upon him. In contrast, most systems theorists assume that symptoms of "craziness" serve some protective function: stabilizing the family by detouring conflict or preventing some threatened reorganization such as marital dissolution or a young person leaving home.

Therapy from this perspective tries to change patterns of interaction which are assumed to be the basis for schizophrenic behav-

ior. Haley and Madanes, for example, regard medicating a schizophrenic family member as reinforcing the very patterns of
dependency that define schizophrenic transactions. Similarly, instead of lowering relatives' expectations by educating them about
a family member's illness, Haley and Madanes counsel parents to
expect normal behavior. They may even redefine "mad" behavior
as "bad" to empower parents to use their own resources rather
than relying upon outside experts.[30]

Treatment approaches that have been found to be effective
don't aim so much to rearrange families as simply to educate
them. The thrust is to help relatives understand schizophrenia as
an illness, underscoring the importance of medication, limited
expectations, and the patient's vulnerability to stress. The relatives are usually taught concrete problem-solving and crisis-man-
agement skills and sometimes they participate in multiple family
support groups. The emphasis is on reducing stress, not curing
schizophrenia, and accomplishing this appears to correlate with
avoiding relapse.[31]

In a recent *Family Therapy Networker* interview, Cloé Madanes
was asked for her view of the psychoeducational approaches that
train families to deal with schizophrenia as a kind of handicap.
Her answer:

> I disagree with a pessimistic point of view that assumes that
> schizophrenia is an incurable physical illness, like diabetes, that
> follows an inevitable course. Also the psychoeducational ap-
> proach is so often just an adjunct to a psychiatric intervention of
> medication. In many cases, medication gives irreversible, neu-
> rological damage. I think it's better to have schizophrenia,
> which is reversible, than irreversible neurological damage.
>
> There is a tremendous emphasis in the psychoeducational
> approach on getting the person 'functioning' back at school or
> at work. I'm not going to give people brain damage through
> medication so that they can go back to work. I think that's not
> ethical. I think there is a lot of confusion about the difference
> between financial expediency and good medical care. A lot of
> the medical intervention in schizophrenia has to do with fi-
> nances. Getting a person to work is partly a financial problem.

Many people are on medication instead of an intensive therapy because medication is cheaper and psychiatrists are not being taught how to do therapy.[32]

Madanes' tone here is reminiscent of R. D. Laing back in the 1960s. Still, many patients would rather endure the discomfort of medication and the side effects than suffer the terror and pain of schizophrenia.

Serious depression or psychosis may require psychopharmaceutical treatment, but the utility of drugs does not mean the family ceases to be important. One family member's symptoms may reflect both that person's disturbance and the family's disturbing influence. In some cases, psychopathology may be the consequence of interactional problems; in other cases, the antecedent. However, in most cases, the best results are obtained by working with, or at least considering, both individual and family problems.

Internalized relationships must be reckoned with as significant determinants of behavior, however much influenced by a matrix of contemporary relationships. Recognizing that the inner world is a mediator of social behavior enables us to render an account of our patients that does justice to a person's full nature. The result is ultimately practical. We cannot reconcile competing impulses until family members disengage sufficiently to discover what is in their own hearts and minds. Acknowledging the self at the heart of the system respects the basic and universal wish to be valued and affirmed as a significant person in the lives of others, as well as the need to be attached in varying degrees of closeness to others while remaining capable of autonomous functioning.

8

Understanding

One of the reasons family therapists abandoned psychology in favor of systems theory is that individuals often seem powerless to control what happens in their families. An 11-year-old girl once ruddy with health now begins to starve herself, yet try as they might her parents seem unable to stop her. A man and woman very much in love marry, but no matter how hard they struggle they cannot seem to make a place for him with her children. In these and countless similar examples we see systems forces at work. The system is powerful, the persons are weak.

We therapists feel the same apparent powerlessness when families interact in our offices. A 16-year-old boy, at war with his mother, is so clearly a stand-in for his father that we want to redirect the hostilities by having the parents fight their own battles. But each time we overcome their great reluctance to participate, the result is the same: endless, senseless bickering, and arguments that never seem to get anywhere. This is one reason for avoiding interaction; it only activates irrational and uncontrollable forces—and, it feels awful.

Families, we know, are expert at avoiding sitting down together to confront their problems. First they tell us, "Johnny is the problem." Then, when we ask to see all of them, they say, "Dad can't come." Later, they find ingenious reasons why the family, or this one or that, can't come tonight. When it comes to avoidance, families demonstrate the kind of ingenuity for which Rube Goldberg was famous. Ironically, family therapy, which was designed to unify and transform families, often accepts, even promotes, this separatism. Some clinicians argue in favor of accepting into treatment whoever is willing to come; others actively encourage subgrouping to fit the treatment unit to their tools.

Murray Bowen, for example, moved toward a progressively smaller unit of treatment (beginning with mass assemblages of families and staff members, to single families, and eventually to adult couples and individuals) to get away from emotionality toward rationality. Bowen developed the most sophisticated appreciation of complex family dynamics, but retained a fairly simple strategy for change. Bowenian therapy is a method of teaching, with only those willing to learn and do their homework invited to class.

Communication *can* be overrated. When they finally do open up, many families become mired in a verbal swamp of quarrelling, faultfinding, and self-justification. When that happens, less talking and more thinking may be in order. However, therapists should be wary of any method that too quickly gives up on working with whole families because they don't work easily together.

When therapists take over, it isn't systems they interrupt but persons, persons who get so stirred up when they talk that they automatically respond in defensive, self-centered, or otherwise unproductive ways. Because these destructive habits get in the way of productive conversation, something has to be done. The therapist may not have to take control, but something has to change.

Refashioning automatic reactions begins with delay. "Automatic reactions" are not involuntary—mindless, perhaps, but mindless in the sense of unstudied and compulsive habit rather than in the sense of a machine that has no mind. Biological systems operate by reflex. Families, also, may behave reflexively, but that means their actions are unconsidered or ill-considered. To break thoughtless chains of interaction, people must pause. Therapists can introduce delay in a variety of ways, beginning with seeing family members alone for individual psychotherapy. Family therapists eschew this strategy, but resort to their own ways of avoiding the complications of family quarrels, including working with manageable subgroups and controlling the meetings by asking questions.

One way family members can stop reacting automatically is to do simply that—pause, check impulsive, reflexive responses, learn to see options, avoid unthinking reactivity, and understand each other. Families become mature and flexible the same way individuals do—by deliberating between action and reaction, substituting thought for thoughtlessness. So, how do therapists get people to pause? One way is by interpretation.

INTERPRETATION

Because interpretation has a bad press in family therapy, family therapists tend to ignore all the rules when, inevitably, they make interpretations. They point things out, using simple descriptions of what they see, or fashion oh-so-clever statements designed to force change by indirection, using words as weapons. Interpretation does not mean simply describing what you see, or giving advice. It means pointing out something of which family members are unaware—especially suppressed emotion, unsuspected motivation, and patterns of reciprocal influence—in a manner that has implications for responsible, self-initiated change.

Interpretation and its effect, insight, are catchwords, so tied to theoretical allegiances that their meaning is clouded with prejudice. Psychoanalysts invoke insight with reverence—the great "Aha." Family therapists reason that insight is not necessary or useful, but they say it with scorn.

Truth may have a wholesome effect, but insight alone cures nothing. Insight gives only greater understanding; personal change and family improvement require putting insight into practice. The idea that interpretation is designed only for knowledge is a legacy of Freud's personal preference. For Freud, the ultimate value was not so much health as truth. He discovered that neurosis often clears up when the residue of childhood misunderstanding is washed away and people see reality clearly. Knowing the truth and facing the truth may relieve us from unnecessary confusion and restraint. Self-knowledge enables people to grope their way out of self-imposed limitations. In the context of psychoanalysis, knowledge implies independence, but there are other contexts, as well. Harmonious family relationships are an equally valid goal, and one that can be furthered by understanding—understanding of interactions, understanding of the need for other people, and insight into the nature of one's self.

Where relief of suffering is our goal, understanding is a means to an end; the therapist is a guide and helper, not just a sage. This is more than an abstract point. It affects how we make interpretations and how we follow up on them. What is called interpretation is often preemptive, presumptive, and prescriptive: "Mrs. Jones, you worry too much about your son. You should back off and let him fight his own battles." This is advice, not interpretation.

The term *interpretation* should be reserved for a revelation. It should go beyond unreflective observation, a priori theoretical statements, and what family members report they are doing. Interpretations should move people toward deeper experience, with acceptance of self and others given equal weight to understanding. Most important, interpretations should be useful. The only "fallacy of understanding"[1] that makes any clinical difference is the fallacy of putting too much weight on the therapist's intervention and too little on the patient's experience.

The impact of an interpretation depends upon the patient's receptivity. Patients in individual therapy are usually willing students. By seeking out psychotherapy they acknowledge that they need expert advice. In addition, if there is a state of positive transference, the patient hangs on our every word, he or she is gratified merely to hear us speak, and even the most banal utterance can have remarkable effects.

Family therapy is quite different. Most of the participants are reluctant to be there; they don't recognize their role in the problem and are therefore unlikely to be receptive to interpretations. Once they do begin to speak, differences of opinion emerge and create an atmosphere of conflict, in which the therapist's interpretations may be resisted as supporting "the other side." Many times, family members announce in the first session their opposition to certain interpretations of their experience. Let me illustrate this with two brief examples:

Mrs. Gronowski was one of those incredibly dominating mothers who turn initial phone calls into marathon diatribes. I don't like to talk on the phone and I am pretty good at keeping calls short. Not with Mrs. Gronowski. She wanted me to see her 14-year-old son who was "addicted to pornography" (he hid copies of Playboy under his mattress). He was "impossible," "unmanageable," "sick," "disrespectful"—you get the idea. His father was no better. He was "a weakling and a coward," "left everything to her," and so on. Before I got off the phone, I had heard at least half a dozen stories illustrating how wrong everyone but the caller was.

In the first session, Mrs. Gronowski again launched into her litany of complaints. But her first barb was all for me. "I took Zachary to a psychiatrist once before, but all that fool had to say for himself was that I was too harsh with the boy and I should give him more freedom. Nonsense!"

I felt a little like an archer after someone cuts his bowstring.

My second example is similar: a family of four, with an overprotective mother who wanted help for her 11-year-old son because he was lonely and depressed. The family could have served as a textbook example of enmeshment. The first thing the mother said was that she had a long history of seeking help for her son, who also suffered from a learning disorder. Because the boy was bright enough to get by in elementary school, countless authorities told her that she should leave him alone. The school ignored her requests for special evaluation, and six (!) different pediatricians told her he was fine. Eventually, however, the school did have an evaluation, and she was vindicated: The boy did have a learning disorder and did need special help at home. "So don't tell me my son doesn't need help!"

How do you tell a mother whose heroic efforts saved her son from academic failure that those same efforts might be interfering with his social success?

These familiar examples of predetermined resistance to explanation illustrate why many family therapists are skeptical of interpretation as a means of influence. Part of the problem is confusing
interpretation with self-evident maxims—content-free generaliza-
tions, based on theory, without considering the specifics of a family's situation. A correct interpretation discloses something new; it
is an uncovering, a revelation. It is, therefore, novel and striking.
In this way, it differs from what is often called interpretation,
namely homespun exhortation, which the patient experiences
rightly as "Just the same old thing," or perhaps, "Oh, yeah, that's
what my mother always used to say." Making an interpretation is
like shining a light in a dark room; what family members choose
to do about it is up to them. It is as if the therapist were saying,
"It's all right if you behave in these (unproductive) ways, but I
want you to know about it."

CONJECTURE AND INTERPRETATION

"Interpretation" is often used to refer to two distinct actions:
developing a hypothesis about a family's problem, and offering
that hypothesis to them. Thus, therapists speak of "formulating
an interpretation," plainly referring to their own understanding.
For clarity, I will use "interpretation" to refer to what a therapist
tells a patient about unsuspected motivations and unrecognized
patterns of interaction, and I will use the term "conjecture" to
refer to formulations in the therapist's own mind. Some therapists
rarely confuse these two actions because they rarely tell patients
what they honestly think; they do not believe in the power of self-
knowledge. Other therapists routinely elide the distinction between conjecture and interpretation because they automatically
tell patients anything they figure out.

Interpretation requires two stages of activity: first, forming a
hypothesis or conjecture; second, communicating this idea to
family members. Both are complicated endeavors about which
much has been written. Here I will add only a few suggestions
about using interpretation in family therapy.

In psychodynamic psychotherapy, patients are expected to

"free associate," to relax their conscious deliberation and say whatever comes to mind. The counterpart to the patient's free association is the therapist's "free floating attention." The ideal of neutral, passive listening—"evenly-hovering attention"—leads us in the direction of openness and receptivity. On the other hand, it suggests a mystical attunement between inner minds, and it obscures the work necessary to formulate conjectures. Understanding requires committed listening. Part of the commitment is negative—letting go of one's preconceptions—and part of the commitment is active—listening carefully and using a knowledge of individual and family dynamics to help create understanding.

Many interpretations come from intuition ("I'll bet this woman was abused"), stock formulas ("Men care more about their careers than about their children"), and psychological clichés ("You have a lot of anger inside"). Worthwhile observations come from a variety of inspirations. The real mistake is interpreting according to a formula.

As Francis Bacon noted centuries ago, once people become wedded to a particular idea or concept, their minds are no longer open. In the course of repeated interactions, family members become wedded to particular viewpoints about their own intentions and the consequences of their actions. For example, a man may believe that children will turn out right if you keep your eye on them and enforce a strict code of behavior. This viewpoint takes them as far as it can until they become stuck. It works fine with small children, not so fine with big ones.

Bacon's judgment applies equally well to family therapists. As a group, we become so wedded to certain ideas that we develop tunnel vision. A common example is the way many family therapists assume that marital conflict is always the root cause of a child's acting out.

Interpreting according to formula reflects what we are taught in training *and* in our personal lives. When I was a young therapist, I naively assumed that most adolescent problems were the parents' fault; they were too strict. Now I know better. It's the kids' fault.

Too many of us see the same conflicts in every person. I, for some reason, am acutely sensitive to adults who are afraid to express their dependency needs.

If we listen from the vantage point of structural family therapy, we will learn a lot about enmeshment and disengagement, just as we will learn about triangles and emotional cutoffs if we listen with Bowenian theory in mind. Interpreting exclusively from one pet theory is like throwing the book at families. This argues for wide learning to inform our conjectures. Ironically, though, experience is a mixed blessing. With experience, therapists tend to develop a narrow outlook without proper regard for alternative approaches. They make too many assumptions and do too little listening. Confidence and conceptual sophistication make some of us prejudiced and not open to surprise. The point is not whether to rely upon intuition, training, previous experience, or personal reflection. Formulate understanding the best way you can, *but* wait before delivering it as an interpretation. Conjectures should always be tentative, tried on for size before they are offered as interpretations. Here is an example of a conjecture that was disconfirmed.

Russell, age 49, and Iris, age 43, sought therapy to help them resolve their constant quarrelling. One of the things they argued about most frequently was Russell junior, who called home almost daily to complain about how rough things were for him at the Naval Academy. Russell senior objected to these long and frequent calls and wanted to discuss the problem of the family's finances. Iris responded angrily, "No! We've always managed to get by. I want to talk about this marriage." The two of them went around and around, getting nowhere. The therapist conjectured that when her husband brings up money, Iris feels threatened and, rather than say so, counterattacks. However, before the therapist made this interpretation, events proved it incorrect. After a prolonged silence, Russell admitted that money wasn't really the issue. He was afraid to talk about the marriage because he didn't want to acknowledge the couple's sexual problems.

Forming conjectures is an active process, involving both conscious and unconscious input. Projection plays a role, unwitting projection as well as deliberate:

I recently saw a couple who came for therapy because the husband complained that life was passing them by. He was 40 years old and couldn't have any fun because his wife wasn't interested in doing anything he liked. I liked this guy, but felt myself growing annoyed. I know from experience, personal as well as professional, how men blame their wives for their own inability to enjoy themselves. And I said so. She smiled, he winced.

But I was wrong. My hasty comment was a projection of my own experience onto theirs. It didn't fit. In fact, this man was not conflicted about having fun, and his wife *did* refuse to do the things he liked (sailing, weekend trips, bicycle riding, tennis). The problem was not something psychological, as I had thought. It was simply a problem of competing interests.

To achieve true understanding, we must hold our own projections in disciplined abeyance. Use projective identification—what you feel as a clue to what family members avoid feeling—but don't make the mistake of assuming that whatever you feel is necessarily caused by them.

What we interpret, and therefore the subject of our conjectures in family therapy, may refer to a pattern of interaction or to one person's concerns. Patterns of family interaction can be quite complex; what we see reflects our own theoretical way of parsing this complexity. Still, I think the essential thing to interpret is *reciprocity*. Family therapy's single most important principle is the way family members' behavior is interdigitated, such that what one does is a function of what others do, and what others do is a function of what one does. Whether you call it "circular causality" or "reciprocity," teaching family members about this aspect of their behavior can liberate them from the helpless feeling of being trapped and help them realize that they can control what happens in the family by changing their own behavior.

I once saw an attractive young professional couple, yuppies, I suppose, but it was before that term was coined. Anyway, they seemed like sophisticates. She wore a tailored suit and an elegant silk blouse. He wore a three-piece suit and an air of authority. I asked them what the problem was and he began: "It's her . . . she's boring." Frankly, I was put off that anyone would say something so unkind, so directly. She didn't get mad, or at least didn't seem to. She wanted him to explain, maybe she could change. The story went like this. They were both lawyers, met and married in law school. They had been married four or five years and had recently made two changes. They moved from an apartment in the city to an old house in the country, and he had moved from a state regulatory agency to a job in a political campaign. He spent his days knee deep in the excitement of an election fight. She stayed home renovating the house.

My first intervention was as follows. "The problem is that she's boring, right?" "Yes." "What do you do that makes her boring?" "What do you mean!" He was clearly annoyed at my suggestion. Nevertheless, as the story developed further, it came out that he felt he was now in the charmed world of politics. With people at work, especially one woman whom he was probably infatuated with, he could talk endlessly about the excitement of the campaign. When he came home he was tired. More to the point, he approached his wife with the attitude that she didn't understand all the political intrigue and probably didn't care. In plain English, he acted as though she were boring. As a result, their interactions were boring. I pointed this out to him, and asked him to imagine how he might approach her if he saw her as a gorgeous, fascinating woman—which, as far as I could see, she was. He accepted my challenge, and together they became more romantic than they had been in years.

Clinicians often overlook the distinction between the theory behind an interpretation—the axioms and hypotheses of psychology and systems theory—and the theory it provides family members. Must both theories be true? I don't know, but I believe the truth value of the latter is more important. Pragmatic fictions— "Big girls don't cry"—can manipulate change, but accurate understanding of self and reciprocal influence have a more liberating and lasting effect. "Getting it" in family therapy is grasping that what they do is a function of what we do. The specifics of the reciprocity vary—nagging begets withdrawal begets nagging; helplessness and passivity beget control, and vice versa—but these observations can be phrased in a common form: "The more you do X, the more he does Y; *and* the more you do Y, the more she will do X." A variation is to make the same observation and then ask either one of them, "Where did you learn that?" This ploy makes it less likely that the person will respond defensively.

When a man grasps that his withdrawal propels the nagging he hates, he can break the cycle *all by himself*. Many counterproductive cycles of behavior can be broken, or at least interrupted, in this way. Sometimes, however, the person who withdraws, or nags, or tries to overcontrol the children cannot seem to stop. They see the pattern but cannot seem to change; something keeps them stuck. That something can be subject to an interpretation. What we shed light on with our interpretations is something unknown to the person—not necessarily deeply repressed, but, in Sullivan's words, "selectively inattended to." These are important aspects of the person and of his or her relations to important people, past and present.

What people don't know about themselves can, and does, fill books. I have already discussed some of this subterranean complexity in earlier chapters. Much of this complex content falls into two themes: unsuspected motivation and enduring, rigid patterns of relating to others. In helping people grope toward an understanding of their own intentions, we can use our knowledge of drives and defenses, and unresolved narcissism. To help them grasp how they misunderstand those around them, we can use object relations theory.

Doctrinaire psychodynamic therapists *know* what to interpret; their theories tell them exactly what to look for. Freudians look for anxiety and depression, which they see as signals of latent, but feared, impulses—to get mad or to seek pleasure. Behind all actions, no matter how rationalized, Freudians see blind drives burning inside. Self psychologists see people longing for attention and admiration, and they interpret defensive self-inflation the same way they do withdrawal: as ways of warding off low self-esteem and insecurity. Without the least wish to disparage these formulas, I would point out that we can think of "the what" to interpret in somewhat more general, ordinary human terms. We interpret—in whatever way we see it—reasons for family members holding back and reasons for them being stuck. This means discovering and pointing out latent individual concerns.

A common objection to explaining what family members really feel is that even if they understand they will not change. "You seem to be angry at your wife." "Yeah, sure." This can be seen as the limitation of insight, or as only partial and limited understanding. Often something is in the way of self-discovery and we have to remove that obstacle, technically called a defense, which we can accomplish with an explanation.

If a man is making every effort to remain unaware of his anger at his wife, it makes no sense to tell him that he looks as though he would like to strangle her. At best he will deny it. At worst, both he and his wife will become upset, he for being falsely accused (or exposed), she for being attacked (she might blame the therapist, her husband, or both). Instead, talk about defenses, and try to make it interactional. This reassures him and neutralizes her counterdefensiveness. "You may be afraid that if you got annoyed at your wife, she couldn't tolerate it. (To her) "You know, a lot of men think women cannot tolerate a man's anger." Calling this "defense analysis" is somewhat misleading because whenever you point out defenses you also call attention to the impulse being warded off.

Bear in mind that the man who is afraid his wife will attack him if he gets angry is probably right. Of course she will, it's only human nature. But her own annoyance is probably not the disaster he fears. "What's so terrible about your wife getting irritated?" This should *not* be a rhetorical question. Understanding is not achieved by telling the man that his anger is okay, or that he shouldn't get so upset if his wife retaliates. If he gets upset, he has a very good reason. Your job is to discover that reason. "If you are *that* afraid of her anger, you must have a reason." This implies that the reason is not necessarily rational—that is, having to do with her—but the remark is not critical or preachy. It leaves the door open for further exploration. What does a woman's anger mean to him, loss of love? Whom does she remind him of?

The art of making effective interpretations is twofold: forming accurate and useful ideas—conjecturing—and delivering these conjectures to the family. The value of the interpretation is in the conjecture; its impact is in the delivery.

DELIVERING INTERPRETATIONS

Interpreting means explaining, not directing. When a couple grows silent, we can ask them what they are feeling or suggest that they continue talking. These common interventions may move the conversation along, but they do so only at the therapist's initiative. An alternative is to interpret the reason for the silence. Even if the interpretation is fairly simple, it still has the effect of helping the couple understand the pattern of their own avoidance. This puts *them* in charge, which not only helps them get past this impasse but also puts them in a better position to do so in the future. For example: "Whenever the subject turns to planning Joshua's bar mitzvah, both of you get anxious and clam up. I think you are afraid to talk openly about your feelings because you think that if you get angry at each other something awful will happen."

Sometimes, of course, it's perfectly reasonable just to prod a couple to continue rather than interpret the reasons for their getting stuck. This can be phrased as a suggestion—"Keep talking"— or as an observation—"Since neither one of you appears willing to listen, neither one of you gets heard."

The possibility of moving things along with just a push brings up the question of timing and the purpose of interpretation. Much has been written about the timing of interpretations—defense before impulse, surface before depth, and so on. Though many of these precepts are good ones, I would suggest a more general rule: Interpret in whatever order and in whatever way seems most likely to further treatment.

Understanding the role of interpretation may help clarify this general rule. In family therapy, interpretations serve the purpose of helping individuals understand themselves better so that they can get on about the business of working together on family problems. Thus, interpretations help family members realize what they want, how they feel, and what they are afraid of. This enables them to sort out who they are and what they want, and, equally important, who other family members are and are not. In general, the time for an interpretation is when interactions get stuck *and* the reasons—individuals' wishes and fears and misperceptions—are close to awareness (preconscious).

Hollywood psychoanalysts deliver their interpretations brilliantly and forcefully, like lightning bolts of wisdom. It makes good theater and gives the audience a chance to escape from everyday feelings of futility by identifying with a powerful figure. Actually, this form of delivery is a perfect example for working clinicians—*of what not to do*. With characteristic wit, Eric Berne referred to this style of interpretation as "NIGYSOB": "Now I got you, son of a bitch!"

Effective interpretations are delivered tentatively. "I'm not sure, but it seems that you are annoyed." "I don't know if this is right or not: I get the idea you want her to pay more attention to you, but you're afraid to ask." "This may seem a little farfetched, yet it's almost as though when she raises her voice you forget that you are 35, and you feel like a little kid. What do you think?" "It may seem dramatic, but I think you are afraid that if you get mad he'll leave you. Does that sound possible?" The tentative delivery invites further thought, leaving open the possibility for discovery and surprise. The alternative, the authoritative delivery, puts the therapist in the role of an all-powerful expert, like a parent, before whom it is possible only to submit or rebel.

Family therapists should also remember that interpreting individual motives and responsibility challenges the cherished view that "It isn't *my* fault!" Behavior is always determined partly by the individual's predilections, and partly by context and circumstance. Therefore, since most people are more aware of the pressure of circumstance, most interpretations should acknowledge that role. An abbreviated example may be helpful. "Obviously your mother feels that she should control you and decide for you things you could decide for yourself. Still, it sometimes seems that you could get more freedom by avoiding these fights. Do you think it's possible that you have some reason for fighting with her other than being free to do what you want?"

The false idea that interpretations are so powerful that they must be absolutely correct leads to paralysis and failure to follow through. In individual therapy, interpretations must be repeated many times. No wonder, when they concern powerful motives and equally powerful defenses against them. In family therapy, an interpretation may have a more potent, immediate effect if it alters an interaction in progress. A man who shuts up "because it isn't worth arguing about" may change his mind if the therapist interprets both his anger and his fear of expressing it. Thus, one interpretation can have an immediate and spiraling impact. Don't, however, expect that a single interpretation will bring about an epiphany of understanding. It isn't any one interpretation, but the sum of the therapist's interpretative efforts that eventually increases family members' self-knowledge and enhances their ability to get along better.

Overemphasizing what the therapist says underemphasizes what clients hear. After making an interpretation, the therapist should look for validation. Direct agreement or disagreement is not sufficient. Some people say yes to almost anything, others automatically say no, at least until they've thought it over. In childhood, saying "I understand" was enough to put an end to an argument with a parent. Similarly, "I'll try," or "I'm trying but I can't help it," is generally acceptable. A valid interpretation is useful, not true. Effective interpretations are followed by fresh material—recognition with surprise, a return of forgotten memories, dreams, fantasies, or strong feelings—due to a diminution of anxiety and guilt, and a relaxation of defenses.

An effective interpretation causes a disturbance; it interrupts the familiar taken-for-granted appearance of things. A good interpretation is likely to stimulate a memory of how and why a personal habit was formed in the person's family growing up. For example, I once said to a mother who was having trouble sharing her husband's time with her teenage daughter, "It's hard sometimes, isn't it? She gets so much attention and you get so little." The woman started to cry and then suddenly remembered an incident from her childhood. "My sister was prettier than I was; she was so popular, and she was ashamed of me. One time she saw me walking down the street and she crossed to the other side, just so her friends wouldn't know I was her sister. The humiliation was terrible. But I was like a boomerang, I would always come back for more."

These memories are a confirmation that carry with them special conviction for the patient. Recovery of memories of the original family confirms the accuracy of the interpretation. These memories are a kind of answer to the question of why the person seems doomed to repeat problematic interactions. And the memories prolong the period of ambiguity and uncertainty. When awareness is opened up for a person, through what we might call interpretive pressure, it becomes much more difficult for that person to continue to act out repetitive and unproductive patterns. When interpretive pressure is released, as it were, after prolonging the ambiguity of self-awareness and uncertainty, the system does not generally return to precisely where it was before. Major changes can occur.

At what level of meaning should the accuracy of an interpretation be judged? What constitutes a correct interpretation? Is it solely at the cognitive, denotative level, the overt meaning of the therapist's intervention, or must we include also the metacommunicational level? (Ironic, isn't it, that in a field that began by investigating levels of meaning, the therapist's metacommunication is so often ignored.)

Interpretation cuts away the self-deception that people use to protect themselves against the truth of their personal experience and their role in family problems. Some of these truths are painful and hard to bear. So, like the rest of us, clients transform painful reality into more palatable versions. Through repression or selective inattention, they seek comfort in not knowing. In the act of interpreting, the therapist uncovers and exposes key fictions. In spite of, or perhaps because of, their correctness, some interpretations sting too much to be heard.

INTERPRETATION AND EMPATHY

What is the relationship between understanding through empathy (compassionate awareness) and understanding through interpretation (knowledge)? Interpretations are usually aimed at elucidating the "truth" about persons, and often this truth is, at the least, a subjectively unpleasant one. The person who is unable to face unpleasant truths is blind and doomed to repeat maladaptive patterns of avoidance. But rubbing somebody's nose in painful truths makes them recoil, not think.

The second most common reason why interpretations don't work is that they are experienced as disapproval, and their truth value is lost to the emotional impact of criticism. (The first reason? Because the "interpretation" does not uncover something new and specific.) Being understood is not the same thing as understanding. What the therapist thinks and says is less important than what the patient "gets." Understanding is only achieved if the patient *feels* understood. If something about a person is truly explained, he or she may feel more deeply understood as a result. But interpretations also have covert messages, hidden behind and within the therapist's words: expressions of love, praise, admiration, or criticism, rejection and demand. "Was your mother a very critical person?" implies that the person is overreacting, acting like a defensive little boy. If that's what you mean, fine, but be aware of the implication.

The nag factor in interpretation is even more important in family than in individual therapy because many interpretations are likely to coincide with what other family members have already accused that person of doing or thinking or feeling. When we say to a depressed adolescent, "Why do you suppose you are drinking so much?" it may be close enough to his father's nagging to blur the distinction. Instead of responding to the question by exploring his motives or allowing his warded-off depression to be felt, he may just feel attacked and clam up. Since the disapproval was not intended, the therapist may mistakenly take it for granted that it was not expressed.

To bring about understanding, therapists must strike a judicious balance between empathy and interpretation. First clarify with and for the patient what he or she is experiencing. Then, and only then, explain what it might mean, especially in relation to what is going on in the family at that moment. What we interpret is often a piece of childishness—a longing for more attention, say, or a tendency to pout when angry. Instead of accusing or rebuking family members, we should demonstrate that we love and care for the child in them. Most interpretations can be "permission oriented"—pointing to an aspect of experience that has been disowned or obscured, and helping family members be more accepting of that experience. I will illustrate with an example.

Regina Parker complained that even though both she and her husband worked, she ended up with all the responsibility for taking care of the house and kids. She tried talking to him about it, but that didn't help. His attitude was that he had an important career. Sure, she worked, but her main job was still taking care of the family. When she asked him to come to therapy, he refused. Surprise. I told her that although she seemed to have tried to get him to do more, still she didn't do whatever it would take to *make* it happen. "You seem to think that something terrible would happen if you demanded that he make some changes." "Well," she said, "I don't want him to leave me. . . . But he wouldn't do that, would he?"

Since it isn't always possible to prevent an interpretation from being misunderstood, it is important to notice when this does happen. A woman once asked me at a workshop, "How do you know if a patient misunderstands what you're trying to say?" I affected a quizzical look. She was puzzled for a moment, then smiled. She got the point. Most therapists have a pretty good ability to read people, and can judge the impact of what they say by studying family members' reactions. Their incomprehension, hurt, embarrassment, or anger is there to see—if you look. Thus, an alert therapist will discover when interpretations have effects that were not intended; an honest one will remember that sometimes "misunderstanding" is a correct reading of what was unconsciously intended.

I recently pointed out to a woman in a family I had been seeing for quite some time that she left out so many details from her explanation of what happened that I couldn't follow. "Perhaps the reason you skip so lightly over the quarrel is that you prefer to think of it as something you just fell into, rather than take a careful look, with the possibility of discovering that you also played a role in it." She burst into tears. I was surprised. I hadn't meant anything like that. But when I thought it over, I realized that her response was a correct interpretation of my frustration and anger. I wasn't aware of it, but I conveyed it—and she got the message.

One final point about the impact of interpretations. Interpreting should not be "done to" patients for specific effects beyond elucidating meaning. A good interpretation is a probe toward understanding, but the understanding is discovered as a product of mutual exploration. In order to interpret effectively, therapists must give up illusions of control and omniscience.

Most family therapists have a pragmatic and action-oriented approach to behavior change. Problems are seen not as a result of unconscious, distorted thinking and buried emotions, but of a person's action and interactions. Action is divorced from inner experience. This is not to say, however, that family therapists are uninterested in cognitive strategies. They are. In fact, in many quarters family therapy has become an intensely cognitive enterprise. Family therapists work to alter their client families' construction of reality, but they are not interested in uncovering the truth. They are interested in creating their own useful fictions through framing and reframing.

THE POWER OF THE WORD: FRAMING AND REFRAMING

Reframing is a useful device that, unfortunately, is often asked to do more than it can. It is a cognitive device in an action-oriented therapy. Words being easier to control than actions, reframing has been elevated from a supporting role to a major part. Reframing means to offer a new description, usually a more positive one, in hopes that a family will alter their viewpoint and change their behavior. Once an adolescent's misbehavior is redefined as "striving for independence," parents may begin to relax efforts to control which only make things worse. Relationships are kept going by certain premises on which behavior is founded. Behavior, from this point of view, is consistent with cognition. Reframing is an attempt to reorganize the premises. Once beliefs shift, behavioral change is expected to follow.

The effectiveness of reframing is based upon two presuppositions: (1) alternative behaviors exist, and (2) they will be carried out if the therapist offers a new perspective. If we change the conceptual viewpoint or emotional valence, families will experience their situation differently. What changes is attributed meaning, and hence action. "What makes reframing such an effective tool of change is that once we do perceive the alternative class membership(s) we cannot so easily go back to the trap and the anguish of a former view of reality."[2]

The problem with reframing, in practice if not in theory, is that it blurs the distinction between what the therapist says and what family members perceive. Moreover, since reframing is thought to include the whole family, many therapists believe that everyone must buy it. An effective reframing is a statement which takes into account everyone's intentions and moves them in a productive new direction. We can aim our words wherever we like, but to be effective they must hit—and move—one, at least one, individual.

The concept of reframing has become so popular that it is now used to refer to a variety of different interventions. The general idea is that it is possible for the therapist to describe something troublesome in such a way that it alters the family's point of view. But this "description" can range from an interpretation ("He acts angry when he is scared") to a statement of personal value and opinion ("A real man helps with the housecleaning") to a tricky manipulative remark ("She can't change because she is too weak"), designed to provoke people to change by insulting them.

Reframing can be used to alter the meaning of behavior, as illustrated by the following example. Leslie Cameron-Bandler was asked at a workshop to help a woman overcome her anger at her family for continuing to mess up her clean house. The thing that bothered her most was their leaving tracks on the carpet. Cameron-Bandler hypnotized the woman and asked her to imagine her carpet all clean and fluffy: "That means you are alone." Then she asked the woman to imagine the carpet with footprints all over it: "That means the people you love are with you."

Virginia Satir once used reframing to suggest that even annoying behavior may be useful in the right context. To a man who complained bitterly about his daughter's stubbornness, Satir said: "You worked hard in bringing her up, and you taught her to be strong-willed like you are. This will help her get ahead and it will be very important on dates when men try to take advantage." No more complaints from him!

Every experience and every form of behavior is appropriate, given some context and some perspective. Positive connotation, a form of reframing, is a way of recognizing this and giving people credit for their good intentions. It helps humanize the actions of anxious and guilty persons, and thus makes it easier for them to accept themselves and not be locked in battle with each other. The danger, from my point of view, is of sliding from support to control. When positive connotation is used as a superficial and disingenuous gloss over unpleasant reality, it is an example of the covert use of words to maintain power over the patient family as the therapist's object.

Gregory Bateson[3] and Erving Goffman[4] defined "frames" as the rules of games people play. Family relationships as "rule-governed behavior" is one of the cherished metaphors of family therapy. Among some family therapists, the "frame," meaning statement of the rules, is often confused with the rules themselves, and therefore the therapist's statements are given undue weight. Even "rules" are an attribution of the observer; people do not obey rules, they behave *as if* there were rules. These distinctions are blurred when people speak of reframing as though it were in the therapist's power not only to *offer* a new perspective, but actually to change the rules, leaving the impression that a clever therapist can label away unpleasant reality.

In their book *Change*, Watzlawick, Weakland, and Fisch say we never deal with reality but only with images of reality, and the nature of those images determines whether our actions are effective or ineffective. Surely this is one of the great truths about human nature. However, just as surely, this logic can be used either to help family members develop new perspectives on their lives—putting them in charge—or as a justification for putting the therapist in charge of provoking change by imposing pragmatic fictions.

It is certainly valid to try to provoke a beneficial change in a family's behavior without (or before) trying to achieve insight. Change achieved in this way may or may not last. A more serious problem with the overuse of reframing is that it fosters the belief that if the therapist is clever enough to find just the right language, the family will be outwitted. When reframing is done *to* families rather than done *with* them, we assume authoritarian control, trying to manipulate families as mechanical systems using words as magic.

One of the results of imitating the great Milton Erickson is an overemphasis on the power of language. Erickson spoke cleverly; it was hard to wriggle out of his attributions. This has led his imitators to search for the best phrasing, the perfect reframing, as though the *mot juste* would disarm all resistance. Erickson himself was a man of extraordinary persuasiveness who changed people because of his powerful personal qualities, not because he phrased his comments in some magical fashion. Yet when I see a group of therapists behind the one-way mirror deliberating about the precise way to phrase a comment to the family, I sometimes get the impression they believe that if they say the magic word, the recalcitrant family will turn into a quivering white rabbit or an array of silk scarves.

I recently observed a family session conducted by an experienced therapist whose work I admire. One thing I don't admire, however, is his overemphasis on the power of his words to reframe the family's reality. The family was a chaotic, working-class family. The young husband, a reformed alcoholic and ex motorcycle gang member, was working hard to achieve middle-class respectability and security. His wife was a borderline personality, an engaging, colorful woman who, between sessions of working on a Ph.D. in psychology, hung out in rough bars and sometimes went home with other men. When this happened, her husband was left with the responsibility for their two small children, and with a rage that he took out on his wife with his fists.

At the end of the session, the therapist reported: "I gave them a new frame. And that is that the wife is a more effective parent when she gets help from her husband, her mother, or a friend. And when she doesn't get help, she feels trapped. She goes off to bars to pick up men or demonstrates her incompetence in order to engage her husband to take over."

This is, in fact, an excellent interpretation and it contains some good advice: that the husband should give help and allow his mother-in-law to help also, and that the wife should ask for help with the children instead of creating a crisis to force her husband to take over. The problem is that when such an intervention is conceived of as a "frame" it is delivered to the family as the therapist's decree—often, as in this case, at the end of a session—rather than as an interpretation which the family has to react to—understand and accept, or challenge, or revise.

Most of the striking exaggerations of the power of reframing are seen in the sessions of novices—you have to be there—but here is one that occurs in print: "A somewhat similar form of reframing can be used with the frequent conflict generated by the nagging wife and the passive-aggressively withdrawing husband. Her behavior can be relabeled as one which, on the one hand, is fully understandable in view of his punitive silence, but which, on the other hand, has the disadvantage of making him look very good to any outsider. This is because the outsider would naively compare his behavior to hers and would see his quiet, kind endurance, his forgiveness, the fact that he seems to function so well in spite of the very trying home situation to which he has to return every evening, etc. It is the very inanity of this redefinition of her behavior which will motivate her to stop 'building him up' in the eyes of others at her expense; but the moment she does less of the same, he is likely to withdraw less, and nothing ultimately convinces like success."[5]

Here is another one: "For example, a wife who was actively psychotic was relabeled as the caretaker and guardian angel by the therapist. He explained to her husband that she actually wanted him to feel more comfortable and not threatened by issues in their marriage. The wife became more lucid and agreed to take care of her husband in a more competent manner."[6]

Come on, now. If these precious remarks were to have any lasting impact, it might be as a confrontation, the force and aggression of which are masked by teasing humor, but they hardly seem like "a new version of the truth that works better."[7]

Neo-Ericksonian therapists continue to make a great deal of the power of the word. For example, instead of asking, "Have you ever been in a trance?" the Ericksonian therapist asks, "Have you ever been in a trance *before*?" Instead of asking, "How many cigarettes do you smoke?" he asks, "How many cigarettes *have you been* smoking?" Or the therapist offers *the illusion of alternatives*: "Would you like to go into a trance now or later?" Or uses language to challenge syntactic presuppositions: "First . . . " (there will be more later); "Are you aware of . . . ?" (. . . does exist); "Not yet" (it will happen); "Fortunately, I know how to solve family problems" (it is a family problem).

Another example of the artful framing of questions is illustrated by Steve de Shazer's technique of asking about *when* change occurs, rather than *if* a change occurs. "What will it be like *when* the problem is solved?" Expecting cooperation and success is fine—manipulative but useful—but the words should come from the therapist's attitude, not the other way round.

Reframing is a powerful tool that works when new ways of seeing lead to new ways of acting. Notice the emphasis: seeing, not saying. Reframing can sometimes be effective when it is purely manipulative (pragmatic fictions)—for example, defining an adolescent's maladaptive behavior as immature by saying, "You will only start to be responsible when you are *really* 16." However, it is a mistake to overestimate the power of the therapist's words. It matters less what the therapist is selling than what the patient is buying. In the long run, people buy what is true and what works. It is a mistake to think that the right reframing statement transforms experience—not for long it doesn't. Effective reframing should be experience-near and must be made forcefully and repeatedly to have a real impact.

CONFRONTATION

One reason family therapists drifted away from working with understanding is that people often don't change when something is pointed out to them. Verbal interventions may not always work, but they rarely work unless they are made with force. We worry too much about upsetting family members, making them angry at us, or driving them out of treatment. Empathy—understanding and showing it—cements a bond that makes it possible to confront family members hard, pointing out what they (as individuals) are doing, what the consequences are, and that only they can change.

Stacy Milstein and John Tessio smiled wanly when I greeted them in the waiting room, but when they came into my office both of them slumped down in the chairs, looking like Christmas shoppers after a long day's shopping. It was Christmas time, but it was 9 in the morning, and they hadn't been shopping. Like a lot of families who come to therapy, they were demoralized. When I asked how I could help, they looked at each other, weary, worn out, hopeless.

Finally, she began: "We've been married six years, and we have a little boy, Benjamin . . . but I think we may be basically incompatible. We come from very different backgrounds. . . . When we were dating I thought our differences were complementary; now I'm afraid they are irreconcilable differences. I'm the boss, I orchestrate everything. He's so passive. . . . When he was a boy, his parents took care of everything for him. Now I take care of him."

According to him, she does too much. "You're frenetic. We both have demanding jobs, but you don't know how to relax. You always have to be doing something, and you're always criticizing me. I wish you'd lay off—lay off me, and lay off yourself."

Stacy and John's dilemma is not exactly unusual. One partner is more energetic and more demanding; the other is passive, an avoider, and always on the defensive. They're both miserable. They think their problems happened to them. Call it bad luck, or "irreconcilable differences." Oh, they've tried—tried to ignore their differences, tried to talk them out ("You demand too much," "You do too little," "You demand too much. . . .")—and now they have lost faith in their own ability to solve their problems. So, they're ready to turn over the reins to a therapist.

My sense of this couple was that they were locked in a pattern of pursuit and withdrawal, and that they might well stay there, therapy or no therapy. Having them "work on their communication" wouldn't solve anything, nor would simply pointing out the pattern. They were bright people and probably had at least some sense of what they were doing to each other. I could work slowly to help them develop insight into some of the underlying reasons why they couldn't seem to change, or I could use a paradoxical approach. An alternative to being clever is being forceful. I pointed out the reciprocal pattern of their relationship, using the terms "pursuer" and "distancer," and I suggested that he probably had reasons for assuming that he couldn't stand up to his wife, and that she probably had reasons for looking to him for most of her satisfaction. I went on to say that they could talk about these things in therapy for weeks, at the rate of $75 an hour, but my impression was that as long as they kept waiting for the other one to change that would be a waste of time and money. Maybe they should go home and think it over, and call me in three or four weeks.

Two weeks later, they called. At first they had been angry at what I had said, but they thought it over and decided that I had a point. Now they were both ready to work hard and take some responsibility for changing their relationship.

With Stacy and John I broke what I consider to be a good rule for using confrontation: Use confrontation sparingly. Wait until family members have committed themselves to therapy and until their self-defeating patterns are clearly evident. Maybe I was just impatient. I hope not.

One of the reasons why understanding has a bad name in family therapy is that people so often understand, but don't change. The fault is not with insight, but with the failure to act on it. Confrontation brings forceful pressure to understand *and* to act on that understanding. In everyday language, "confrontation" carries the image of combat; it is a bellicose and brave word, meaning to stand up to someone in bold opposition. Antagonistic confrontations occur in family therapy, but they are not therapeutic *and* they more often result from indirection than direct and honest forcefulness.

What I mean by confrontation is similar to Minuchin's use of "intensity," but with a difference. Intensity means putting pressure on family members to get past the point where they usually break off conversations before resolving them. Intensity can be generated by affect—telling people forcefully what are the consequences of not finishing what they started, by repetition, or by duration—prolonging the time when two people talk, which may enable them to get past giving up. One of my favorite illustrations of intensity is an edited videotape of a session I once had with a conflict-avoiding couple. They began the session by saying that they wanted to talk about cleaning up the basement, but then they kept switching the subject to talk about their children. In the edited version of the tape, you see me interrupting them to say, "But what about the basement"—19 times!

Intensity puts interactional pressure *between* family members, where it belongs most of the time. Confrontation is really between the therapist and (usually) one family member. It is as if the therapist were saying, "*I* insist that *you* face what you are doing, or not doing." Later, with the couple in the example above, I confronted their interactional defense of ruminating about the children to avoid talking about their own relationship. Obsessional individuals and couples often use up week after week ruminating about a particular subject, tempting us to join them in a search for its solution. Sometimes, however, it is better to think about what they are avoiding.

I think most family therapists use confrontation in one form or another. Sometimes it is done artfully, using restraining or paradox. But saying to people, even with meek tones, that they cannot change is really a way of confronting them. A more direct form of confrontation is used to pressure family members to carry out tasks, and to rebuke them when they fail to do so. One variant of this is "the devil's pact," telling them you have a suggestion but won't tell them until they agree to carry it out.

What I often say when I assign tasks is that I don't often do so, but in this case I think it might be a good idea. If they would like to try, fine, but if they don't want to do it, simply tell me now. I don't want to waste my time or theirs giving tasks that they won't carry out. In fact, I do use tasks sparingly. More often, I confront people to face their own agency. This means to face up to what they are doing or what they could be doing, as in the following two examples.

After several weeks, Mrs. Wright (and her therapist) were worn out by the siege warfare with her disturbed, borderline adolescent son. Most of the time I saw her alone, because she had too little control over her son to force him to attend. Few parents would have been able to live under the same roof with this boy, but Mrs. Wright had adopted him when he was 15 and she was 39, and she was an extraordinarily tolerant person. Besides, there were times when the boy was so charming and loving that he lit up her life. The rest of the time, however, he was a constant trial. He stole, not occasionally, but anytime there was money lying around, inside her bureau, in her purse, in the glove compartment of her car. He also stole checks, either from the back of the checkbook or from the extra boxes of checks, if he could find them. He lied, and he did it so well that it was hard to tell the lies from the truth. He also had a violent temper, which he gave her a full dose of when she accused him of lying or stealing. And he was moody and self-destructive. Once when she refused to let him borrow her car—he had smashed the one she gave him—he went out into the barn, climbed up to the rafters and attached a rope to a beam, then got on a chair and put a noose around his neck. She saw him go out into the barn, followed him, and begged him to stop.

So, the boy continued to follow his chaotic impulses, unchecked. Mrs. Wright knew she should put her foot down, but couldn't seem to. I knew she should put her foot down, but I also knew she was worn out, and I thought there might be some reasons—motivation I had yet to understand—why she hadn't. Then he came home with an unloaded gun. His grandfather was dying and wanted the boy to have the .22 caliber rifle that the two of them used to hunt with. Mrs. Wright knew the gun meant a lot to the boy, but she said, "You're not bringing that into this house!" He grabbed her arms and threw her against the wall, stalked upstairs, and put the gun in his closet.

Mrs. Wright's failure to confront her son effectively may serve as a model for the therapist to avoid. Failure to confront dangerous or destructive behavior constitutes implicit sanction. When she told me this story, I acknowledged how worn out and frustrated she was. Then I confronted her. "When will you draw the line? After the next time he loses his temper and shoots you, or gets moody and threatens to shoot himself? I know you are afraid of a confrontation. But you have been controlled by his 'vulnerability,' and you have been controlled by his temper tantrums. That's what his threats really are. If you don't put your foot down now, you *never* will. You might as well forget about being in charge of your own life."

She did put her foot down. She went home, walked up the stairs into his room, went into his closet, grabbed the gun, and took it to a neighbor's house. That night the boy burst into her room. "Where's my gun!" "I put it away for safekeeping." He screamed at her, called her a bitch and a whore: "You're always putting me down. That gun belonged to my grandfather. It's the only thing I ever cared about." Then he stormed out of the house. The next day he was calmer. He told her how much the gun meant to him; he just wanted to have it. "Someday," she said.

The drama of the preceding example may obscure my point. Everybody intervenes in an emergency. To me, the most important reason for confronting someone is not to accomplish something, or to pressure them to accomplish something, but to push them to face their own responsibility and to act on it. My own tendency is to intervene with force when I can see clearly a way to resolve problems and I think the person sees it as well, but just doesn't act. That, I think, is every bit as tragic as most emergencies. I believe, and I sometimes say to the people I work with,

"Life is complicated enough. Most of the time we don't know what to do. But when you do see something that would help, it's a damn shame not to do it."

Although my confrontation pushed Mrs. Wright into acting, the aim of confrontation is not merely to get someone to do something; the validity of a confrontation is confirmed through freshly discovered self-awareness. Mrs. Wright's failure to act evoked both interpersonal conflict—for all his destructive behavior, the boy did side with her against her husband—and intrapsychic conflict. For her, standing up to someone meant: (a) massive retaliation, and (b) total emotional rejection. (The son was an expert at playing on both of these fears.)

A woman in another family I had been seeing for weeks called me recently to tell me that there was a family crisis. She told me how badly everyone in the family was doing, and ended by saying, "I wish you'd tell me what to do." My response was: "No, you don't. You are a very headstrong woman, and you already know what you intend to do. You say you want my advice; well, frankly, I don't believe it. You act as though there is no alternative to keeping on doing what you have been doing, regardless of what other ideas come out of our sessions. You will do what you always do, with or without my advice. For you there are two overriding agendas: number one, controlling your son; number two, trying to feel you are right and everybody else is wrong. You do not seem willing to compromise for the sake of peace, and even more than that you do not seem willing to even consider the possibility that you are trying to overcontrol your son."

Does this use of confrontation contradict what I have said about the importance of empathy? No. Confrontation *is* a forceful way to make people see what they are doing; it *is not* misunderstanding, ignoring, or invalidating them. In fact, the most effective confrontations are often coupled with empathy. Using both—respectful understanding and honest pressure—frees a therapist to wrestle effectively with what keeps family members stuck. Consider the following brief vignette.

After slogging through several weeks of cranky grumbling, the student therapist was growing disgusted with a whiny wife. When she responded to her husband's latest effort to help out more by saying, "I want you to be more consistent," the therapist said, "Oh, he wasn't perfect?" The therapist's sarcasm was an understandable product of built-up annoyance and frustration. But it didn't help. Sarcasm is bad manners, as well as a technical error. The therapist could have been more direct *and* more understanding. He might have paired a confrontation with empathy: "Yes, you want him to do more. And you feel rejected when he doesn't. But when you nag him that way, it doesn't help. It only drives him away."

As in the previous example, confrontation is often a form of scolding: "See here, this is what you're doing." But not always. Confrontation can also be a form of inspiring: "Look what you might be doing." The subject of confrontation is personal responsibility—personal causation, self-control, will, effectance—but the context can be possibility instead of failure. Self-knowledge need not only apply to current shortcomings and past mistakes; it can also be knowledge of possible selves. This is a type of self-knowledge that pertains to how individuals think about their potential and about the future. "I am now . . . but I *could* be . . . " These fantasies are very powerful, even though they may be only dimly perceived.

Possible selves can be extremely liberating because they foster hope that the present self is not immutable. At the same time, negative possible selves can be powerfully imprisoning because their negative affect and expectations may stifle attempts to solve problems and function more effectively.

EXPLAINING

Like all good clinicians, family therapists avoid giving advice in order not to accept clients' definition of their problems and because people don't usually follow advice. Nevertheless, as I will explain, there is a role for teaching in family therapy. We may not solve problems by teaching, but we can solidify change with understanding, and there are a variety of useful ways in which we can share our expertise and experience with patients. Explaining works best when it does not support the opinion of one of two antagonists, when family members' anxiety is low, and when advice is solicited.

The way explaining is done may be more important than what is explained. Give advice sparingly. Ignored advice is worse than a waste of time. Advice conveys a parental attitude toward the family, and when the advice is ignored, so is the parent.

I am full of advice (ask my poor children), but I try to limit the advice I give to things I know well. Maybe six or eight things. I know, for example, that young parents have to work to make time alone for themselves. I know that a good trick for controlling children is to permit them as much freedom as you possibly can; enforce few rules, but do so consistently and powerfully. And I think that it is a good idea for many two-paycheck families to spend more than they do paying someone else to do some of their drudgery. Many of you know more than I do, certainly about things with which I have little experience—raising adolescents, for example. Timing is also very important. A good time to give advice is after a positive change has been made. You can fortify the change by explaining it. This may involve a little teaching and preaching, but it is preaching to people about why they have succeeded, not why they are failing.

The following is an example of the uses and misuses of explaining.

Mrs. Burns was an extremely bright woman who dropped out of college to get married. When her first child was born, she projected all her ambitions onto him. She gave him tremendous attention, and he became an excellent student. He was smart, but hooked. Now when he was 11, his mother went back to school and was naturally less available. He couldn't stand it. And he learned to get attention by misbehavior.

A behaviorist would have had a field day with this family. They were nice people, but when it came to discipline they did everything wrong: They ignored the boy when he was good and paid attention to him when he was bad, the only discipline they seemed to use was criticism, which may have hurt his feelings but his behavior was immune to it, etcetera. Teaching the family about positive control and time out and so on would have done little, however, to reverse the pattern of enmeshment (mother and son) and disengagement (father and son, husband and wife).

The therapist, a student, did an excellent job of getting the father more involved with the son so that he talked to him in the session and spent time with him at home. Then she started working on the husband and wife relationship, also in the session and at home. Following a breakthrough tearful session between the parents, the boy acted up all week. The parents were upset and they dumped on the therapist. "These sessions aren't helping, we need your advice about how to handle him. What should we do?" Their pressure exerted a tremendous pull on the therapist to drop the strategy of working on the couple's relationship and give them some advice about how to control the boy. So, the therapist asked the parents what the boy had been doing, and then spent the rest of the session discussing ways to discipline a teenager. The therapist also tried to explain that the boy's misbehavior was a way of getting attention, but the explanation carried less weight than the therapist's actions— namely, giving the attention.

Two weeks later, following supervision in which the supervisor pointed out that the therapist was inadvertently reinforcing the pattern she was trying to change, the therapist was prepared to withhold explanation until after the parents had completed a successful transaction. Once again, the parents described all the ways the boy had misbehaved during the week. The boy argued, but seemed to enjoy the attention. So, the therapist asked the parents to discuss between them what they should do. As soon as they began to talk, the boy interrupted. The therapist waited—and held her breath. Fortunately, the parents did tell him to shut up and stay out of their discussion. Then the therapist intervened, congratulating them for acting in charge and not allowing the boy to butt in. Since they had successfully completed a transaction, the therapist felt free to offer an explanation of what was going on.

There is no holy writ that says explanations are effective only to solidify change and therefore should be given only *after* a successful transaction. The point is that explanations are not particularly effective ways to change behavior. Advice—general axioms about family life—should not be confused with interpretations. Interpretations, unlike advice, contain a "because clause," a statement of why it makes sense from a family member's point of view to behave as he or she does. Making that clear helps the person let go of ineffective habit; just telling him or her to do so rarely helps.

There are some areas so sensitive that I assiduously avoid giving advice. These include decisions about separation, affairs, and divorce. Oh, one exception here. If they ask, I tell divorcing spouses that in my experience getting legal advice—*two* lawyers—is good protection. Couples often underestimate how much acrimony crops up when it comes to division of the spoils. I also have two lists of divorce lawyers. On one list is "the barracuda"; on the other list are two men and two women who seem to be knowledgeable and flexible. Probably, you have different opinions than some I have expressed, and perhaps you can see some personal bias in my advice. Remember, when you feel like giving advice, that we are all biased.

Sometimes explanations are useful and help people resolve a dilemma, usually a minor one. Often things turn out to be more complicated. That's why Ann Landers, Leo Buscaglia, and Scott Peck have not driven us all out of business. Advice can play a role in family therapy, but only a minor one. Therapists who do rely on good advice to help families solve problems underestimate the power of family dynamics, psychodynamics, and resistance to change.

9

Resistance

David Rutnik was frantic when he called. The woman he was living with had finally asked him to move out after a long series of battles about disciplining her children. "You don't know how miserable I am," he said. "I'm an attorney and since this thing happened I can't concentrate at work. Please, can you see me as soon as possible?" Yes, I said, and I offered him an appointment in three days. "Oh please, this is *urgent*. Can't you see me before then?" So I agreed to meet with him the next morning, which was Saturday. I also told him it was essential that I meet with both of them. "Fine, we'll be there."

Mr. Rutnik showed up alone, explaining that he wanted me first to "get all the facts" before he invited Mary Ellen. Once I used to insist that all the major parties to a family problem be present; no family, no session. Now, like most of my colleagues, I try to work with whoever shows up. If Mr. Rutnik was afraid to bring his girlfriend, or if she was reluctant to come, I would try to understand; rather than insist, I would endeavor to overcome their reticence. For the time being, then, I was willing to listen to his story, attempt to make sense of what was going on, and try to empathize with his position. It wasn't easy.

At every step of the way, he opposed my efforts. To begin with, he let me know he had a low opinion of therapists. "I should tell you, my posture coming in is negative." He made this point emphatic by telling me the story of a therapist who had refused to testify in defense of one of Mr. Rutnik's clients, a man who had broken into a woman's apartment and stolen several pairs of her panties. Obviously, from Mr. Rutnik's point of view, this man had a problem. And just as obviously, he should not be punished because of it.

The rest of the hour went by in a hurry. He told me about his two-year relationship with Mary Ellen. At the start, things were great. The trouble was, though, she was "bull-headed about her children." She "insisted on doing things her way," and wouldn't listen to reason (him). "She spoils them something rotten." Even worse was her stubborn refusal to handle her ex-husband, Ed, in "a rational manner." Mr. Rutnik wanted her to be tough and sue him for alimony and court costs, as well as for child support. Mary Ellen didn't want to. She was afraid of alienating her children from their father, as her mother had done to her.

As he talked, Mr. Rutnik's face reddened and his voice rose to a high-pitched whine. At frequent intervals he mentioned how stupid the people who disagreed with him were. Though he didn't know me, he insisted on calling me Mike—to avoid putting me in a position of authority, I suppose. At the end of the hour (actually, well over an hour), he bombarded me with frantic questions: "Should I leave her?" "Should I represent her?" "Am I doing the right thing?" If it was an exam, I could have guessed the answers he expected (no, yes, yes). I tried to reserve judgment, saying that I knew how urgent these questions were but didn't feel I could answer them until I had a chance to talk with both of them. He thanked me profusely for seeing him on such short notice and left. I never saw him again.

Here, in spades, is what every family therapist is all too familiar with: resistance. Mr. Rutnik contested on many levels my efforts to help. He resisted me, he resisted therapy, and he resisted taking into account his girlfriend's point of view. Resistance refers to anything clients do to subvert or slow the process of therapy. In family therapy, resistance is the rule, not the exception. Families resist coming in, they ask for but resist alternative explanations for their problems, they resist challenge to familiar ways of behaving, and above all, they resist our efforts to get them to change their ways of interacting. Every family therapist deals with resistance—from the families who week after week come late or miss appointments, to the angry teenagers who refuse to talk to us, to . . . well, you get the idea. Yet, what exactly is resistance?

To avoid *abstractitis*[1] (placing abstract words in command, thus putting persons and what they do in the background) let us take the verb form—to resist—so that we can ask what the subject of this verb is and who its object is. In family therapy, resistance is often thought to be a property of families or of family systems. But resistance is not a property of systems; resistance is not a *property* of anything. It is an *action*. Systems don't resist and families don't resist; individual persons resist. As to the object of resistance, whom or what do they resist? They do not resist "therapy." This, too, is an abstraction consisting of various specific operations, some of which are easy to accept, some of which are not. They resist the therapist's pressure, they resist meeting together, and they resist behaving differently. Of all of these we may ask: Is it reasonable to do so? When I put it this way, the obvious answer is yes. Yet our usual understanding of resistance is burdened with two unfortunate implications: that resistance is a product of the way systems function, and that resistance places families and therapists in an adversarial position.

NAMING AND BLAMING

Family therapists discovered resistance the moment they tried to challenge how families interact. As I described in Chapter 1, family therapy was launched as an "undeclared war" against families who seemed bent on maintaining someone in the sick role and who steadfastly opposed attempts to change them. Two of the most influential pioneer family therapists, Don Jackson and Jay Haley, led the way in naming families as resistant and then blaming them for it.

It was Jackson who described families as *rule-governed systems*, and who emphasized their conservative tendencies. In the process, however, his descriptions were elevated to causal determinants. The observation that families are destabilized by change—even positive change—in one of their members, led Jackson to say that the essential function of symptoms is to maintain the homeostatic equilibrium of family systems.[2] He concluded that "pathology inheres in the system as a whole."[3] Thus was established the traditional family therapy view of resistance: Families are "homeostatic systems" that respond to change as "negative feedback"—that is, as a threat and a signal to change back.

When I first started treating families in the late 1960s, I found this model elegant and informative. What I didn't notice were its implications. Consider what this model explains and what it fails to explain. It explains the human tendency to fear the unknown and to avoid taking chances. But it fails by ascribing resistance to the family—the patient—rather than to the interaction between the therapist and the family. The explanatory powers of this model are best when it is applied to families in transition, notably to the problems associated with a young person leaving home. It is less useful when applied to the complexities of long-standing patterns, which are based not merely on habit but on the personalities, in some cases the psychopathology, of the participants.

Jay Haley paid more attention to the family-therapist interaction, but it was a decidedly one-sided analysis. Just as family members struggle to achieve control over one another, so do patient families struggle to control what happens in therapy.[4] On the plus side, Haley's analysis led to the development of ingenious strategic tactics for outwitting resistance. A negative consequence was that in some quarters families were conceived of as objects of intervention and as opponents to be outwitted, rather than as partners in a collaborative effort.

We are coming now to familiar ground, namely the story of family therapy's artful gamesmanship, the strategic orientation that can be seen as gimmicky and manipulative or as enlightened pragmatism, depending upon who is doing the looking. I have no intention of rehashing this stale debate. What I do intend is to take a quick survey of some of the problems associated with how we

have conceived of resistance, and then get on with some suggestions for what to do about it. To begin with, it is important to
remember the *context* in which Jackson and Haley worked. They
weren't just any family therapists and they weren't working with
just any families. They were exploring pioneers, and therefore
they were necessarily somewhat naive (by today's standards), and
they were deliberately directive.

The fact that Jackson and Haley were among the first family
therapists has a significant bearing on how they viewed resistance, because a family's resistance is different from an individual
patient's resistance. The person who comes alone for psychotherapy is, in the nature of things, in a one-down position (calling
patients "clients" doesn't alter this). Except for those few individuals who are coerced into coming, the act of seeking therapy
carries with it the implication that the person has failed in some
way and needs expert help. With families it is altogether different.
Most family members resent coming and, unlike individual patients, generally do not accept the therapist's right to change
them. So they resist—naturally.

Given family members' inherent reluctance to accept their role
in the family's problems and their distrust of the therapist's intentions, it is instructive to remember how the early family therapists
approached families. On the one hand, they expected automatic
resistance to change—"homeostasis"—and then they provoked it.
First, they announced to families prepared to defend themselves
against blame that "everyone in the family is involved in the patient's symptoms," and that *the* problem is a family problem.[5]

This bluntness was soon abandoned. In its place there grew up
a directive behavioral approach. Like behaviorists, the early family therapists had no use for insight, only for changing behavior—
"interrupting vicious feedback circles."[6] But unlike behaviorists,
family therapists did not assume rational cooperation. In fact,
they assumed the opposite. And they got it.

Following Milton Erickson, Haley led family therapy in the use
of crafty directives to usurp patients' control. Thus was created a
spiraling process of assuming resistance, assuming lack of cooperation, and therefore becoming directive and not acknowledging

the therapist's point of view or the direction that interventions would take.

Just a minute. Before I go on to discuss recent efforts to rethink the idea of resistance, let us remember one thing: Most of the families Jackson and Haley were working with were extremely disturbed families with schizophrenic members. Saying that these families are resistant is like saying that 26.2 miles is a long way to run, or that having a baby is difficult. Families like these are always on the brink of such chaos that they fight, as though for survival, against anything that threatens their stability.

My point is simply that not all families are this way; many are willing to try new options *if* these options make sense *and* if they are explained reasonably. Moreover, even when families *do* cling tenaciously to familiar routine, resistance is not an affliction of some autonomous entity (the system), nor is it an inability to change; it is something that individual family members do, and do for a reason—namely that they are confused and afraid.

Resistance implies obstinacy. It is a combative term, one that suggests that families (or persons) fight against something (someone). But, as we have seen, the someone they fight against often harbors a condemning, accusatory attitude toward those who do not cooperate with his or her wishes, and then charges them with being willful, defiant, and obstinate. "Don't" cooperate is shifted to "won't" cooperate. "Won't" is judgmental; it assumes its own explanation, and leads to attack, anger, or, more subtly, deviousness. "Don't" is descriptive; it suggests looking for reasons.

Though they would surely reject the parallel, many family therapists push their own agendas on patient families as though it were an oedipal struggle with patriarchal authority. Terms like "resistant," "defiant," "refractory," "noncompliant," and "oppositional" leave little doubt about who is grown-up and who is not.

THE DEATH OF RESISTANCE

Recognizing that the term "resistance" is accusatory and combative, some therapists have suggested scrapping it. William Lewis and Jerry Evans believe that since the idea of resistance carries the implication that clients are our adversaries, we should no longer use the expression. They prefer to talk about "defensiveness" and "fearfulness" in an attempt to humanize the way we think about therapy.[7] Steve de Shazer recommends dropping "resistance" in favor of "cooperating."[8] The concept of resistance, he says, is based on the linear notion that the therapist and the family are separate systems, one pushing for change, the other resisting. This way of thinking sets up a contest between the two supposedly separate systems. In fact, according to de Shazer, family and therapist are actually part of the same system—a therapist-family suprasystem. Therefore, what appears to be resistance on the part of the family is actually a product of the therapist-family interaction [so far so good] *and* behavior that is commonly called "resistance" can usefully be redefined as "cooperating": "Each family (individual or couple) shows a unique way of attempting to cooperate, and the therapist's job becomes, first, to describe that particular manner to himself that the family shows and, then, to cooperate with the family's way and thus promote change."[9]

Attempts to repeal resistance by fiat may seem harmless, even benign, but by clouding the issues involved this approach may do more harm than good. Efforts to do away with resistance by renaming it, as Susan Stewart and Carol Anderson have pointed out, only allow it to live quietly under an assumed name.[10] And as Lyman Wynne so nicely stated, "resistance is a thorn that by any other name pricks as deep."[11] It is not the word "resistance" that is responsible for the us-against-them attitude of many therapists. It is something else.

When psychoanalysts speak of resistance, they have a tendency to give patients all the credit, modestly ignoring the role of their own interventions: ill-timed interpretations, "unavoidable" latenesses that precede the patient's "resisting" by coming late, and so on. Robert Langs has taken his colleagues to task for this one-sided, holier-than-thou attitude, pointing out that therapist errors are often responsible for negative patient reactions.[12] His solution: First, make fewer errors by adhering to a strict and austere version of analytic neutrality; second, acknowledge that a patient's resistance may be based partly on a legitimate response to the therapist's errors, as well as on the patient's own overreaction. Notice the underlying canon here. Instead of blaming patients for resistance and then confronting them ("You're late"), Langs's approach is to understand *and* interpret resistance. How does this relate to family therapy?

Although there is, as I have said, a role for interpretation in family therapy, family therapy is primarily a therapy of action. So, the point is not that we should interpret resistance, but that we should begin to understand our own role in provoking it. This much is obvious, and most sophisticated discussions of family therapy take this into account. de Shazer, for example, recommends certain techniques to promote cooperating and changing. These include creating positive expectations and accepting any response to assigned tasks as a family's way of cooperating. Instead of asking what will happen *if* things improve, de Shazer suggests asking what will happen *when* things improve.[8] This is old wine in new bottles. It may be subtle and artful, but it is only an example of the calculating approach—overcoming resistance by means of indirection.

In their fine book, *Mastering Resistance*, Anderson and Stewart recommend thinking of resistance as negative behavior—behavior that impedes change—potentially residing in all parts of the therapeutic system: the family, the therapist, even the agency where therapy takes place.[13] This approach gets us away from blaming and helps break down the adversarial stance. But there is a problem. This redefinition blurs the distinction between resistance and "not changing." It isn't resistance if a family doesn't change, because the resistance is directed against therapy, not against change. If resistance means anything—and I think it does—we should limit the concept to behavior that resists, or fails to cooperate with, the process of therapy. For not changing long-standing patterns of behavior we might better use the term persistence, as Lynn Hoffman suggests.

"Resistance," "persistence," what's the difference? Plenty. The way we view resistance, whether as not changing or merely as not cooperating with the process of therapy, has important practical implications. As long as we remain confused about who resists, and why, we cannot escape the adversarial us-against-them position. We only mask it.

My aim is not to get fussy about language or to legislate how family therapists talk about resistance. Since we are interested in change, resistance (to therapy) is part of a larger problem—persistence of maladaptive behavior. My point here is only that we should recognize the difference between opposing the process of therapy (and the therapist), on the one hand, and not resolving problems on the other.

WHO RESISTS, AND WHY?

It is people who resist, not families and not systems. The fact that so many people resist family treatment so energetically has much to do with how we approach them. As long as we ignore the selfhood of persons in families we treat, we fail to discover why they resist relating to each other in new ways. As long as we usurp their responsibility for change, we continue to provoke them to resist us.

Using the metaphor of the system to describe what goes on in families is no less legitimate than using psychological explanations. In fact, it is the basis for much of the power of family therapy. Families *do* resist change. It is the means by which they maintain stability and cohesion. But as long as we ascribe resistance to "the system," we limit our ability to influence individual family members, and risk absolving them of responsibility for changing their own behavior. Resistance may serve to perpetuate group patterns, but this abstraction lives in the actions of individual family members. Mr. Jones harps on his teenage son: "You hang around with a bunch of losers; you waste your time in school; and you never help out around the house." In response, (surprise) the son continues to rebel and defy his father. The boy's behavior is not independent; it is provoked and it is provocative. Together, their actions preserve a structure whose time is passing—a family with young children, where parents and children are thoroughly involved with each other. The resistance of the father-and-son pattern to therapeutic efforts to change it might be said to be systemic since the system is stuck in transition. But who nags and who rebels?

By now you know what my answer to this rhetorical question is: individual family members. This leaves us only to ask *why* family members resist our treatment efforts.

Families who come seeking desperately for help soon bend every effort to defeat the help we offer. They miss sessions, "forget" homework assignments, and accuse us of taking sides if we as much as acknowledge competing points of view. Beginners often see this resistance as being directed against them. With experience, we come to see it as a fear of changing and a fear of disturbing the peace.

The underlying theme of most resistance is never looking at things in more than one way. Resistant family members take a steady and exclusive view of what therapy sessions should be about. The controlling father doggedly insists that "The only thing to discuss is how to make this boy behave!" A couple comes in to work on their relationship following one spouse's brief affair, and the only thing the injured party considers important is forcing the spouse to apologize. A disengaged father attends family sessions, reluctantly, but steadfastly avoids voicing his disapproval of how his wife handles the children. Moreover, this rigidity turns out to be the way some people run their lives—safely within the well-worn grooves of habit. Even those admirable people who seem so unafraid, so flexible, are usually rooted to habit in certain areas. The salesman whom everybody admires for his warmth and ability to get along with so many people may yet continue to dwell in an emotional cocoon at home. The attorney who is known for her forceful attacks on social injustice nevertheless may absolutely refuse to lay down the law to her teenaged son.

Although I have rejected the mechanical and biological model of systems moved by forces and energies in favor of a model of the person as agent, notice how my explanation of why people resist is similar to the homeostatic explanation: saying that people are afraid to change, like saying that systems are homeostatic, is a *negative* explanation. Resistance also has a positive side. When they resist, people are doing something active, not just not doing something.The father who refuses to attend family meetings may be maintaining his composure and self-esteem; the wife who refuses to discuss her reasons for wishing to leave her husband may be getting revenge for all his bullying; the teenager who consistently lies to a therapist about her drinking may be preserving a sense of differentiation and integrity.

"Positive connotation" (or "ascribing noble intentions") recognizes the positive features of apparently negative actions, but usually points exclusively to group aims ("Your daughter is trying to preserve your marriage by starving herself"), while generally neglecting personal ones. Acting affirmatively is not necessarily cooperating or "being constructive"; it can also be acting greedily, aggressively, or in a deliberately self-destructive manner.

In a therapy that aims to put people in charge of their own lives, the therapist asks steadily, though not necessarily out loud, "What is this person doing? What is that person aiming at? Why is he or she doing such and such?" If we are pursuing increased flexibility, sooner or later, resisting unconsciously (or automatically) becomes resisting consciously (or deliberately). Here is a brief clinical example to illustrate the value of bringing out the positive accomplishments of resistance.

The presenting complaint in the Dusard family was a clue to the family's dynamics. Mrs. Dusard called to say that her 17-year-old son, Jay, was getting into trouble. He was on the phone every night for half an hour, "talking to *girls*," and two or three times a week he was *at least an hour* late coming home from school. Clearly, this was a woman exquisitely attuned to her son's behavior. She was enmeshed. Unfortunately, family sessions with the Dusards regularly degenerated into shouting matches. I wanted to work with interaction; they wanted to work each other over. So I began meeting with separate subgroups, first the parents, then the two boys, once or twice with Mrs. Dusard alone, and then several times privately with Jay. These separate sessions were very effective in calming things down, at home as well as in my office. After a couple of months, though, Jay and Mrs. Dusard started violating the cease-fire. Just about once a week the two of them would get into a brouhaha, ending with her ordering him to leave the house.

At this point, my sessions with Jay were deliberately strategic in that my overriding purpose was to guide him to keep the peace long enough for him to graduate from high school. I didn't really care how I did it, but I knew that my meetings with him had a nontherapeutic stabilizing effect: Seeing him alone supported Mrs. Dusard's position that he was the problem while at the same time allowing him to complain to me about how bitchy she was. Together, we conspired to outwit his enemy. I taught him about the family triangle: how his mother fought with him as a stand-in for his father, who stayed in the background. I explained how his mother would continue every fight until she made him wrong and herself right. And I made him understand that by propitiating her he would get more control and more freedom. Sometimes this meant avoiding her. But since this was not always possible, it also meant learning to say, "Yes, Mom, you're right."

This strategy worked for a while, but then Jay started "forgetting" what we had discussed, and "not getting around to" apologizing. Things got worse at home and I got mad. I pointed out that what he called "forgetting" must accomplish something indirectly that he could not do openly. I was thinking that he would not let go of his fights with his mother, but his response surprised me. What he said was that he was angry at me. (Moi?) "You're making *me* do everything. You're on her side!" (Amazing.) Jay's "resistance" was a refusal to submit to my will and manipulations. Without words, he was saying to me, just as he had said to his mother, "I will be manly toward you—the way I learned from my father."

The moral of the story is that when family members resist we should not turn first to more subtle and clever techniques. That *may* turn out to be a useful solution, but first we need to find out what the problem is *from their point of view*. We should ask ourselves both "What is he or she afraid of?" and "What is he or she aiming at?" Understanding that resistance is the action of individual persons and that it has both negative and positive aims has immediate practical implications. I will discuss these in reference to a familiar topic, joining, and a less familiar one, the contract.

CONTRACT

Why is it that we who are so adept at solving problems for other people's families are often so inept when it comes to solving problems for our own family and friends?

Four years ago my mother quarrelled with my brother's wife, and they haven't spoken since. Both of them are cut off from a friendship that once meant so much; my parents are cut off from my brother, who out of loyalty to his wife doesn't come around much; and three little children are unable to see their grandparents. Anyone who has ever been party to a similar feud knows how much everybody suffers. I pride myself on being a skillful family therapist, a solver of much stickier problems than this one. Yet, despite all I have tried, I have been totally unable to make a dent in this impasse. Do I have some secret motive for failing to heal the breach—sibling rivalry? hostility toward my mother? laziness? No, I don't think so. What I have is no contract to act as mediator.

A contract, according to Webster, is "an agreement between two or more people to do something." In psychological therapy, contract is an old-fashioned concept, not much discussed anymore.[14] Too bad, because it is important. If you could have only one precondition for doing therapy, have a contract.

Family therapy, like other forms of treatment, is transactional and contractual in the sense that a sufferer petitions a therapist for help and assumes the obligations of a client or patient. He, she, or they contract to cooperate and to compensate the therapist for professional services rendered. The therapist contracts to provide skilled assistance. And together they proceed in total cooperation until the job is done. Well, not exactly. Unfortunately, the usual contract in family therapy is implicit and unnecessarily vague, which begets misunderstanding and lack of cooperation. "Resistance"—lack of cooperation—is often a function of an unclear contract, a lack of agreement about what to do in the first place.

Family therapists' contracts with their clients are inherently problematic because the party of the first part wants and expects something quite different from what the party of the second part wants and expects. Most family members are convinced that the source of their difficulties is external to themselves; some are not even convinced that there *are* any difficulties: "I think my wife is blowing this whole thing all out of proportion." Furthermore, almost all families are resistant to the idea of being treated as a unit. Therapists usually begin expecting to find the source of the trouble precisely where family members don't think it is—in themselves—and they intend to treat the family as a unit. No wonder, then, that our customers are never so sure of just what they want or of what they get.

It will not do simply to say that family therapists should announce their intentions openly at the start and ask for informed agreement. We tried that and it didn't work. Unfortunately, family therapists have made too much of this discrepancy, promoting a difficulty into an impossibility. Instead of trying to make the clearest possible contract at the outset, and then later clearing up as much of the discrepancy as possible, family therapists often give up altogether on the possibility of enlisting families as informed and willing allies in a joint enterprise. Failure to establish the clearest possible contract is a by-product, also, of the mechanical systems model. As long as we treat the people we work with as "homeostatic systems," we are likely to begin with an unnecessarily weak and fuzzy contract. And as long as we neglect the self in the system, we are likely to ignore some of the individuals in the family when we do make our agreements.

The less we accept the importance of clarifying what people expect and agreeing upon a course of action, the more likely we are to fumble preliminary arrangements. Here is an example.

Mr. and Mrs. Stoughton came together, but they were miles apart. He was depressed. When his wife found out that he was having an affair, she threw him out. Now he was sorry. He would do anything to repair the marriage. She didn't want him back but was willing to talk. So, the therapist started to work on "the relationship." What relationship? After two months of desultory treatment, the therapist sought supervision. The first thing the supervisor did was suggest that the therapist clarify what each of them wanted. Mr. Stoughton wanted to move back with his wife. She wanted a divorce. She had no intention of ever letting him back into her life. Why had she put up with couples therapy? She felt sorry for him, a little guilty perhaps. It sometimes happens that one or more parties to the contract don't know for sure what they want. The way to find out is to ask them.

When you go to get your hair cut, you tell the barber or hairdresser what you want, and then you sit there (and hope for the best). Psychological therapy, in contrast, is not a passive submission, but a give-and-take, a mutual exchange. Patients don't just sit there; they actively cooperate and they actively resist. But the patient alone doesn't *do* resistance, any more than the therapist alone does the therapy. A clear contract helps reduce one of two types of resistance: conscious and deliberate opposition. The other type of resistance—opposition that occurs despite the best of intentions—is largely a product of anxiety. That, too, can be reduced if we sharpen up our agreements.

A therapeutic contract is a service contract, not a sales contract. Nothing material is given or taken away. The patient or client does not pay money for relief. Relief is what they want, but they are paying only for the professional services of the therapist. The contract is not usually for "cure" or for solving problems; that's why we like to get paid by the hour. The first step is taken when a patient or family seeks out a trained consultant whose title or professional affiliation announces that he or she is prepared and willing to render expert assistance. The therapist listens to the prospective client's complaints and then decides whether he or she can justifiably accept the responsibility of attempting to help this person as a patient (*attempt* to help). Effective therapists are eager and able to help a wide variety of clients, but they know their own limits and they freely refer those they don't think they can help or are not interested in helping.

After listening to the complaints, the therapist formulates a plan of action and offers a recommendation. I suggest that, whenever possible, you reserve your decision to take on a case until after at least one, sometimes two, sessions. If you offer to take a family into treatment only when you feel strongly that you can help, you will save a great deal of trouble. If you think you can help, say so: "I think you were wise to seek treatment, and I believe I can help you." This is the first step to negotiating a contract.

A treatment contract has four elements: (1) definition of the problem, (2) determinants of the problem, (3) goals, and (4) the rules of therapy. The more of these elements you can spell out and secure agreement upon, the more likely therapy is to succeed. How a therapist makes contracts is, of course, related to the therapist's theoretical position. The more transparent the therapist—behavior therapists, for example—the more concrete he or she is likely to be about setting goals. The more controlling the therapist—say, brief, strategic therapists—the more explicit he or she is likely to be about setting a specific number of sessions.

My intention here is not so much to tell readers how they should make contracts, but to spell out the relationship between contracts and resistance, and to develop the implications of remembering that every individual in a family has a separate version of reality. In discussing these elements, I will leave out much—including, for example, money, "the last taboo"—in order to concentrate my suggestions on dealing with the individuals that make up the family.

1. Definition of the Problem

This is usually the simplest element in the contract. They say the problem is that Susie wets her bed; we have no reason to disagree. But notice the example I picked. Behavioral problems are the easiest to define, and when parents complain about a young child, there is unlikely to be much effective dissent from the child.

Contracts are usually spoken of in two-party terms—a customer and a vendor. It is, however, misleading to think of a contract between a therapist and a family. Families don't make contracts, only individuals do. True, sometimes there is only one client, in the sense of there being one person who wants the therapist's services. This may be a mother worried about her child, a husband who drags his wife into couples therapy, or someone outside the family, such as an agency worker or a probation officer who initiates therapy and sometimes is the only one who really wants it. The initial contract is made with "the customer," the one who wants the therapist's services. But as long as the contract goes no further, there will be little or no cooperation from the other family members.

Occasionally, our patients are involuntary clients, referred by the courts or other legal authority. When a judge says, "Therapy or jail," or a spouse says, "Therapy or I'll leave you," or a college dean says, "Therapy or you'll have to leave school," both the therapist and the patient are in an unhappy predicament. My personal position used to be that I don't work with involuntary clients. Unless they have—acknowledge—a problem that I as a therapist can help solve, I will not see them.

When I was working at a university health service, the dean would occasionally sentence troubled students to the psychologist (a variation on the insanity plea). My policy was to ask these students why they had come. When they said, "The dean sent me," my response was, "Okay, you've come." Since my agreement with the dean was only to let him know whether or not these students showed up, that's all I told him. Once they felt free of compulsion, some of the students elected to become patients, some just walked away. Many people believe that if you are clever enough you can *make* people do things for their own good. Perhaps, but I'm not very good at it.

At the other extreme are those clinicians who regularly and freely accept involuntary clients. Some have to. They work in agencies that have an arrangement with the court to treat sex offenders, drunk drivers, wife beaters, and so on. Other therapists underestimate the problem of working with clients who don't want to be patients. They think they can manipulate any situation to their advantage. I believe that many clinicians err by accepting too many referrals, rather than limiting their caseloads to clients who want their help *and* whom they have good reason to believe that they can help. Nevertheless, I have modified my own position somewhat with regard to unwilling clients. One reason for this is that since I have become more aware that families are not units but collections of unique individuals, I have realized that almost every family has involuntary clients.

I still don't like forced referrals, and I do not accept them readily. But I have become more sympathetic with the plight of those people caught in a bind between what they think and what they feel compelled to do. I try to recognize their hostility, to see it and let them know I see it, and I try to avoid becoming another coercive force. For example, when someone is sent to me by a probation officer, I *assiduously* avoid asking questions about what the client has been up to. To ask such questions is to become like another probation officer. Instead, I try to make myself available to listen to whatever the person wants to bring up. Perhaps, the client will eventually come to trust me enough to start using therapy as a place to work on problems, rather than merely a place to check into once a week. If not, I become like a benign jailor who tries to make the period of incarceration as hassle-free as possible. At this point I might list some examples of where I have converted involuntary clients into effective cases. Unfortunately, I can't think of any.

Sometimes we begin therapy assuming that we have an agreement about what the problem is, and later discover that we do not. When this happens, we have two choices: to continue working as before, trying to achieve our ends without family members' full awareness, or to stop and attempt to negotiate a clearer agreement. A brief example may clarify this option.

A husband and wife were referred for couples therapy by a psychiatrist who was treating their daughter for anorexia nervosa. The psychiatrist had seen the whole family a few times, but felt that the couple should work on their relationship with a different therapist while he continued to try to help the daughter. The couple welcomed this suggestion, because both of them were tired of always worrying about their daughter. Nevertheless, the couples sessions were dominated by discussions of how to treat the daughter. The father thought they should be "tolerant and understanding," while the mother thought they should "be firm and set limits." They were at an impasse.

There are a number of techniques that might help bring them closer to a united position, such as Minuchin's "unbalancing" or Selvini Palazzoli's "invariant prescription," to name but two. Acting as consultant, I chose a different task—to reopen the contract. My first thought was that trying to get this couple to change the way they related around this specific issue of how to treat their daughter was the toughest place to get leverage, because they were frozen into relatively inflexible complementary positions. Then it occurred to me that though they had been referred for couples therapy, they made it "parent therapy," not marital therapy. *If* they had had an agreement with the therapist to work on their marriage, the therapist could have pointed out that their preoccupation with their daughter was resistant—that is, it diverted them from other issues in their relationship. But there was no such agreement. In fact, lack of agreement to talk about other marital issues was both cause and effect of their impasse.

I advised the therapist to say that he noticed that they talked of little other than how to discipline the daughter. Although they had reason to worry about her and this was obviously an important subject, still it seemed to have the effect of narrowing down not only what they discussed in therapy, but probably their whole relationship as well. What did they think, and would they be willing to broaden the focus to include other aspects of their relationship?

Their response was revealing—and counterintuitive. The mother, who stood for strict control, said yes, she did want to talk about the marriage. But as the weeks went by, she continued to be preoccupied with her daughter. Her strictness had more to do with enmeshment than with boundary making. The father was not only more lenient, but also somewhat less worried about his daughter. Although he was initially reluctant to talk about the marriage, as the weeks went by it was he who focused more on the couple and less on the child.

2. Determinants of the Problem

This is the least frankly spelled out part of our agreements. We're not about to tell them what we really think. Well and good. My only point is this: If we remember that we are treating a group of persons, not manipulating "a system," then we will try, tactfully, to eventually help each one of them recognize their own role in the family's problems and their ability to make a difference by changing what they do. Until a peripheral father accepts that his distance is part of the problem and that changing his behavior will make a difference, then he has no reason not to resist and persist.

Remembering that each member of the family has a unique perspective, we should ask each one for his or her view of the problem. This is, of course, standard practice. However, it should not be done with an attitude of arrogant superiority: expecting that their views will be incorrect, but asking for them mainly in order to know what kind of misperceptions you have to work around. Rather, the therapist should try honestly to understand each person's opinion *and* consider it. True, these opinions will often be self-serving and counterproductive; sometimes, however, they may be correct, or at least useful. It is not a good idea to move too quickly to redefine viewpoints that we think are not useful. However, few family therapists err in the direction of being too blunt. It is much more common to be more dishonest than necessary—by withholding what you think—than to be overly confrontive.

Don't just ask each person perfunctorily what he or she thinks. Spend some time talking to each of them. Stay with them. Accept and acknowledge each one's version. But sometimes you can add a gentle challenge to your clarifications: "So, you think he's the one? If he stopped doing (whatever), things would be better?" This lays the groundwork for later trying to make explicit agreements with individuals to try to improve things by changing what they are doing.

3. Goals

Therapists vary quite a bit in terms of how explicitly they try to define the goals of therapy. Those who emphasize specific goals are usually behavioral and directive; nondirective therapists often say little more than, "I think I can help." Such general statements leave open the possibility of expanding the clients' initial concerns into a broader form of self-improvement, but unless some attempt is made to spell out goals, the clients' expectations are likely to remain vague and unrealistic.

Be careful what you promise to deliver. You cannot promise cure. You cannot even promise relief. Simply not promising won't do either, because even if cure isn't promised it is implied. You can promise only to try to help family members with their problems. My point is not to counsel making little speeches, but to suggest that promising too much may be a cover for being anxious about being able to deliver anything worthwhile. Although clients may initially be pleased to hear promises because it enhances their idealized fantasies of a rescuer, most of them have often been disappointed by broken promises and they soon become distrustful.

If you are an engineer trying to retool a mechanical system, it makes sense for you to decide what's wrong and how things need to be improved. But if you are a family therapist working with a group of autonomous individuals, do not overestimate your ability to set goals for them. They all have individual goals, some of which they are aware of and may be willing to voice, others of which are covert. I suppose the ideal would be to have a mutually agreed upon goal between the therapist and every member of the family, and to have these goals subordinate to a joint family goal. However, since we work in the real world, at least try to be aware that each person may have different goals, and that many of these agendas may be hidden.

4. Rules of Therapy

There is no possibility of *not* making a contract, only the opportunity of making it more or less explicit. Some things should be very explicit; other things are better left open. From my point of view, most discussions of contract are too explicit about goals and not explicit enough about the conditions of treatment.

The ground rules are the simplest element of the contract and the one that should be the most specifically spelled out. These include fees and when they should be paid, how long the sessions are and how frequent, and who is expected to attend (which may vary from session to session). Sometimes, you may wish to clarify what you expect family members to do in session—"talk over these problems"—but I do not recommend trying to explain your theory of therapy. The point is merely to let them know what you expect of them. People cannot cooperate unless they know how to cooperate, and what we expect of our clients may be different from what their past experience has led them to expect. Take the matter of keeping appointments and coming on time. Clinic patients often come late and frequently miss appointments. Are they resisting? Perhaps, but many clinic patients have been conditioned to expect to be kept waiting in doctors' offices. Spell out the basic conditions of treatment *and* look for acknowledgment and agreement. Here is an example.

Harry and Silvia Green came to the clinic because they weren't getting along. After talking with each of them about how he or she saw the problem and then observing what happened when they tried to talk together, the therapist could see that they did have trouble getting along, and he thought he could help. So he offered them a treatment contract. "I can see that you do have a problem getting along, and I think I can help. The clinic's fee is 55 dollars a visit, and I expect you to pay that at the start of each month. If you have health insurance, I will be glad to fill out the forms, but I expect you to pay the fee directly to me. Our sessions will be once a week at this time and will last for 50 minutes. In order to work effectively, it is important that we meet regularly; I expect to meet with you every week and I will hold you responsible." (If you charge for missed sessions, say so. But even if not, do not suggest that they may not attend by telling them to call if they aren't coming. Expect them to come; handle not coming when it arises.) After stating these guidelines, the therapist studied the couple's faces to see if they understood (they seemed to) and he asked if they had any questions (they didn't).

It is not always possible to have a clear agreement about ground rules, at least not in the first meeting. Sometimes a first session ends with the therapist still maneuvering for leverage. When you aren't sure they will return, it is not the time to make conditions. If they are obviously not ready to agree to anything, say only enough to ensure that they will return for a second visit. "I can see how serious things have gotten, but I will need one more meeting before I know for sure what should be done. So, I want all five of you to come back once more at this time next week."

By the way, nowhere is it carved in stone that therapy sessions must occur at weekly intervals and last for 45 or 50 minutes. These are part of a standard set of rules that usually make sense. But therapists should feel free to experiment with the rules. You may discover that longer or less frequent sessions are useful in some cases. Though I have trouble sitting still for more than 50 minutes, I have sometimes had very good results from marathon sessions. Most of the time, however, I see families weekly for 50 minutes. Part of the reason for this is that this format is convenient for *me*. It helps to clarify that in your own mind.

The essential point about ground rules is to work toward getting as clear and explicit an agreement as possible. Strike a balance between the vagueness of professional disdain for cooperation and the appearance of rigidity and uncaring that creates the impression that the ground rules are more important than the clients' welfare.

Sometimes, when we state the rules of therapy, they do not agree.

A way that many clients express initial resistance to treatment is by fighting the ground rules. This may take the form of arguing about the fee, refusing to be videotaped, or insisting that they can come only at odd hours. We all have scheduling problems, but flexibility is a measure of a sincere desire to do what is necessary to get help. These and other forms of initial resistance are commonly seen as the system's inflexibility, and the usual response is joining—accepting the family as they are.

JOINING

Let us return to the case of the Dusard family, presented earlier in this chapter. Mrs. Dusard called the crisis clinic after her son had walked out in the middle of an argument, gone to his room, and slammed the door. She went after him and ordered him to pack a bag and leave the house. That was two days ago and she hasn't heard from him since. Now she wants to know, "What should we do?"

We could assume that our responsibility is to get the boy back home. If so, we should probably avoid directly suggesting that the mother find him and bring him back because of the likelihood that the mother—this mother—will resist the suggestion. Or we can assume that our job is only to help the family work on the problem. Incidentally, this does not mean that we should tell a defensive mother, bluntly, that she'll have to make some changes, although that is an honest possibility. The problem here is joining, the relationship the therapist has created, not resistance—a property of them.

"Joining" is a term introduced by Minuchin for something that all therapists recognize as important, establishing rapport. But Minuchin did much more than simply relabel something that we all do anyway. He taught us that joining is an essential precursor of restructuring, that before a family will accept anything approaching a radical revision in the way they do business they must already trust and accept the therapist. Moreover, this is not a linear process; we do not join once and for all, then spend the rest of our time inducing the family to change. We join once and then rejoin again and again each time our confrontations and challenges threaten to alienate the family or one of its members. Joining is the grease that makes reorganization possible.

Joining consists of making friendly contact with family members and accepting the family's organization and style. The first is a person-to-person action; it involves thinking about each individual. What does this person think about the presenting problem? And how does that person feel about being here? Joining means understanding each person's point of view and telling each of them that you understand. The second aspect of joining is systemic. The therapist figures out how this system usually functions—perhaps father is the spokesman, but mother makes all the real decisions—and accommodating to that.

In principle, joining comes before changing. How much time need a therapist spend in joining? Fifteen or 20 minutes, or several sessions, or 10 seconds. Join until you sense they are with you, trust you, and are ready to cooperate. This may happen automatically or may take a great deal of doing and redoing.

A couple once came to see me from a distant state. They had heard that I was an expert on "midlife crisis," and the husband was having one. Their willingness to go to all that trouble was a measure of the extent to which they were willing to cooperate. In this case I could have begun immediately confronting or challenging them with little fear of driving them away. As it happened, I didn't feel any need to confront or challenge. Instead, the first several sessions were spent in a meticulous exploration of why the husband was unhappy. To what extent was it a function of his marriage, and to what extent was it his own conflict about having fun?

In about the fourth session I became aware of how little attention I was paying to the wife. Since I had noticed what a stylish dresser she was, I complimented her on her outfit. She smiled and thanked me. I judged from her easygoing response that she wasn't annoyed or jealous of all the time I was spending with her husband. Two weeks later the wife called to say that her husband would no longer come to therapy. He felt that I was too biased in favor of his wife; my complimenting her proved I was on her side.

The point of the story is that you can never tell how much joining a particular person may require. The story also demonstrates another problem with joining, not with the idea, but with how it is put into practice. Sometimes therapists confuse empathy and acceptance with phony and ingratiating remarks, like my comment to the woman above. I'm not sure that my remark alienated her; I don't think she felt I was stereotyping her. But the casual compliment is not what joining is about. In this case, I might better have asked her how she felt about my spending so much time talking to her husband.

I think we playact joining, that we pretend to understand and accept people in order to get on with rearranging them, when we think too much about problems and dysfunctional interactions, and too little about persons. Let's be honest. Sometimes we do play along with a family's way of seeing things even though we disagree. My point is simply this: Joining becomes a sham if it is nothing more than that, nothing but pretense.

Diana and Sam Kirschner call it "bonding," a term suggesting genuine connection of real people. But they go on to suggest a very calculating strategy, including imitating the patient's manner of speaking. Even: "Nonverbally, the practitioner must use similar vocal tones and expressions, and mimic the behavioral movements and breathing patterns of each spouse."[15] There's a big difference between imitating and trying to understand. Once again I want to point out the danger of assuming, and creating, an overly central role for the therapist. One way this is done is by taking up a calculating, directive and manipulative stance. It is obvious that this can provoke resistance. But so, too, can an overemphasis on joining. The too-active therapist who works too hard at joining accepts responsibility to eliminate resistance.

Resistance is the expression of defense, and defense is important; it is not just something to get out of the way, but something to be understood. Resistance assumes forms which accord with the level of family members' object relationships. "Unmotivated" individuals may want help, but may have negative aggressive internalizations, which are played out in the family *and* between family members and the therapist. Whether or not you delve into why some people are so negative, their negativity is apparent.

The same may not be true of those people whose inner objects lead them to an overly confident expectation of a benign experience or to idealized fantasies of an omnipotent therapist offering a magical cure. Actually, this is the poorest kind of motivation because the family that gives themselves over freely to the therapist may be giving up their own function. Instead of taking over, a therapist might comment on this readiness for rescue: "Since you are so ready to put yourselves in my hands, you must have become totally baffled. We'll have to try to figure out why your own attempts haven't worked out."

One of the implications of not joining in a phony way is to avoid responding to unusual requests literally or to demands impulsively. Talk them over. When clients make unusual requests, the therapist should remember that clients are handling themselves in the best way they know how. They need understanding and empathy, but you don't have to accede to every request in order to demonstrate understanding.

What happened to the man who felt that I was on his wife's side? I decided that I must have ruptured the empathic bond between us. His annoyance at my compliment may have been only a sign of that. So I wrote a letter to him, telling him that I thought I must have misunderstood him and that I was sorry. But I did think I could help, and I asked him to return to discuss it with me. It turned out that he was very jealous of his wife and sensitive to other men's glances. Moreover, he felt that I was unduly suggesting that his unhappiness was his problem rather than a problem of the marriage. I told him that he was right, I had thought that, and we then proceeded to talk more about his life and her life, with me following more and leading less.

As we have seen, resistance is an interactional phenomenon depending as much on the therapist as on the family. Since discussions of resistance usually focus primarily on clients, there is little mention made of the therapist's feelings—anxiety, frustration, impotence, anger, disdain, or helplessness—when dealing with difficult cases. When such feelings are alluded to, they are often treated as automatic by-products of dealing with difficult families, and the usual remedy is to apply more and better techniques. The alternative is to recognize and modify the therapist's contribution to resistance. Resistance always occurs in relationship to the therapist, and is heavily influenced by the therapist's interventions, empathy or lack of empathy, sensitivity or insensitivity, understanding or provocativeness, and blind spots. I have already discussed altering what the therapist does deliberately: contracting and joining. Now I would like to look at what the therapist does inadvertently.

INDUCTION AS COUNTERTRANSFERENCE

When family therapists are drawn into playing out a missing role in the families they work with, we call it "induction." Here's how it works.

Susan McCarthy had been seeing the Jacksons for about six months. Shelly (age 14) got into frequent arguments with her mother, and these often ended in a slapping match. The other children, Lee (19) and Brian (11) were "no problem." The therapist had been working with Mrs. Jackson to set firmer limits on her daughter, making her go to bed by 10 o'clock on school nights and finish her homework before watching television. This was a way of putting the mother more clearly in charge and helping the daughter feel more secure. After about five months of steady improvement, the arguments grew less frequent and the hitting stopped. Shelly was doing better in school, and was making more friends. Then things started going downhill again. The therapist was puzzled and sought out a consultation.

The consultant asked to observe the next therapy session to see what was going on. Before the session started, he asked for a brief summary of the course of therapy. The therapist repeated what I have written above, and added that the mother had separated from her alcoholic husband three years ago. When the family was a few minutes late, the consultant asked if they usually came on time—"Oh, yes"—and how frequent the meetings were. They had been meeting weekly for about five months; then, since things were going so well, the therapist had spread out the meetings to two- or three-week intervals. Hmmm.

Apparently the therapist had been providing a missing role in the family. As long as she met regularly with them, things were fine, but when she tried to pull away, the problems resumed. This is induction. When the family showed up and the session got underway, the consultant observed that the therapist seemed to be on target with how to respond effectively to a 14-year-old girl, but tended to speak to the girl herself, rather than help the mother to do so. She was, in other words, playing out the role of a competent parent. Once a week for about an hour is about as much time as many fathers spend talking to their children about problems.

Induction is one of the most useful concepts in family therapy. Whatever goes on at home will be replayed in therapy, with the therapist playing a significant role. Therapists cannot avoid induction by playing strategic tactician. They can try, but it won't work. The important factor is not the therapist's ability to avoid the family's pull or avoid the temptation to react emotionally to them, but rather the ability to recognize when he or she is trapped and immersed in the system, and to work his or her way out. To do so, it is useful to remember that induction is a human, not a mechanical process.

Induction is a useful concept, but it rests heavily on the metaphor of the family as a mechanical system. Sometimes it is useful to say that a therapist was inducted: The family members felt they needed a competent parent to control the children and they covertly induced the therapist to play the role. The limitation of this mechanical notion, however, is that it treats the family as a unit and the therapist as a cipher.

A therapist's response to a family is more complicated and more personal than the notion of induction suggests. For example, the therapist's identification with family members may result in two alternative modes of reaction. The first is concordant: The therapist resonates to the family's needs and responds in harmony with them. The second possible reaction is complementary: The therapist rejects and opposes what the family seems to want. This is not necessarily a form of disciplined neutrality, or even conscious stubbornness; it may be a form of identification with an internal object. If a family member carries around an internal persecutor, expecting that authority figures will be persecutory, he or she may create this response in the therapist. If this process is played out consciously, it might go something like this: An adolescent complains that "the stupid teacher made me stay after school," and you, the therapist, sympathize with the teacher. You don't have to say anything, it will show.

The point is simply that the dynamics of the therapeutic relationship are more complicated than we usually think, and are as much dependent upon the therapist's emotional reactions as on the family's. The name for the therapist's personal reactions is *countertransference*. Family therapists often ignore, or at least deemphasize, countertransference because they believe that the therapeutic relationship is less important in family therapy than in individual therapy. Maybe.

The presence of the real family in the consulting room makes it less likely that therapist and clients will live out an ersatsz family relationship. On the other hand, countertransference feelings are stirred strongly in family therapy because of the likelihood that some of the painful issues the clients are wrestling with were (are) also present in the therapist's family. Moreover, the greater activity in family therapy makes it harder to monitor and control the therapist's personal reactions. There's not much time for self-reflection when a family is clamoring for you to *"do something."* If a therapist has problems with arguing, discipline, intimacy, independence, control, flexibility, or any other dimension of family life, these problems may interfere with his or her capacity to be objective, feel empathy, and render effective therapeutic help.

The therapist is always contributing in some meaningful way to the presence of resistance in family members and there is at least some element of countertransference in every intervention. This is true whether we accept the nice distinction between countertransference as *inappropriate* attitudes and interventions, or simply as any reactions.[16] What to do?

Most of the writing in family therapy about the therapeutic relationship recommends that therapists stay neutral and maintain enough distance to be objective. Exceptions to this advice, found in the writing of experientialists like Carl Whitaker, are just that, exceptions. In family therapy, the therapeutic relationship is undoubtedly less intense than in individual therapy. Transference, though not absent, is less powerful, not only because the real family is present, but also because other family members make better objects of transference than the therapist. Countertransference, on the other hand, may be *more* important in family therapy than in individual therapy.

Maintaining therapeutic neutrality probably is the best protection against undue countertransference. But this is easier said than done. Therapeutic neutrality is a highly complex achievement. It involves, as is widely recognized, a kind of impartiality, and evenhanded openness to every member of the family. It also involves—and this is more controversial—a willingness to let the family discover and choose their own way out of their difficulties. Once I was treating a family, who lived in the deep South, with a school-phobic child. As a result of the therapy, the parents rekindled the spark in their marriage, and they united in concern for the child. They took their son out of the public school where he had been afraid and sent him to a segregated, all-white school. It was not my way, but it was not my business.

The best way to be neutral is to see your role as helping the family figure out why they can't solve their problems, what is dysfunctional about the way they are operating, and why they are stuck. Then you can help them change to a more effective way of solving their own problems. The neutral therapist eschews determining how families *should* behave in favor of helping them discover what is right *for them*. This implies in the therapist a state of receptivity, an inner neutrality that is the achievement of a frame of mind, not just a pose.

When the therapist is at an appropriate distance and maintains neutrality, his or her response to the family's behavior should be trial action—that is, thought—rather than impulsive reaction. Do not respond to patients' productions in kind. This means not meeting anger with retaliation or appeasement as, for example, by trying to control a family by taking a "one-down" position. Sometimes this seems like a useful strategy, but often it is only acting out a need for control. Beginning therapists often have an excessive need to be loved by their clients; experienced ones often develop an overweening need to be in control.

Therapeutic overactivity is as often motivated by a need to discharge the therapist's own anxiety as it is to help the family. Of course, patient families do stir our feelings and make us impatient to do something. But if we can metabolize, contain, the induced feelings, we can learn to scrutinize what we are feeling—to think before we act.

It is also possible for countertransference to eventuate not in action but in immobility—excess inaction. When awareness of one's own personal emotional reactivity is exaggerated to oversensitivity, as in the work of Robert Langs, for example, it can lead to a fearful passivity. Like a child who is afraid of getting yelled at, the therapist who is overly concerned to avoid personal contamination of the therapeutic relationship may end by sitting in mute silence, creating an atmosphere of strained distance which, ironically, itself becomes a conspicuous and controlling stimulus. Don't be too afraid of making mistakes. We're not that powerful.

I once treated a family in which the main problem was conflict with an adopted teenaged girl. She stayed out as long as she liked, whenever she liked; she didn't do her schoolwork, and she stole money and checks from her parents. The parents had strongly differing views about what should be done. The mother was for discipline; the father was for understanding. To complicate matters further, the parents were emotionally alienated, and father and daughter were carrying on a sexual relationship.

I remained, or so I thought, admirably neutral. I encouraged the parents to talk over their differences and I encouraged the daughter to get involved with kids her own age. All to no effect. And so I began to think of them as resistant. But because of my own revulsion and anger at the sexual involvement, I was unable to maintain a state of inner neutrality. Because of my feelings, I worked overtime at being "neutral." I became not only a neutral therapist, but a determinedly neutral one, afraid in the face of my own angry feelings to be very forceful, lest the anger show. Unfortunately, I was so busy being not-angry, I wasn't doing much of anything else.

While it is wise to be neutral and maintain professional distance, it is a mistake to overlook all that goes on beneath the surface. The swirling undercurrents of feeling that families stir in us tempt us to push them where we want to go but are afraid, or to hold them back from doing what we ourselves are afraid of. A male therapist, for example, may encourage female patients to be more sexually adventurous. The same therapist, however, may avoid confronting passive men to speak up to their wives or mothers. A female therapist might push her women patients to be more assertive and self-interested than the therapist herself dares to be, or than the patients themselves wish to be.[17]

Instead of projecting our annoyance back onto the family, we can observe our reactions and use them as a clue to what may be going on in the family.

It is possible to distinguish two sources of countertransference:

(1) the therapist's own personal and idiosyncratic response, stem-
ming from unresolved conflict and constituting a potential unde-
sirable bias, which client families should not be burdened with;
and (2) the therapist's natural and valid reaction to important
messages, unconsciously transmitted by family members. Rafael
Springman has called these "therapist-induced countertransference," and "client-induced countertransference."[18] This is a useful distinction, but in practice one that only a Solomon could
make.

Those, like Robin Skynner, who recommend using the feelings
stirred in the therapist as a clue to what is going on in the family
often advise sharing these feelings with the family.[19]

Humanistic therapists were the first to advocate honest disclo-
sure from therapists as well as from patients. Sidney Jourard went
so far as to say that the therapist's "self-disclosure" was the primary vehicle of cure.[20] From this perspective, the unflappable analyst was not only unresponsive, but unfeeling. Among family
therapists, Carl Whitaker is the most well-known proponent of
this kind of openness. Like other experiential family therapists, he
believes that *existential encounter* is the essential force in the psy-
chotherapeutic process. Walter Kempler insists that these encoun-
ters be reciprocal:

> In this approach the therapist becomes a family member dur-
> ing the interviews, participating as fully as he is able, hopefully
> available for appreciation and criticism as well as he is able to
> dispense it. He laughs, cries and rages. He feels and shares his
> embarrassments, confusions and helplessness. He shares his
> fears of revealing himself when these feelings are part of his
> current total person. He sometimes cannot share himself and
> hopefully he is able to say at least that much.[21]

By being "real," experiential therapists believe that they can
teach family members to do the same. While this is an attractive
(and liberating) point of view, it may be more effective in the
hands of wise and experienced therapists like Carl Whitaker.
Those of us who are younger and not yet certified as wise might
do well to avoid overestimating the salutary effect of our personal
disclosures.

Since the 60s we have entered more sober times and the trend among humanistic therapists has moved away from the extremes of open expression on the part of therapists. Alvin Mahrer, who is in the vanguard of the humanistic tradition, recommends that therapists minimize their personal influence on their patients.[22] According to Mahrer, therapists should enter the patient's experience, not vice versa. I agree.

Over the years I have realized that my own countertransference reactions are affected by the context within which I am working. Very often, when I interview families in front of a group of observers—students or workshop participants—I feel a certain pressure to perform. I used to respond to this pressure by becoming a little more dramatic and flamboyant. This was not all bad. My awareness of the audience energized me and probably made my work more focused and direct than on my sleepy days. Many times, though, my self-consciously forceful interventions took the form of vigorous confrontation of one or another family member.

Looking back, I'm ashamed to say that it was usually somebody's mother that I confronted. Maybe I was using these women as scapegoats to work out unfinished business with my own mother, or maybe I just hadn't developed sufficient empathy for what it means to be a mother. In any case, when I find myself getting angry at somebody's mother now, I tell myself: She's behaving in a way that makes me uncomfortable, being bossy or uncaring; she must have a good reason, not necessarily conscious; I need to figure out what that good reason is, which may lead me to a better awareness of what others in the family are doing, or to experiences in the woman's background that taught her to behave this way.

Whether or not you work with observers, be aware not only of your reactions to various (classes of) family members, but also of the effect on your work of other things going on in your life. Sometimes we are tired, conflicted, or distracted. At these times, we should be wary of sinking into passivity. Remember: There is a big difference between allowing families room to work things out and being frozen into prolonged passivity because you are depressed or discouraged. It isn't easy to assess the impact of our personal lives on our professional conduct, but we can try. When I find myself telling the same stories or using a small number of metaphors regularly, I ask myself why. What am I working over? Sometimes, and this is hard, I find that my own injured narcissism makes me impatient with families and tempts me to put manipulative pressure on them. "I'll succeed here, goddammit!"

The ache for specialness and recognition doesn't disappear when we act as "helpers." We may hide away our pride and longing for admiration, but they are there. Wisdom lies in trying to let go of our own narcissistic needs for families to perform. But it also rests on acceptance of our own limits and on acceptance that, just as family members are who they are, not who we want them to become—we are who we are.

Many people ask if personal therapy for the therapist is the best inoculation against countertransference. That was, of course, Freud's wish: that well-analyzed therapists would be immune to the complicating influences of their own emotions. I don't know. I don't think so. Perhaps the most useful prevention of countertransference is approaching families without needing anything from them—an impossible task, but a standard to aim for. Not needing for them to like you, not needing for them to get better, and not needing for them to act in any particular ways. Bion's felicitous phrase for this was "freedom from memory and desire."[23]

When your feelings do get stirred up, the first thing to do is to notice them. Try to be neutral, but face what you do feel. A phobic attitude toward your feelings leads only to denial. Countertransference can be useful if you begin to understand it, what it says about the family, about you, and about the therapeutic relationship.

Do not act rashly on the dictates of your feelings, but do not beat yourself up either: "I *shouldn't* be angry!" Think of your reaction as a temporary trial identification and not necessarily an enduring aspect of your self. I only rarely tell family members what I am feeling toward them. Instead, I try to see if someone else in the family is reacting similarly, and then I try to understand why I am feeling the same thing or the complement of what that person is feeling. I feel that my age and experience make it more useful now to share my feelings than it once was. But that still isn't much.

Once in a while clients come in cooperative and stay that way. But not too often. Resistance is usually part of their unhappiness, a sign of the inflexibility that led to their getting stuck in the first place. They resist without clearly realizing what they are doing. It really *is* hard to change. The therapist's job is to show them that *hard* doesn't mean *impossible*.

Epilogue

The family as a system has always stood at the center of family therapy. This view made possible enormous advances in understanding with respect to such puzzling phenomena as one family member getting worse when another one gets better and a child's symptoms often clearing up when his parents' relationship improves. This increment of understanding has in the past depended upon thinking of the individual person primarily as part of a larger whole. Not that all of a person's life is controlled by what goes on in the family, but enough is so that therapy can usefully proceed by concentrating on the interconnections in the family. It is through this vision of life that family therapy accomplishes so much, alleviating many forms of human misery more quickly and more effectively than otherwise possible. Unfortunately, while concentrating on the interworkings of the group, we have tended to forget the considerable extent to which interactions are personal actions. As a result, the view of persons as actors has remained the slighted and undeveloped dimension of family therapy.

This book began with a critique of family therapy's deliberate deemphasis of personal experience and individual psychology. By elevating the metaphor of the system to dogma, we have lost sight of the richness and complicating influence of personal feeling, motivation, and conflict. The result has been a tilt toward the quick fix, along with a host of mechanical interventions for a mechanical patient: the system. The systems metaphor has been overdone, leading to esoteric theories of human behavior without humanity, at times verging on the ridiculous—as, for example, when some people deny that psychopathology exists and must be reckoned with.

More important by far than what we write about, our over-elaboration of the systems model can be detrimental to effective clinical practice. The inappropriate application of the metaphor of a biological organism to a group of persons has led some family practitioners to treat family members as dumb appendages of something they cannot understand and cannot willingly change. Some of the techniques we use to push and prod families work, but only in a very shortsighted sense. When we put a premium on manipulation, we treat people like puppets on a string who may stop dancing when the strings are no longer pulled.

In conducting this lengthy exploration of the self in the system, I have tried to show that the self is curiously conditioned by the social context, and yet, in some respects, is independent of the context.

Family therapy, as we are fond of saying, is a therapy of context. That is, we try to understand behavior not solely as the actions of isolated individuals, but also as the result of converging influences of time and place and other persons. The same kind of thinking can be applied to ourselves. The context in which family therapy first emerged was quite different from the one in which we find ourselves today. Once we were a new discipline, struggling to define ourselves and create an alternative approach to treatment. Now, we are an establishment, with entrenched interests and entrenched ways of thinking. Then, it made sense to break away from tradition, to strike out boldly in new directions, and to concentrate on what is unique in our new approach. Today, we have less need of narrow orthodoxy.

Family therapy has come of age. Like an adolescent who once

turned her back on her parents, family therapy has now grown strong enough and self-confident enough to reconcile with the once rejected ideas of individual psychotherapy. Contemporary family therapists see family life in a broader perspective than pioneers like Bateson and Jackson did. Not having discovered the system and built family therapy on it as a foundation, we can never value it as much as they did. And so, without really slighting the importance of this discovery, we are free to bring back the psychological life of individuals and to take a more inclusive view than the pioneers did. After all, we are standing on their shoulders.

Although my argument is in part a critique of the field as a whole, my real message is to practicing clinicians, many of whom, perhaps, have had experiences similar to my own. The initial excitement of seeing families soon gives way to confusion—how to understand what's going on—and frustration—how to have an effect on it. For me, the discovery of systemic concepts and techniques was as clarifying as turning on a light in a dark room. ("Discovery" is probably not the right word for someone fortunate enough to have studied with Salvador Minuchin, Jay Haley, and Murray Bowen.) I think many family therapists must have a similar experience. Things get very clear very fast when you learn to see triangles and enmeshment and disengagement where formerly you saw only chaos and confusion. These concepts carry us a long way. In my own practice I had a great deal of success and satisfaction. But over the years I discovered that, for me at least, something was missing. I was bothered by the Mr. Templetons I couldn't understand, and the Mrs. Sullivans I couldn't get through to.

I had studied and taught psychology in universities and in a psychoanalytic training program. But I always kept this work separate from my family therapy practice. (Like most men, I am pretty good at compartmentalizing my experience.) When I saw individuals I used all the knowledge of social learning theory, catharsis, and psychoanalysis that I could muster. But when I saw families, I stuck to systems concepts and methods. With many families this was enough; but with others I began to suffer boredom and burnout. As a therapist, I think I took myself too seriously and the people in the families I was seeing not seriously enough. My shift to becoming a more complete therapist consisted of paying more attention to individuals—as simple as that—and giving myself permission to use some of the psychological insights that I had been reserving for psychotherapy with individuals. This dual emphasis on system and psyche brought new excitement and effectiveness to my work. I hope that expanding your thinking to include more attention to the self in the system will enrich your work as well.

But how? Once we get beyond abstract statements about "the self in the system," and "the dignity and worth of individuals," the question remains: How do we translate this commitment into clinical practice?

One answer to this question is to practice psychoanalysis (or behavior therapy, or experiential therapy) in the context of the family. Many have done this. Some continue to. These hybrid approaches offered insight into the individual and (in some cases) to the interactional dynamics of couples, but with few exceptions they had little to say about the family as a system—or, to put it more specifically, little appreciation of triadic interactions.

For the most part, these earlier approaches lacked a sophisticated understanding of family systems theories and techniques, and therefore could not compete with structural and strategic approaches. I have called for a deeper appreciation of the self in the system, but there is a risk in this. Some therapists propose to create a synthesis of psychoanalytic therapy and family therapy. Although I have already criticized this idea, I wish to reemphasize what I consider the danger of losing the power of family therapy by reverting back to an overemphasis on psychodynamics. We have theories of the psyche and theories of the system. Like the quantum and wave theories of light, both are useful for their own special purposes. They may be reconciled some day, but for now, why not use them both at the appropriate time and place. This means shifting back and forth, not trying to create a homogenized model which loses the oomph of its constituent elements. The two perspectives complement each other, but they don't merge into a single, synthetic approach.

Systems, as we know, must grow and change. But they must also resist dissolution. In order to endure, a system must withstand disruptions that threaten its essential character. This is true of families and it is true of family therapy as a discipline. In my enthusiasm for incorporating more psychological ideas into our work, I do not wish to encourage anyone to reject or discard the systemic ideas that are the basis of family therapy. Psychodynamic (and behavioral and experiential) theories and techniques can be incorporated to enrich family therapy, but should not, I believe, be allowed to dominate it. If I have devoted more space in this book to the psyche than the system, it is offered as an antidote to our current unbalance in the opposite direction—it is *not* meant to replace interactional concepts with intrapsychic ones.

What is it that we forget when we neglect the individual dimension? Quite a bit. Feelings and memories and opinions and expectations and motives and conflicts. These realms are so complex that we can get lost in them. When we do, we are at risk of losing sight of interaction—the essence of family therapy. When we incorporate something new—or old—into our work, we must not lose sight of what should endure.

So, while I have argued for a greater appreciation of the self, I have tried to demonstrate how this appreciation can be incorporated into a genuinely interactional brand of family therapy. These brief guidelines may not always have been as explicit as some readers would like. This is largely deliberate. Recognizing that something needs to be done is often more important than worrying about the details of how to do it. It is that clarity of purpose that inspires women to lift up cars that have fallen on top of their husbands, and makes firefighters do almost anything to rescue people from burning buildings. When I teach family therapy I often avoid, or at least delay, answering such questions as: "How do you quiet down two people who are screaming at each other?" or "How do you get a parent to control a child who is running around the room?" The main thing is to know, very clearly, that you must do it. This clarity of purpose will help you find a way.

Although I have introduced several topics that I think are useful ways to understand the psychology of individual family members, I think it matters less how much a clinician knows about psychodynamics or psychopathology than that he or she begin to pay careful attention to the individuals in family treatment. Really, most of us want to anyway. Much of what I have tried to do in this book is encourage family therapists to do what their common sense and humanity urge them to do.

Therapy is an art whose general principles can be described but whose specific interventions are the products of intuition and inspiration. As a family therapist you have an enormous responsibility, not to take over for families, but to be as helpful to them as possible. Because this work involves persons and their interactions, it is exceedingly valuable to know as much about both as possible. And because the act of conducting therapy with families is an act of courage, you have my admiration.

Notes and References

Chapter 1: Finding the Family and Losing the Self

1. Christopher Lasch describes a massive erosion by public schools of the family's educative function and an appropriation of parental functions by the "helping functions" in the first 25 years of the twentieth century. His *Haven in a Heartless World* (New York: Basic Books, 1977) is a telling analysis of the American family besieged by "the guardians of public health and morality."

2. For a detailed history of the beginnings of family therapy see Guerin, P. *Family Therapy: Theory and Practice*. New York: Gardner Press, 1976; Hoffman, L. *Foundations of Family Therapy*. New York: Basic Books, 1981; and Nichols, M. *Family Therapy: Concepts & Methods*. New York: Gardner Press, 1984.

3. Goffman, E. *Asylums: Essays on the Social Situation of Mental Patients and Other Inmates*. Garden City, N.Y.: Doubleday Anchor, 1961.

4. Jackson, D. The question of family homeostasis. *The Psychiatric Quarterly Supplement*, 1957, *31*, 79–90.

5. Bateson, G., Jackson, D., Haley, J. & Weakland, J. Toward a theory of schizophrenia. *Behavioral Science*, 1956, *1*, 251–254.

6. Haley, J. (Ed.) *Conversations with Milton H. Erickson, M.D. Volume III.* Washington, D.C.: Triangle Press, 1985, pp. 64–65.

7. Bateson, G. Foreword. In C. Sluzki & D. Ransom (Eds.), *Double Bind: The Foundation of the Communicational Approach to the Family.* New York: Grune & Stratton, 1976, pp. XII–XIII.

8. Laing, R. D. Mystification, confusion and conflict. In I. Boszormenyi-Nagy & J. Framo (Eds.), *Intensive Family Therapy: Theoretical and Practical Aspects.* New York: Harper & Row, 1965; Brunner/Mazel, 1985.

9. Jackson, D. Family interaction, family homeostasis and some implications for conjoint family psychotherapy. In J. Masserman (Ed.), *Individual and Family Dynamics.* New York: Grune & Stratton, 1959, p. 140.

10. Weakland, J. Communication theory and clinical change. In P. Guerin (Ed.), *Family Therapy: Theory and Practice.* New York: Gardner Press, 1976, p. 121.

11. Coyne, J. A brief introduction to epistobabble. *The Family Therapy Networker,* 1982, *6,* (4), 27–28.

12. Liddle, H. & Saba, G. Systemic chic: Family therapy's new wave. *Family Therapy News,* July 1981, *9,* 12.

13. Bateson, G. *Steps to an Ecology of Mind.* New York: Ballantine Books, 1971.

14. Hoffman, L. Deviation-amplifying processes in natural groups. In Haley, J. (Ed.), *Changing Families.* New York: Grune & Stratton, 1971.

15. Dell, P. Researching the family theories of schizophrenia: An exercise in epistemological confusion. *Family Process,* 1980, *19,* 321–335.

16. Auerswald, E. Families, change, and the ecological perspective. In Ferber, A., Mendelsohn, M., & Napier, A. (Eds.), *The Book of Family Therapy.* New York: Jason Aronson, 1972.

17. Keeney, B. Ecosystemic epistemology: An alternative paradigm for diagnosis. *Family Process,* 1979, *18,* 117–129.

18. de Shazer, S. *Patterns of Brief Family Therapy: An Ecosystemic Approach.* New York: Guilford, 1982, p. 5.

19. Hoffman, L. *Foundations of Family Therapy.* New York: Basic Books, 1981.

20. Dell, P. Beyond homeostasis: Toward a concept of coherence. *Family Process*, 1982, *21*, 21–41.

Chapter 2: The Problem of Change

1. This example was taken from a September, 1986, conference, entitled Neutrality versus Provocation. The review is found in Nichols, M., The Fox and the Bear: Gianfranco Cecchin and Maurizio Andolfi. *The Family Therapy Networker*, 1987, *11*(1), 59–62.

2. The phrase "breaking the symptomatic cycle" is from Lynn Hoffman's *Foundations of Family Therapy*.

3. Watzlawick, P., Weakland, J. & Fisch, R. *Change: Principles of Problem Formation and Problem Resolution*. New York: Norton, 1974.

4. Fromm, E. *Escape from Freedom*. New York: Holt, Rinehart and Winston, 1941; and Campbell, J. *The Hero With a Thousand Faces*. Princeton, N.J.: Princeton University Press, 1949, pp. 9–10.

5. Elkaim, M., Prigogine, I., Guattari, F., Stengers, I. & Deneubourg, J. Openness: A round-table discussion. *Family Process*, 1982, *21*, 57–70.

Chapter 3: Interaction

1. Selvini Palazzoli, M., Boscolo, L., Cecchin, G. & Prata, G. Hypothesizing—circularity—neutrality: Three guidelines for the conductor of the session. *Family Process*, 1980, *19*, 3–12.

2. Penn, P. Circular questioning. *Family Process*, 1982, *21*, 267–280.

3. Selvini Palazzoli et al., op. cit., p. 8.

4. Selvini Palazzoli et al., op. cit., p. 8.

5. Penn, op. cit., p. 272.

6. Minuchin, S. & Fishman, C. *Family Therapy Techniques*. Cambridge, Mass.: Harvard University Press, 1981.

7. Bowen, M. Theory in the practice of psychotherapy. In P. Guerin (Ed.), *Family Therapy: Theory and Practice*. New York: Gardner Press, 1976, pp. 75–76.

Chapter 4: Empathy

1. Schafer, R. Generative empathy in the treatment situation. *Psychoanalytic Quarterly*, 1959, 28, 342–373.

2. Kohut, H. Introspection, empathy and psychoanalysis. *Journal of the American Psychoanalytic Association*, 1959, 7, 459–483.

3. Greenson, R. Empathy and its vicissitudes. In R. Greenson, *Explorations in Psychoanalysis*, New York: International Universities Press, 1960.

4. Madanes, C. From an interview by Richard Simon: Simon, R. Behind the one-way kaleidoscope. *The Family Therapy Networker*, 1986, 10(5), 29.

5. Fliess, R. The metapsychology of the analyst. *Psychoanalytic Quarterly*, 1942, 11, 211–227.

6. Fenichel, O. *The Psychoanalytic Theory of Neurosis*. New York: Norton, 1945, p. 511.

7. Rogers, C. *Client-Centered Therapy*. Boston: Houghton Mifflin, 1951. Rogers, C. Therapy, personality, and interpersonal relationships. In S. Koch (Ed.), *Psychology: A Study of a Science. Volume 3*. New York: McGraw-Hill, 1959, pp. 184–256.

8. Fliess, op. cit.

9. Schafer, op. cit.

10. This family is also described in Minuchin, S. & Fishman, C. *Family Therapy Techniques*. Cambridge, Mass.: Harvard University Press, 1981.

11. Minuchin & Fishman, op. cit., p. 85.

12. Minuchin & Fishman, op. cit., p. 167.

13. Jacobson, N. Problem solving and contingency contracting in the treatment of marital discord. *Journal of Consulting and Clinical Psychology*, 1977, 45, 92–100.
Patterson, G., Hops, H. & Weiss, R. A social learning approach to reducing rates of marital conflict. In R. Stuart, R. Liberman & S. Wilder (Eds.), *Advances in Behavior Therapy*. New York: Academic Press, 1973.
Stuart, R. An operant interpersonal program for couples. In D. Olson (Ed.), *Treating Relationships*. Lake Mills, Iowa: Graphic Publishing Company, 1976.

14. O'Leary, K. & Turkewitz, H. Marital therapy from a behavioral perspective. In T. Paolino & B. McCrady (Eds.), *Marriage and Marital Therapy*. New York: Brunner/Mazel, 1978.

15. Jackins, H. *The Human Side of Human Beings*. Seattle: Rational Island Publishers, 1965.
Jackins, H. *Elementary Counselor's Manual*. Seattle: Rational Island Publishers, 1962.

16. Strean, H. *Clinical Social Work*. New York: Free Press, 1978.
Perlman, H. *Persona: Social Role and Personality*. Chicago: University of Chicago Press, 1968.

Chapter 5: Assessment and Reassessment

1. Watzlawick, P., Weakland, J. & Fisch, R. *Change: Principles of Problem Formation and Problem Resolution*. New York: Norton, 1974.

2. Fisch, R., Weakland, J. & Segal, L. *The Tactics of Change: Doing Therapy Briefly*. San Francisco: Jossey-Bass, 1982.

3. Masters, W. & Johnson, V. *Human Sexual Inadequacy*. Boston: Little, Brown, 1970.

4. Haley, J. *Strategies of Psychotherapy*. New York: Grune & Stratton, 1963.

5. Rohrbaugh, M., Tennen, H., Press, S., White, L., Raskin, P. & Pickering, R. Paradoxical Strategies in Psychotherapy. Symposium presented at the American Psychological Association Convention, San Francisco, 1977.

6. Duvall, E. *Marriage and Family Development*. New York: Lippincott, 1977.

7. Carter, E. & McGoldrick, M. (Eds.) *The Family Life Cycle: Framework for Family Therapy*. New York: Gardner Press, 1980.

8. Shapiro, D. *Autonomy and Rigid Character*. New York: Basic Books, 1981, p. 14.

9. Ibid., pp. 14–15.

10. Minuchin, S. *Families and Family Therapy*. Cambridge, Mass.: Harvard University Press, 1974.

11. I am indebted to Allan Cooper and Earl Witenberg for their discussion of the "bogged down" treatment in psychoanalysis: Copper, A. & Witenberg, E. The "bogged down" treatment: A remedy. *Contemporary Psychoanalysis*, 1985, *21*, 27–41.

Chapter 6: Interactional Psychodynamics

1. Haley, J. *Strategies of Psychotherapy*. New York: Grune & Stratton, 1963.

2. Dicks, H. *Marital Tensions*. New York: Basic Books, 1967.

3. Kohut, H. *The Restoration of the Self*. New York: International Universities Press, 1977.

4. Freud, S. (1926) Inhibitions, symptoms and anxiety. *Standard Edition*, Volume 20. London: Hogarth Press.

5. Kohut, H. *The Analysis of the Self*. New York: International Universities Press, 1971.

6. Kohut, H. *How Does Analysis Cure?* Chicago: University of Chicago Press, 1984.

7. Mahler, M., Pine, F. & Bergman, A. *The Psychological Birth of the Human Infant*. New York: Basic Books, 1975.

8. Chessick, R. *Psychology of the Self and the Treatment of Narcissism*. New York: Jason Aronson, 1985.

Chapter 7: Object Relations and Psychopathology

1. Laing, R. D. *The Divided Self*. New York: Pantheon Books, 1960.

2. Pearce, J. & Friedman (Eds.) *Family Therapy: Combining Psychodynamic and Family Systems Approaches*. New York: Grune & Stratton, 1980.

3. Sander, F. *Individual and Family Therapy: Toward an Integration*. New York: Jason Aronson, 1979.

4. Slipp, S. *Object Relations: A Dynamic Bridge Between Individual and Family Treatment*. New York: Jason Aronson, 1984.

5. Scharff, D. & Scharff, J. *Object Relations Family Therapy*. New York: Jason Aronson, 1987.

6. Kernberg, O. *Borderline Conditions and Pathological Narcissism*. New York: Jason Aronson, 1975.

7. Balint, M. *The Basic Fault*. London: Tavistock, 1968; New York: Brunner/Mazel, 1979.

8. Bowlby, J. *Attachment*. New York: Basic Books, 1969.

9. Fairbairn, W. *An Object Relations Theory of the Personality*. New York: Basic Books, 1952.

10. Greenberg, J. & Mitchell, S. *Object Relations in Psychoanalytic Theory*. Cambridge, Mass.: Harvard University Press, 1983.

11. Guntrip, H. *Schizoid Phenomena, Object Relations and the Self*. New York: Basic Books, 1969.

12. Jacobson, E. *The Self and the Object World*. New York: International Universities Press, 1964.

13. Kernberg, O. *Object Relations Theory and Clinical Psychoanalysis*. New York: Jason Aronson, 1976.

14. Mahler, M., Pine, F. & Bergman, A. *The Psychological Birth of the Human Infant*. New York: Basic Books, 1975.

15. Modell, A. *Object Love and Reality*. New York: International Universities Press, 1968.

16. Schafer, R. *Aspects of Internalization*. New York: International Universities Press, 1968.

17. Segal, H. *Introduction to the Work of Melanie Klein*. New York: Basic Books, 1964.

18. Stolorow, R. & Lachmann, F. *Psychoanalysis of Developmental Arrests*. New York: International Universities Press, 1980.

19. Winnicott, D. *Collected Papers: Through Paediatrics to Psycho-Analysis*. New York: Basic Books, 1958.

20. Maturana, H. Biology of language: The epistemology of reality. In G. Miller & E. Lenneberg (Eds.), *Psychology and Biology of Language and Thought*. New York: Academic Press, 1978.

21. Haley, J. *Leaving Home: The Therapy of Disturbed Young People.* New York: McGraw-Hill, 1980, p. 11.

22. Haley, ibid., p. 12.

23. Lansky, M. *Family Therapy with Major Psychopathology.* New York: Grune & Stratton, 1981.

24. Minuchin, S., Rosman, B. & Baker, L. *Psychosomatic Families: Anorexia Nervosa in Context.* Cambridge, Mass.: Harvard University Press, 1978.

25. Dell, P. From pathology to ethics. *The Family Therapy Networker*, 1983, 7(6), 29-31, 64.

26. Doane, J. Parental communication deviance and attentive style. *Archives of General Psychiatry*, 1981, *38*, 685-697.
Falloon, I. Family management in the prevention of exacerbations of schizophrenia. *New England Journal of Medicine*, 1981, *306*, 1437-1440.
Goldstein, M. (Ed.) *New Developments in Interventions with Families of Schizophrenics.* San Francisco: Jossey-Bass, 1981.
McFarlane, W. (Ed.) *Family Therapy and Schizophrenia.* New York: Guilford, 1983.

27. Leff, J. A controlled trial of social intervention in the families of schizophrenic patients. *British Journal of Psychiatry*, 1982, *141*, 121-134.

28. Goldstein, op. cit.

29. Rohrbaugh, M. Family therapy and schizophrenia research: Swimming against the mainstream. *The Family Therapy Networker*, 1983, 7(4), 29-30.

30. Haley, op. cit.

31. Beels, C. & McFarlane, W. Family treatments of schizophrenia: Background and state of the art. *Hospital and Community Psychiatry*, 1982, *33*, 541-556.
Leff, op. cit.

32. Simon, R. An interview with Cloé Madanes. *The Family Therapy Networker*, 1986, *10*(5), 64-65.

Chapter 8: Understanding

1. For a profoundly thought-provoking discussion of the limits of intellectual insight in the context of interpersonal psychoanalysis, see: Levenson, E. *The Fallacy of Understanding*. New York: Basic Books, 1972.

2. Watzlawick, P., Weakland, J. & Fisch, R. *Change: Principles of Problem and Problem Resolution*. New York: Norton, 1974, p. 99.

3. Bateson, G. *Mind and Nature*. New York: E. P. Dutton, 1979.

4. Goffman, E. *Frame Analysis*. New York: Harper & Row, 1974.

5. Watzlawick, et. al., op. cit., pp. 103–104.

6. Kirschner, D. & Kirschner, S. *Comprehensive Family Therapy: An Integration of Systemic and Psychodynamic Treatment Models*. New York: Brunner/Mazel, 1986, p. 71.

7. Wachtel, E. & Wachtel, P. *Family Dynamics in Individual Psychotherapy*. New York: Guilford Press, 1986.

Chapter 9: Resistance

1. The term "abstractitis" is Fowler's (*A Dictionary of Modern English Usage*), and the analysis of resistance as an action borrows from Roy Schafer's *A New Language for Psychoanalysis*. New Haven: Yale University Press, 1976.

2. Jackson, D. & Weakland, J. Conjoint family therapy: Some considerations on theory, technique and results. *Psychiatry*, 1961, 24, 30–45.

3. Jackson, D. The question of family homeostasis. *The Psychiatric Quarterly Supplement*, 1957, 31, 79–90.

4. Haley, J. Control in brief psychotherapy. *Archives of General Psychiatry*, 1961, 4, 139–153.

5. Jackson, D. & Weakland, J., op. cit.

6. Watzlawick, P., Weakland, J. & Fisch, R. *Change: Principles of Problem Formation and Problem Resolution*. New York: Norton, 1974.

7. Lewis, W. & Evans, J. Resistance: A reconceptualization, *Psychotherapy*, 1986, 23, 426–433.

8. de Shazer, S. The death of resistance. *Family Process*, 1984, *23*, 11–17.

9. de Shazer, S. *Patterns of Brief Family Therapy: An Ecosystemic Approach.* New York: Guilford Press, 1982, pp. 9–10.

10. Stewart, S. & Anderson, C. Resistance revisited: Tales of my death have been greatly exaggerated (Mark Twain). *Family Process*, 1984, *23*, 17–20.

11. Wynne, L. Foreword. In C. Anderson & S. Stewart (Eds.), *Mastering Resistance: A Practical Guide to Family Therapy.* New York: Guilford Press, 1983.

12. Langs, R. Interactional and communicative aspects of resistance. *Contemporary Psychoanalysis*, 1980, *16*, 16–52.

13. Anderson, C. & Stewart, S. *Mastering Resistance: A Practical Guide to Family Therapy.* New York: Guilford Press, 1983.

14. There are, however, exceptions to the rule that family therapists don't talk much about contracts. Anderson and Stewart's book (ibid.) contains an excellent discussion of negotiating contracts in family therapy. Another source of useful information on contracting with families for treatment is the work of Nathan Epstein and his colleagues, e.g., Epstein, N. & Bishop, D. Problem-centered systems family therapy. *Journal of Marital and Family Therapy*, 1981, *7*, 23–32.

15. Kirschner, D. & Kirschner, S. *Comprehensive Family Therapy.* New York: Brunner/Mazel, 1986, p. 64.

16. Annie Reich's differentiation between "healthy" and "pathological" countertransference has not been incorporated into the vocabulary of the field. Reich, A. On countertransference. *International Journal of Psychoanalysis*, 1951, *32*, 25–31.

17. The important and sometimes contentious question of how much family therapists should promote feminist principles in their treatment was the subject of an entire issue of *The Family Therapy Networker*, 1985, *9*(6).

18. Springman, R. Countertransference: Clarification in supervision. *Contemporary Psychoanalysis*, 1986, *22*, 252–272.

19. Skynner, R. *Systems of Family and Marital Psychotherapy.* New York: Brunner/Mazel, 1976.

20. Jourard, S. *The Transparent Self.* Princeton, N.J.: Van Nostrand Rheinhold, 1971.

21. Kempler, W. Experiential psychotherapy with families. *Family Process*, 1968, 7, 88–98.

22. Mahrer, A. *Experiential Psychotherapy: Basic Practices.* New York: Brunner/Mazel, 1983.

23. Bion, W. *Second Thoughts: Selected Papers on Psycho-Analysis.* London: Heinemann, 1967.

Name Index

Subject Index